Moments of Cooperation and Incorporation

Moments of Cooperation and Incorporation

African American
and
African Jamaican Connections,
1782–1996

ERNA BRODBER

THE UNIVERSITY OF THE WEST INDIES PRESS
Jamaica • Barbados • Trinidad and Tobago

The University of the West Indies Press
7A Gibraltar Hall Road, Mona
Kingston 7, Jamaica
www.uwipress.com

A catalogue record of this book is available from the
National Library of Jamaica.

ISBN: 978-976-640-708-7 (print)
978-976-640-709-4 (Kindle)
978-976-640-710-0 (ePub)

Cover image: Osmond Watson, *Two Drummers*. Private collection, reproduced with
permission from the Estate of Osmond Watson.
Book and cover design by Robert Harris
Set in Arno Pro 10.5/14.5 x 27
Printed in the United States of America

Contents

Acknowledgements

I must acknowledge the support given to me in a number of forms by a wide number of agents in getting this work to this stage. It had long struck me that the preoccupation with Britain as our socializing agent was misplaced, obsolete or had run its course. In the 1960s days of black power slogans, we replaced Britain with Africa as our socializing agent. I did not find myself on that train for I thought that our real connection in Jamaica was with the United States. More than Britain or Africa, the United States touched the consciousness even of people in the remote village in which I was raised: men sung songs as they walked on the road, which I recognized to be the work of Ella Fitzgerald and Nat King Cole. The new churches, with their boxes of second-hand clothes, were American, and so was the first white man we had ever seen visiting a thatched-roof place of worship in my village. America was the place to which farm workers went on short stays and came back home with record players, records, and fashionable shoes and trousers. Deeper reflection showed me that the mother of the national hero Norman Manley had sought succour there on the death of her husband. It seemed to me that America was even in our parochial politics: I was beginning to see that politicians schooled in England, usually at the London School of Economics, had a different perception of our way forward as a nation from those who had been schooled in America, working at several jobs to pay their way through, as was the style.

It was not until the 1990s that I determined to research what I called the "American Connection". By then, I was an independent scholar with no source of income. My first approach to the Fulbright got the response that this study was so important that any university would want to support it, and therefore there was no need for a Fulbright. But there was no university offering me a place. I turned to fiction. I would use this medium as a kind of hypothesis, a guide to a framework for the social-scientific non-fiction work which I would tackle whenever I got the chance. This framework, my fiction told me, would have to include religion, music and migrant labour, among other things. I did get a Fulbright in 1990, but it was just for six months, and I was only able to work on the people of my Louisiana in my St Mary, Jamaica, and Louisiana, United States, the two places showing signs of cultural resemblance. Even then, this was fiction because I could not afford to buy the time to pursue, through historical and anthropological research, the hypotheses that I had formed about the relationship between the two places.

No offers of enough time and money came to allow me to move on to this work of non-fiction. With a growing reputation as a novelist, I got invitations to go to places where I would be offered accommodations. I need to thank the very many universities and colleges whose invitations to spend a year, a semester or three days gave me enough money to sustain myself while I approached such holdings: the Schomburg in New York, the Public Records Office in London, the holdings in Washington, DC, in Hampton University, the libraries in Richmond, Virginia, the University of the West Indies library, and the National Library of Jamaica. The librarians were very helpful, but I want to mention those at Duke University in North Carolina and the Georgia Historical Society, who heeded my request for material and sent this by mail; the librarians at the Jamaica Archives, who had to lift the heavy records of slave returns and other official records for me so often; and the librarians in the map section of the National Library, where I spent many quiet hours. Thanks, too, to the persons who offered beds free of charge: Esther Vassar in Hampton, Virginia; Pearline Blackwood in New York; Sarah White in London; Mumbi Carter in Washington; Calvin Forbes in Chicago; and my sister, Velma Pollard, in Kingston. I need to thank, too, the Sir Arthur Lewis Institute for Social and Economic Research, which gave me a fellowship for a year, allowing me to sit in an office and read journal articles on the Internet.

I want to name and thank some individuals who made me feel that what I was doing was important. I name Howard Johnson, formerly professor of history at the Univesity of Delaware, and Auburn Nelson of the Schomburg, who answered my queries by email promptly and, when I actually reached the holdings, gently guided me through the several reels of microfilm. Thanks to Vladimir Lucien, who listened; to Judith Anderson, who drove me from Richmond, Virginia, to Suffolk, Virginia, to visit the headquarters of the Church of God and Saints of Christ; and to Olive Senior, who accompanied me to the dreaded office (not so dreaded by the time we reached it) of the De Laurence Company in Chicago, where we both happened to be for readings. Many thanks to Andrea Davis and Lucille Brodber, who, when my computer crashed or went berserk, made their spares available to me. I need, too, to thank the Drake Committee of Vanderbilt University, Tennessee, for the invitation to interact with their students and, in particular, for the gift of the apprenticeship of two of their students, Petal Samuel and Ann Margaret Castro. It was these two students who conducted the interviews on which much of chapter 5 is based. Carolyn Allen was "Jim Dandy", coming to the rescue several times for this computer illiterate writer: How do you indent? How do you get to the journal?

I have to acknowledge, too, my guiding spirit, very active in 2003 when I was the Whichard visiting professor at East Carolina University. In the office assigned to me in the history department was a journal article describing the campaigns in Georgia–South Carolina during the War of American Independence and written in such a way that I could see and be inspired by the presence of African Americans in that struggle. I was later to meet the author, Lawrence E. Babbit, through whom I was able to identify loyalist battalions that had served in Georgia–South Carolina and seemed to have taken up the offer of the British government to settle in the Bagnolds, the part of St Mary where I grew up and whose connection with America I had imagined and confirmed through the slave registers. A chance eavesdropping on a conversation in the library at East Carolina University brought home to me the fact that South Carolina is called the "palmetto state", but the estate in St Mary which the slave registers said had a fairly high number of slaves born in America was the Palmetto Grove estate. What was the historical connection here and how to find it to finally do a creditable socio-historical study of the relationship between African Jamaicans and African Americans? While in the stacks in the library at East Carolina University, a pamphlet fell at my feet, in which I read that Alexander Wright, the son of Sir James Wright, the last loyalist governor of Georgia, a man born in South Carolina and who had properties there, had settled in Jamaica after the War of American Independence. This gift facilitated the research and writing of the first of these essays. Thank you.

I leave Kevin Meehan for the last. Meeting his book *People Get Ready: African American and Caribbean Cultural Exchange* (Jackson: University Press of Mississippi, 2009) had me wondering why I hadn't just sat around reading detective stories and left the young to do the business of writing and research on the African Jamaican and African American connection. Looking at his work more closely two years ago, I wondered whether I should throw away what I had been thinking about and finding time to research and write from my meagre store of funds since the 1990s. The title of his book and its framework come from his comparisons of Bob Marley's "One Love" and Curtis Mayfield's "People Get Ready". As Meehan points out, he had long been aware of the connection between the two musicians and their work and knew that Marley had credited Mayfield with co-writing the lyrics as well as designing the structure of the song, but what amazed him more recently and inspired his book were the emotional similarities that so closely linked the hopes and desires of the African Jamaican Marley with those of the African American Mayfield. "What had my efforts added?" I asked myself, until I met the line: "The Mayfield-Marley intertext suggested ... the need to look 'lower' rather than 'higher' in the social pyramid of art forms for a principle of coherent inter-American cultural resistance." In his volume, Meehan looks at the works of publicly validated African Caribbean and African American literary artists. In my work, I look at those lower in the social pyramid: labourers, healers, non-established religious organizations, politicians and literati on both sides of the black Atlantic.

Shivaun Hearne is helping me for the third time with the birthing of a project. She has been patience itself. This document is larger than the others and calls for a greater degree of patience, and she has given this.

Introduction

IN THE LAST DECADE, THERE HAS BEEN A SIGNIFICANT volume of work on the black Atlantic, a sociographic area peopled in large numbers by descendants of Africans enslaved in the New World. These works have together painstakingly described the circumference of this area; most have selected African America as the point from which to begin drawing the circle; some have gone on to describe an arc pointing from African America to other areas on the circle. Some, like Dixon and Pamphile, have linked African America to Haiti.[1] Others, like Putnam, have not differentiated but chosen to see the Caribbean as an entity on the circumference and made the link with African America from that point.[2] Nwankwo is among the few whose arrow leads not just from African America to another point but has the arrows going two ways, and who puts Spanish-speaking descendants in the circuit, eventually creating an arrow which goes from them to African America and from African America to them.[3] These scholars have selected points in time in which to look at the relationships in the selected arcs. The nineteenth century was popular; Polyné extended it to the mid-twentieth century, and Putnam concentrated on the "jazz age".[4] Mary C. Waters's work on black identities, which, through interviews, compares identity construction of West Indians and African Americans, moves into the post-1965 period and happily shares a conclusion of this work concerning West Indians' (African Jamaicans') hesitancy in the late twentieth century to self-identify as African Americans.[5]

The writers mentioned above have come to their study for scholarly reasons; they have looked at published work and determined to fill gaps. Putnam, for instance, was moved by comments of another scholar that to understand the black Atlantic – "black internationalism" as she prefers to call it – requires that scholars look not just at literary and political figures, as Gilroy, in her view, has done, but also at the voiceless and unlettered. Gilroy himself came to study the black Atlantic, which has fathered others, through his interest in "modernity" and his students. He says: "*The Black Atlantic* developed from my uneven attempts to show these students that the experiences of black people were part of the abstract modernity."[6] Nwankwo stands alone as one who was moved to write by the circumstances of her upbringing. All, whether by newspapers, speeches or published work of the elite, have built their arguments on archival data. Putnam has gone beyond this: she used the lives of the parents of Malcolm X to make her point that the existence of the black international owes as much to the lowly Caribbean migrant as it does to the published philosophers of the Caribbean and of black America; and Waters uses the responses from questionnaires.

I came to this project not from scholarly but from private and political motives. From as early as I can remember, I have seen myself as a descendant of Africans enslaved in the New World; I have been very moved by our past and present condition and have wondered what I could do towards amelioration of the present conditions. The New World group of the 1960s guided me to the fashioning of an instrument. This group was composed of university lecturers and researchers employed to the local University of the West Indies. They hoped to be of use to their territories, which were achieving or about to achieve political independence. They felt, like me, inept, for we had all been trained in curricula which had taught us little about our societies. Out of this group reflection came the notion that we should begin by seeing ourselves as workers, out to build our new world; we differed from other workers such as plumbers and painters in that our skills were intellectual. We were "intellectual workers", and our business was to find out what was collectively real to our people, for "what is collectively real is what is politically significant. To arrive at that and then make it common public property is our task," wrote Lloyd Best, one of my mentors.[7] For me, this meant working among the common, usually unlettered, of our society to discover what is real to them, and then making this common knowledge by publishing it.

One listening to call-in radio programmes in Jamaica or listening to talk at a bus stop realizes that "America" is one of the things that is real to the Jamaican. R.T. Smith, an Englishman and one of the early researchers and opinion makers in Caribbean intellectual circles, concurs. He now rues the neglect of "the crucial importance of the North American influence in the shaping of Jamaican and West Indian society".[8] Like Nwankwo, my personal experience of growing up in my society has propelled me towards the creation of this work. My America was African America of the 1950s and 1960s. African America was the point to which my school friend vanished during this time to become a *Jamerican*; this was the point to which cousins, not bright enough for scholarships to English universities, went, came back with degrees and sat on the pages of the newspaper in gown and cap. This was the point from which barrels of not-so-new but still-in-style clothes came, as well as the pop songs and singers: for example, the Platters, in which the lone female looked like the girl next door whom we had known all our lives. It was a day to hold our heads high when we saw that Frankie Lymon and the Teenagers, of the popular song "Why Do Fools Fall in Love", all looked like us Jamaican fifth formers, making it clear to us that despite our black skin, we could have successful singing careers. It was African American movie stars such as Sydney Poitier and Dorothy Dandridge who confirmed our elevation to celluloid. We saw them as cousins, and the whole movie house would shout with glee "Cous!" when one of these black faces appeared on the screen.

My special paper for my undergraduate degree was a study of the Reconstruction in South Carolina. I wept for my lynched brothers and sisters, but a trip with them to Somalia and Egypt in 1984 shook my roots: they did not recognize me as a sister but as a stranger, not even Jamaican but "Caribbean", someone from the islands. Later readings of Harold Cruse and Melvin B. Rahming opened my eyes more fully to the possibility that these African Americans did not see me as a sister.[9] I also had to admit, after discussion with some Jamaicans who had been brought up or worked in America, that they themselves had purposely lived with a distinction between themselves and African Americans. But, I argued, in a time when the descendants of Africa enslaved in the New World are once more seeing the connection with Africa as the way forward, doesn't it make political sense for us of the diaspora to work together and face Africa together? My task as an intellectual worker was now, it seemed, to convince the diaspora to work together. I could only manage two groups – African Americans and African Jamaicans. My determination to study and make public work that could meld the two groups together was born. I would show these two groups that they had incorporated themselves in each other's spaces and had cooperated successfully with each other. Now an independent scholar, and without institutional support, my first intellectual efforts were the novel *Louisiana* and the non-fiction work *The Continent of Black Consciousness*.[10] In these works, I described, mostly from imagination in the case of the novel and mostly from secondary sources in the case of the non-fiction work, a past of cooperation between African Americans and African Jamaicans. Meanwhile, to the extent that I could get financial support, I did the research towards writing this collection of essays, which I felt would be a better tool than a work of fiction or a collection of essays built from secondary sources.

This work, *Moments of Cooperation and Incorporation: African American and African Jamaican Connections, 1782–1996*, like those academic works mentioned above, sits upon the circumference of what Gilroy named the "black Atlantic" and Putnam the "black international". Its time span is longer than the others: it covers the period from 1782 to 1996. Unlike most of the others, it does not privilege the point on the circumference where African America sits but, like Nwankwo's work, has arrows pointing in both directions, in my case from African America to African Jamaica and back again. While, like most others, the work is based on archival sources, it uses interviews as well. The work is presented in six essays. The first is "African American and African Jamaican Meeting in St Mary, Jamaica, as Slaves of Governor Wright and His Family". Using archival sources, I list the enslaved persons brought from Georgia–South Carolina to the governor's plantation in Jamaica and, through interviews, try to follow them and their descendants into the present time. The second chapter, "The African American in Jamaica in the Mid-Nineteenth Century", also privileges the African American. In the post-emancipation dearth of plantation labour, the Jamaican authorities tried to attract African Americans to fill this slot; a few came. This chapter describes the negotiations related to their migration, lists the migrants and guesses at the nature of their lives in Jamaica.

The third chapter, "Marcus Garvey and the African Americans", privileges the African Jamaican. Here, we look at the needs of the African American community as expressed in their newspapers and at the programme that Marcus Garvey, an African Jamaican, devised to respond to these needs. The fourth chapter, "African Jamaican and African American Religious Cooperation and Incorporation: A Case Study", traces a religious organization, the Church of God and Saints of Christ, from its founding place in the United States to its establishment in Jamaica. A great deal of the fifth chapter, "African American and African Jamaican Encounters Mainly in the Florida Sugar Cane Fields in 1943–1996", is based on interviews with Jamaican men who have served as "farmworkers" in the United States. The final chapter is "The Transformation of a Jamaican Healer into a Black Jew by African Americans". This essay consists of a verbatim interview with a Jamaican healer who was invited by some African Americans whom he met in Jamaica to visit their country to attain knowledge which they thought he needed in order to upgrade his skills as a healer and mystic. From African American newspapers and secondary sources, I compare the world of spirit healing in African Jamaica and African America.

The social psychologist George Homans early established that frequency of interaction leads to heightened sentiment. This sentiment could, of course, be negative or positive. This collection of essays has continued the task of establishing that there is a "black international", a "black Atlantic", adding Jamaica as a point on the circumference. But is there sentiment enough to support a working structure? Was the Jamaica Hamic society, mentioned in chapter 2, which hoped to build a commercial association with their counterparts in African America, able to do so? Were the conditions right in the late twentieth century for a mini Universal Negro Improvement Association? What of the twenty-first century? The afterword, which ends this work, faces this question.

{CHAPTER 1}

African American and African Jamaican Meeting in St Mary, Jamaica, as Slaves of Governor Wright and His Family

THE EARL OF DUNMORE, GOVERNOR OF THE COLONY OF Virginia, on 7 November 1775 invited enslaved blacks, among others, to forsake their American masters and to join the cause of their opponent, the king of England.[1] For this, they would get their freedom after service. "To be free is very sweet," said Mary Prince, and her peers and elders would have concurred, for enslaved black people knew of freedom, having watched their masters in their enjoyment of this sweetness.[2] Several of these enslaved people understandably took up the offer and deserted their American masters. The desire for freedom was contagious: desertion encouraged desertion, even in the states where no emancipation offer had been made. This desertion, and the absence of immediate social control which came with it, naturally brought a significant degree of instability to the world of those fighting the War of American Independence. Add the fact that the enslaved workers of loyalists, the king's men, could as easily be spirited away as those of the patriots, the Americans, and we find a population of Africans of the diaspora enslaved in what is today called the United States of America, particularly in its South, who were in a great deal of social and geographic mobility, running to freedom and masterlessness, slave today, free tomorrow – but also free today and slave tomorrow, slave of the king's side today and slave of the patriots tomorrow.

John Cruden, commissioner of sequester lands in 1780, felt the instability.[3] It was hard enough for him to feed the loyalist refugees, but on top of this, he had to take care of the "slaves" flocking to Charleston, South Carolina, in the hopes of evacuation from the Americans and from slavery. Lieutenant Governor William Bull, also of South Carolina, felt the impact of this instability upon the polity that it was his business to govern. Writing to Lord George Germain of the Colonial Office on 22 March 1781, this loyalist, whose Virginia colleague had six years before offered freedom to the enslaved, commented, "the slaves have been ungovernable", and went on to show us how important enslaved labour was to the theatre of war. His comment continues to describe the consequences of this "ungovernablenness": which, he adds, "with the want of draught animals, is disadvantageous to the planters".[4] Clearly, with the flesh of cows and bulls needed to feed a fighting army supplemented by recruits, and with the horses needed for a war in which the cavalry was key, that part of the population, the planters, whose contributions to the war effort would be to provide food, badly needed people to do, in addition to what workers normally did, the moving of heavy loads normally reserved for draught animals.[5] Obviously, the freedom the Euro-Americans invited African Americans to take was a freedom only from the perceived enemy – the Americans – for it was Governor Bull's hope, as he continues in his communication to Germain, that in "two or three years of peace", apparently with blacks more governable and evidently able to be used as draught animals and more, "plenty" would be restored. African Americans and their labour were crucial to the course of the war, the players threatening each other from time to time with the loss of it.

So crucial was this labour, in fact, that peace talks between General Matthews of the Americans and his loyalist counterpart stalled on the issue of who had a right to it, the Americans of South Carolina threatening to seize all debts and marriage settlements due to the evacuating loyalists if "Negroes" claimed by persons in the state were carried away from Charleston.[6] Until a clause was written into the truce agreement against the removal of "Negroes or other American property", hostilities remained. And even after this, to the annoyance of General Alexander Leslie, the British officer charged with the evacuation of loyalists from Savannah and from Charleston, the Americans insisted on searching the evacuating boats to ensure that their precious "labour" did not leave the state.[7]

On these boats sailing from Savannah, Georgia, to Port Royal, Jamaica, on 20 July 1782 and arriving on 15 August 1782 were fourteen hundred enslaved blacks.[8] Months later, in January of 1783, twenty-six hundred arrived in twenty boats from Charleston, South Carolina.[9] Wallace Brown adds thirteen to this figure.[10] Most were established, by Matthews's men before they set sail, to be bona fide slaves of the refugees. Among them were some blacks who had actually borne arms against the Americans. The labour of these latter the Americans did not want, but they did insist that they be compensated for their loss from the workforce.

Nathaniel Hall, paymaster of the Georgia militia, took on the trip to Jamaica 56 enslaved workers for himself; 217 for Sir James Wright, former governor of Georgia; 102 for William Kerr; 32 for Sir James Wallace; and 5 for Thomas Cuthland.[11] It was arranged with Archibald Campbell, governor of Jamaica, who had in 1779, only three years before, served in Georgia as lieutenant colonel, that the evacuated slaves would be put to work at a stipulated price per day, this payment going to their masters. Transported from the American South to Jamaica, these Africans of the diaspora were clearly fingered by the administration to be the financial support of the refugees. And so important were these enslaved Africans of the diaspora to the resettlement plans of the British government concerning its loyal citizens that prior arrangements were even made for them to be fed, as we learn from correspondence between Leslie, the officer charged with supervising the evacuation of those loyal to the British Crown from Charleston, South Carolina, and Savannah, Georgia, and Sir Guy Carleton.[12]

Wright's slaves brought over by Hall, most likely coming from the family's Richmond and Kew plantations in South Carolina, apparently went to his property in Palmetto Grove, St Mary, for on the 1817 slave list for that Jamaican estate we find forty-six enslaved persons who were listed as Americans.[13] Wallace Brown rues the fact that "apart from George Lewis, the loyalists slaves remain largely 'inarticulate' to historians".[14] It is to fill such gaps in history, as well as to explore this moment of meeting between Africans of the diaspora born in the United States and those in Jamaica, that we examine Wright's American enslaved population and their descendants living on his Palmetto Grove estate in St Mary in 1817. Those who survive in 1817 are listed in table 1.1.

Table 1.1. List of African Americans on the Palmetto Grove Plantation in 1817

Name	Born	Colour
Females		
Amoreltha	1777	Negro
Mary Bennett	1780	Negro
Honoria Brice	1780	Negro
Sophy Collinridge	1780	Negro
Lucretia Dance*	1777	Negro
Selina Douglas	1780	Negro
Dorothy	1772	Negro
Eve	1768	Negro
Lucy Germaine	1772	Negro
Sukey Germaine	1780	Negro
Nancy Johnson	1777	Negro
Sukey Lynch	1780	Negro
Elizabeth Lloyd	1753	Negro
Dolly Martin	1767	Negro
Jane Roberts	1777	Negro
Ruth	1777	Negro
Bell Simpson	1780	Negro
Maria Thompson	1780	Negro
Bessy White	1758	Negro
Ann Wright	1754	Negro
Nancy Wright	1773	Negro
Maria Williams Wright	1761	Negro
Diana Wright	1780	Negro
Arabella Wright	1780	Negro
Phillis Wright	1758	Negro
Old Judy	1740	Negro
Total females: 26		

*Sometimes listed as African

Name	Born	Colour
Males		
Daniel Blake	1775	Negro
Benjamin Bolingbroke	1769	Negro
John Brice	1775	Negro
Edward Cosens	1780	Negro
David Douglas	1779	Negro
Joseph Germaine	1779	Negro
Stephen Hall	1777	Negro
Benjamin Hearsel/Hume	1774	Negro
Matthias	1767	Negro
Peter	1780	Negro
Robert Edwards Pollack	1767	Negro
George Simpson	1779	Negro
James Wallace	1777	Negro
William Clarke Watson	1779	Negro
Jacky Wright	1767	Negro
William Fisher Wright	1767	Negro
John Wright	1780	Negro
Alexander Wright	1763	Negro
Thomas Wright	1780	Negro
James Wright	1780	Negro
Total males: 20		

Source: Derived from Return of Registration of Slaves, 1817 and 1820 (St Mary), Jamaica Archives, Spanish Town, Jamaica.

PALMETTO GROVE: THE GEOGRAPHIC SPACE

A diagram which shows a tract of five hundred acres of land being subdivided for Christopher Frey shows above this area and on the Rio Sambre a tiny place named "Palmetto Grove", as we can see in figure 1. I have circled the area. The diagram was prepared in 1753 in the case of *Cunningham v. Needham*. Could Palmetto Grove have been a property with a name since then? It continues to exist as per figure 2. That diagram, produced by George Neilson in 1774 for

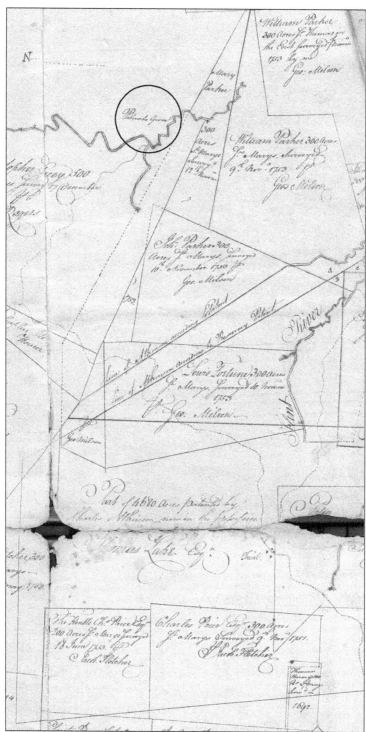

Figure 1. St Mary 1385, showing the location of Palmetto Grove in 1753. Courtesy of the National Library of Jamaica.

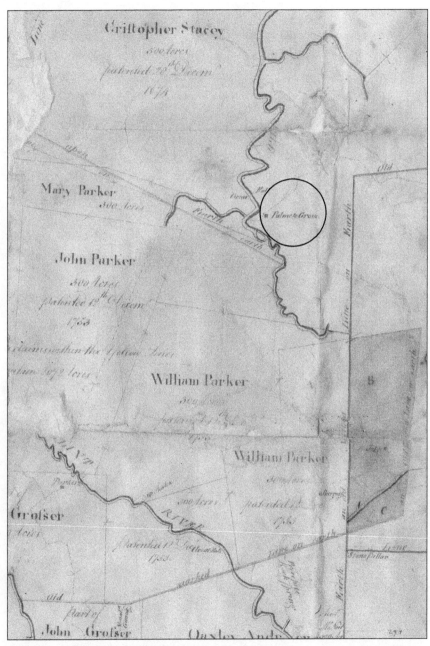

Figure 2. St Mary 1436, showing the location of Palmetto Grove in 1774. Courtesy of the National Library of Jamaica.

William Parker and Louis Fortune, shows Palmetto Grove. I have circled this space on the diagram. This place, part of the parish of St Mary, is bounded on the left by large acres of lands belonging to Mary Parker, John Parker and William Parker. Clearly, Palmetto Grove existed in 1753 and 1774. South Carolina is called the "palmetto state". Sir James Wright, though governor of Georgia, belonged to South Carolina, having been born there to the chief justice, and himself having served there as attorney general for several years. Sir James had landed property there; he also had landed property in Jamaica. Wallace Brown indicates that Sir James Wright was known to have "substantial interests" in Jamaica by 1782 and the evacuation of those loyal to the British Crown from Charleston, South Carolina, and from Savannah, Georgia.[15] Might Palmetto Grove be one of his interests, then, named to romantically reflect his engagement with South Carolina or chosen and bought for that reason? It is not until 1786 and William Smellie's detailed diagram (figure 3), in the case of *Beckford v. Shryer*, that we actually see the name "Wright" on a St Mary diagram. The name

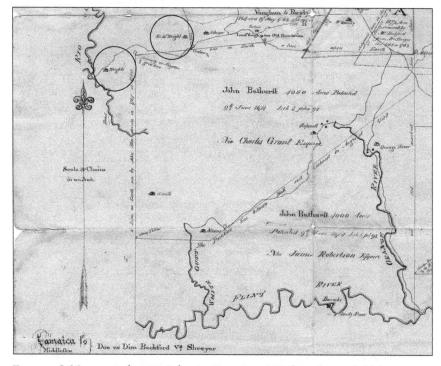

Figure 3. St Mary 1208, showing Palmetto Grove in 1786. Where the words "Palmetto Grove" had been in 1753 and 1774, we now see the word "Wright's". To the right of this, there is a property with the words "Sir Jas Wright". Courtesy of the National Library of Jamaica.

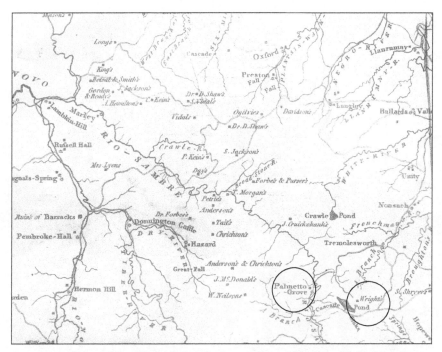

Figure 4. Robertson's map shows Palmetto Grove in 1804 with the words "Palmetto Grove" where the word "Wright's" had been in 1786 and, to its right, the word "Wright" where the word "Sir Jas Wright" had been. Courtesy of the National Library of Jamaica.

"Wright" is on this 1786 diagram where the name "Palmetto Grove" was on the 1753 diagram, and the words "Sir James Wright" further away and close to that of the defendant, Shryer. I have circled these names.

Settled areas are usually denoted on survey diagrams by the image of a house. There are sketches of houses where we see the name "Wright", as well as where we see the name "Sir Jas Wright". Were there two families of Wrights? Robertson's 1804 map (figure 4) has the words "Palmetto Grove" in the place where they were on the 1753 diagram and where the name "Wright" was in the 1786 diagram. Sir James Wright and perhaps other Wrights surely were by 1786 owners of a property called Palmetto Grove. These two pieces of land, one on the Rio Sambre and the other close to a pond, are separated from each other by the "cascade" and "sinks". There seems to have been another piece associated with the Wrights. In figure 5, we note a description of part of the Woodside plantation as "bounded northerly on a road leading from Parkersvale to Palmetto Grove and west on land laid out for Alexander Wright". This survey was done by Robert Leslie

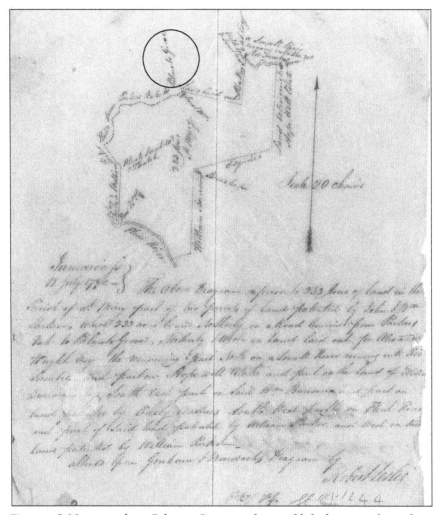

Figure 5. St Mary 1244 shows Palmetto Grove as a place established in 1790 to be used as a descriptive marker. It also shows that Alexander Wright, the son of Governor Sir James Wright, could have owned more land in the area than Palmetto Grove. Note the circled words. Courtesy of the National Library of Jamaica.

on 7 December 1790. Note that "Palmetto Grove" is distinguished from "land laid out for Alexander Wright". Clearly, this property "laid out for Alexander Wright" is not the one called Palmetto Grove, which is close to the Rio Sambre. It is also not that which is close to the Broughton River, for the Hopewell estate then separated this property from Woodside, one of the boundaries of this land "laid out for Alexander Wright".

Sir James did not join his slaves in Jamaica after the evacuation of 1782: he went on to England. Data from the Georgia Historical Society state clearly that his son Alexander, whom we know to have been involved with General Leslie in the evacuation of Savannah-Charleston, did settle in Jamaica for some time.[16] Indeed, he is listed in the *Jamaica Almanack* as being a judge here in 1789.[17] The third piece of land referred to above might have been his compensation for his war efforts. Given the fact that a part of the Neilson's plantation (later to be known as "Woodside") comes to its 1819 owners through the Wrights' default on mortgage held by William Peterswald, who is the post-1804 owner of lands marked on that map "Harrison and Hart" – land which is between Woodside and Palmetto Grove – it stands to reason that what is referred to in the description of the diagram mentioned above is a third piece and that this third piece had linked a part of Woodside to Palmetto Grove. This third piece could have been that marked "Harrison and Hart" and which eventually becomes the property of Peterswald, which he called "Petersfield". There is no evidence, however, that this piece of land was ever called "Palmetto Grove" or even given a name by Alexander Wright, though it is clear that the land had belonged to him at some time.

The physical area called "Wright's" and "Sir Jas Wright" on the 1786 diagram (figure 3) – bounded by Charles Grant's purchase of thousands of acres from Bathurst by Edward Broughton's property, which had a river running through it, by Tremolesworth and by some hundreds of acres belonging to Bolt – is the same as that called "Palmetto Grove" and "Wright's" on Robertson's 1804 map (figure 4) – an area bounded as well by the Crawle and Tremolesworth plantations at one point, by the Hopewell plantation at another, by Neilson's land and by W. Neilson's land, by the part of the Rio Sambre, which was near to land once owned by Bolt, but which now seems to have been taken over by Anderson and Chrichton, by McDonald and Neilson, and by "Harrison and Hart's", today's Petersfield. This area in the 1880 map (figure 6) looks much the same, except that what was in 1786 two distinct areas called "Wright's" and "Sir Jas Wright" are now one, with areas on the edges alienated to small settlers, such as the 103 acres close to Tremolesworth, which I have circled on the diagram and which is to the right above that place marked "Palmetto Grove" and that marked Tremolesworth. This 103-acre plot is Kilancholy. A map of the early 1950s (figure 7) gives us two Palmetto Groves and a Dean Pen in this space which

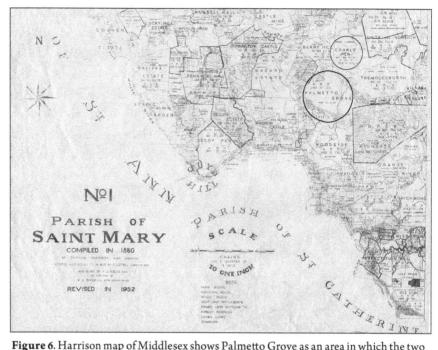

Figure 6. Harrison map of Middlesex shows Palmetto Grove as an area in which the two pieces called "Wright's" and "Sir Jas Wright" seem to be integrated, and pieces on the outskirts seem to be alienated to small settlers, one such piece being Kilancholy, which is near to Crawle and Tremolesworth. Courtesy of the National Library of Jamaica.

covers polling districts 55, 59, 60, 61 and 62, an area described by the Government of Jamaica's electoral office as bounded by Hampstead, Crawle and Unity, by the Broughton River and Tremolesworth, and by Hopewell and by Woodside.

It is in this area, most of it now called Kilancholly, using the names of voters on the polling division lists, that we search for the descendants of the Americans brought from the South of what is today called the United States to serve and to live with other descendants of enslaved Africans and with enslaved Africans in the late eighteenth century. (See figure 8.)

Some properties on the 1786 map (figure 3) have the house symbol as well as the word "works". Some, if you look closely, also carry the windmill. These are properties which are developed businesses. The 1786 Wright properties have only the house symbol; they were probably not yet established businesses. Black blocks on the 1804 map (figure 4) denote ownership and settlement. Some properties, like Hopewell, Hazard and Tremolesworth, carry that second symbol, which

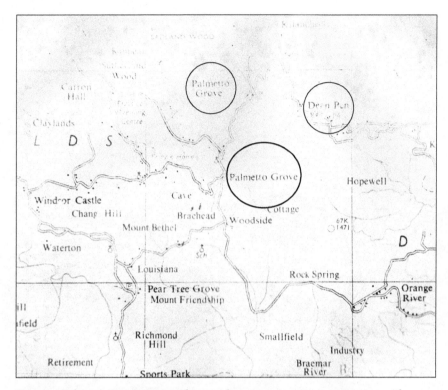

Figure 7. Palmetto Grove in 1952 is shown to be once more two separate areas, with Kilancholy above it to the left. Kilancholy is the village in which we did most of our search for the descendants of the enslaved whom we think the Wrights brought with them from Georgia–South Carolina. Courtesy of the National Library of Jamaica.

appears to denote economic development. The space called "Palmetto Grove" and which is on the Rio Sambre carries this additional symbol – an asterisk – on the 1804 map, though, that with the word "Wright's" does not. It seems very likely then that the Wright's 217 enslaved workers were indeed taken to Palmetto Grove in 1782 to make it into the economic enterprise it was by 1804. Note that by 1799, seventeen years after the exodus from Savannah-Charleston, it produced 226 hogsheads, 50 pounds of muscovado sugar and some rum. These, the first available figures, were presented by its overseer, Robert Anderson.[18] The output increased in 1800: at that point, there were 242 hogsheads and 100 pounds of sugar, plus some rum. The transported people, accustomed to planting rice in Georgia–South Carolina, seemed to be developing skills at growing and processing sugar. Two years later, the output decreased to 70 hogsheads and

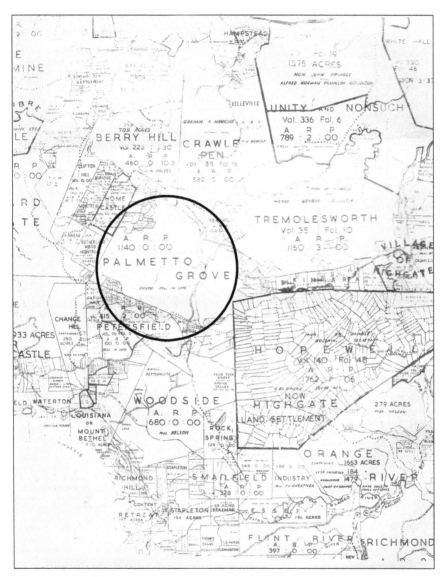

Figure 8. Shows Palmetto Grove in contemporary times (2011), in which the polling districts 5, 59, 60, 61 and 62 are found. It is from the voters' list that we pulled the surnames seen on the slave registers of 1817, 1820, 1823 and 1826. Courtesy of the National Library of Jamaica.

125 pounds of sugar.[19] The overseer then was John Thompson. By 1807, he had been replaced by Thomas Tucker, who seems to have diversified the plantation's trading partners and sources of income. He registers that he was shipping sugar to London via the *Orpheus* and the *Blessing* and selling to neighbours – Walker, Pollock, Burnett, the Woodside plantation and Mrs Burrowes, among others – but he had shipped only 104.53 pounds of sugar. He was also renting out the services of the enslaved workers.[20]

Though Alexander Wright is listed in 1811 in the *Jamaica Almanack* as the owner of Palmetto Grove and its 243 slaves and 126 stock, it is possible that neither he nor his heirs lived there. Thomas Tucker's records indicate that in 1804, the great house and the lands attached to it were rented out to a Mrs Campbell. Efforts to make the estate pay must have been in vain, for by 1817, Hibbert, Fuhr and Purrier had foreclosed on the property of "Alexander Wright deceased".[21] Until 1832, when there are no more returns of slaves listed by owners in the *Jamaica Almanack*, it is James and, later, John Deans listed as owner or trustee for the Palmetto Grove estate – the "estate" being sometimes distinguished from its "pen".[22] By 1832, Palmetto Grove had joined the list of failed St Mary estates. But whether the estates failed or were succeeding, the enslaved population remained *in situ*. Under James Deans, in 1821, the property listed its estate and pen as two separate entities, the estate having 241 enslaved workers and the pen 20, with 111 heads of cattle. In 1826, the stock increased by 33, and the workers on the estate, some perhaps transferred to the pen, decreased to 232. By 1832, and the recognition that the business had failed, the distinction between the pen and the estate had ceased. In this year, Palmetto Grove had 223 enslaved workers.[23]

No one plans to run his estate with teenagers and babies. The enslaved Americans whom Deans bought from the Wright estate in 1817, males as well as females, were born between 1767 and 1780, except for Alexander Wright, who was born in 1760, and Old Judy, who was born in 1740. This means that they were at most fifteen years old, except for Alexander Wright, who was about twenty-two, and Old Judy, forty-two, in 1782, when they would have come to Jamaica. Clearly, the majority of this forty-six who remained in 1817 had come over to Jamaica with their parents. There were very few mother-child units remaining in 1817, though. David Douglas, born in 1776 to Maria Williams Wright; Edward Cosens, born a year later to Nancy Tharpe; Sophy Collinridge, born to Jane

Roberts in 1771; and Dorothy, born to Old Judy, were the only mother-child units which would have crossed the Atlantic from Savannah-Charleston to Palmetto Grove, St Mary, Jamaica.

Old Judy was in 1817 the oldest person on the plantation. She was seventy-seven years old and was by far the oldest woman. The Africans, Lissy MacDonald and Harriet Thomas, were the next oldest, and they were sixty-six years old. Will, alias James Hamilton, an African brought into the plantation with the new owners in 1817, was the oldest male, at sixty-one years old. Males and females on the Palmetto Grove estate tended to be forty-five years and under; only five men and six women apart from the two just mentioned were fifty or over. As everywhere, women lived longer than the men. On several estates, Woodside, for instance, there was a greater percentage of people over fifty than here in Palmetto Grove. Of Woodside's 150 enslaved persons, eleven men and fifteen women were fifty or over.[24] Why were Palmetto Grove's slaves so young, and what happened to the bulk of the 217 enslaved persons who we assume came to Palmetto Grove? Whatever became of the parents of those in the 1817–32 lists of enslaved persons, beside whose name is listed "American" in the "African or Creole" column, and who must have left America as infants? The same question can be asked of the thousand or more enslaved workers transported to Jamaica in 1782 and 1783 to be the financial support of their masters. Very few of them are listed in the general slave returns for 1817 and later. The adjustment was perhaps too much for them and they died.

B.W. Higman notes that between 1817 and 1820, St Mary, the parish in which we find Palmetto Grove, had one of the highest mortality rates in Jamaica at 29.5 per 1,000 of the enslaved population, compared with, for instance, Kingston's 17.8 and St Elizabeth's 18.2.[25] But what caused these parents to die so young, so soon after arrival in Jamaica? My guess is that they had little time in which to establish their own provision grounds, and with hostilities between Britain and the United States, Jamaica's largest source of foodstuffs, these people died of malnutrition. Governor Sir James Wright's complaint, "we were hurried away with our Negros without the least notice and had not provisions for six weeks in hand for their nurture and their subsistence", supports this guess.[26] Wright blames the haste with which Britain sought peace from the rebels, a foolish move in his estimation, for this lack of provisions. Lieutenant General Alexander Leslie, charged with the evacuation, puts another gloss on this lack of provisions, which could have resulted in the early death of the adults brought to Palmetto Grove estate. In his private letter to Sir Guy Carleton, he says:

> I apprehend you may have letters from some of the loyalists going from here to East Florida and to Jamaica complaining (as they term it) of scanty allowance of provisions given them, as directed by Mr. B. Watson of the commissary here, (vizt.) six months to those going to East Florida, three months to those embarking for Jamaica, besides being fed on their passage. I must ~ your Excellency (in secret) assure you there is no bounds to the unreasonable demands of all sorts of people (I don't even except the officers of the Crown). I will venture to affirm the greatest part of the provisions going to Jamaica for the use of the slaves will, on its being distributed, be sold for the benefit of the owners.[27]

So the owners could have sold the provisions meant for the enslaved leaving them to die of starvation. The absence of adults possibly through death could also be blamed on smallpox. Ellen Gibson Wilson tells us that smallpox raged among the African Americans who had run away to Charleston, South Carolina. She mentions its occurrence too in Savannah.[28] These people enslaved in Palmetto Grove, St Mary, could have brought this disease in their system and, with the trauma of transition to Jamaica, starvation and their bodies already weakened by the exigencies of the war, succumbed to the emergence or re-emergence of this contagious and highly deadly disease.

In the three years after Deans assumed ownership of Palmetto Grove and its forty-six African Americans, there were very few deaths, but in a population of 243 enslaved persons, there were only nine births. All survived. There was possibly an epidemic between 1820 and 1823 and a great deal of weeping, for in the tri-yearly estate report, ten children are said to have died. The old must die, and the young may die, but the young did die, for along with the babies, there were young people eighteen, twenty-one and twenty-two years old in the twenty-one deaths which the estate reported for the period 1820–23. The 1826 tri-yearly report listed eleven deaths: four were babies under three years old. In 1832, there were eight deaths, of which four were children under seven years of age. The estate, as noted earlier, was moving into decline. Did its economic woes visit themselves upon the care of the population of Africans of the diaspora, and especially those under three years old?

Palmetto Grove is part of the Bagnolds district, nearly two thousand acres of which were made available by the British Crown for the settlement of loyalists.

One such settlement was Pembroke Hall, and one such loyalist was Mrs Gibb.[29] Here lived with this slave mistress the African American slave preacher George Gibb and his wife. Brought to Jamaica as an eslaved person, Gibb continued, as he had done at home behind the British lines, to proselytize among his people. No doubt he was very well known to his countrymen on the Palmetto Grove estate. His would not have been the only Christian influence on the Americans in Palmetto Grove, for their 1799–1800 overseer, Robert Anderson, belonged to a distinctive Protestant sect which swore on the four Holy Evangelists, and there were others in the Wrights' business set who did so in Georgia–South Carolina and carried this religious tendency with them to Jamaica. Nathaniel Hall, who could have been the one who brought Wright's enslaved workers to Palmetto Grove, was similarly involved with a peculiar Christian sect associated with the countess of Huntington and her good works.[30] Palmetto Grove's enslaved workers were clearly in a Christian environment.

In addition to what they might have learned on their own in Savannah-Charleston and in Palmetto Grove from Gibb and from overseer Anderson was what they could have learned from the Quaker friends of their masters. Sir James Wright was known to be partial to the Georgia Quakers. In fact, they named their village in Georgia "Wrightsborough" in recognition of his kindness to them. In St Mary, there were Quakers among Wright's neighbours, choosing to "aver" rather than to "swear" with respect to the truth of their slave returns. Did the Wrights help these Quakers migrate to St Mary? Whether or not this is so, the Christian influence on Palmetto Grove's enslaved workers existed. It manifested itself in their names, the estates around Palmetto Grove being outstanding in Jamaica for the fact that so many of the enslaved workers had first and last names – Christian names and surnames. Quite likely, these African Americans enslaved in Palmetto Grove, St Mary, had even been involved enough in the Baptist faith of Gibb to help to build the church at Braehead, which we know was in existence in the early decades of the nineteenth century.[31] Braehead is, as the crow flies, less than a mile from Palmetto Grove – an easy walk. By 1818, the Anglicans had begun to proselytize among the enslaved people. More than thirty of Palmetto Grove's slaves, two of whom we know to be American, joined them between 1818 and 1831. The two are Dolly Wharam and Bessy Issard, both women and both sixty years old in 1817, omitted for whatever reason from the 1817 slave list but appearing on the 1820 list. To submit to baptism at this age signifies serious reflection on religious issues, especially when having the choice of joining the American Gibb's Baptists.

The Christian influence seemed to stop at mating behaviour. Mating with one person for life is a rule in many Christian denominations; Palmetto Grove's African Americans did not take this seriously: no woman's set of children all had the same surname. If surnames indicate "father of the child", as it does in the Christian tradition, then no women with more than two children mated exclusively with one man, as we see from the list of mothers and children in table 1.2.

If we assume, as we have done here, that surname denotes paternity, then not only do women have multiple fathers for their children, but they also mate outside of their national group; an examination of the names of males born in America shows that only in the cases of Mary Bennet, Lucy Germaine and Nancy Wright, American-born, were there men living on the estate with them who shared the surnames of their children and, thus, given our assumptions, could be fathers of their children. Of course, it is quite possible that the fathers could have been American and died before 1817 and therefore not be on the 1817 slave list. It is possible that some had "baby fathers" among the Africans and the creoles; for example, Amoretha's son carries the surname "Wildy", and there was a forty-three-year-old African on the estate with the surname Wilds (a spelling mistake?) when her child was born in 1817; Sukey Lynch might have produced Jafrey Lynch in 1824 by the African Patrick Lynch, who was born in 1774. I have concluded that the women and their daughters quite likely mated with creole men on the estate or on neighbouring estates. The American Jane Roberts might have found a mate at Dove Hall estate among Bryan Edwards's or Zackary Bailey Edwards's many slaves carrying his name; among Patience Hermit's small collection at Carpenter's Hut; or among Dr Hugh Edwards's collection at Top Hill to make with her the creoles Markland Edwards, Janette Edwards and Susan Edwards, born in 1801, 1799 and 1797, respectively.32 Her daughter Susan could have found a mate on the estate in one of the creole brothers Charles and Henry Lee, one born in 1782 and the other in 1793, to make Selina Lee, born in 1813. So could Maria Thompson have made Phillis Thompson in 1813 with John Thompson, born in 1790, and Nancy Wright with the African Richard Wilson, born in 1764, to make James Wilson in 1810. Besides Maria, Phillis and Nancy, no other American-born women produced children

Table 1.2. American-Born Women and Their Children[1]

Mothers[2]	Children	Year of Birth
Amoreltha	Ned Wildy	1817
Mary Bennett	George Hibbert	1800
	Alexander Wright	1804
Sophy Collinridge	Frank Nattie	1805
	Adeline Walker	1792
	Flora Gale	1801
	Lucinda Gale	1803
	Susannah Thomas	1808
	Mary Walker	1813
Dorothy	Richard Drayton	1790
	Louisa	1794
Eve	Dick	1801
Lucy Germaine	Ralph Issaua/Issard	1786
	Henry Germaine	1803
	Isaac Germaine	1806
	Peggy Germaine	1802
Sukey Germaine	George Dyke	1800
Nancy Johnson	Thomas Courice	1811
Sukey Lynch	Jannette (?) Clarke	1800
	Margaret Ann Campbell	1803
	Jafrey Lynch	1824
Jane Roberts	Major Simpson	1717
	Markland Edwards	1801
	Mary Ann Clarke	1785
	Sophy Collinridge	1774 [American-born]
	Susan Edwards	1797
	Jennet (?) Edwards	1799
Maria Thompson	Neptune	1815
	Cecily	1812
	Phillis Thompson	1823
Nancy Wright	Elias Wright	1799
	William Wright	1804
	James Watson	1810

Table continues

Mothers[2]	Children	Year of Birth
Maria Williams Wright	David Douglas	1776 [American-born]
	Robert Johnson	1796
	George Neilson	1788
	Cecelia Williams	1806
Diana Wright	Hagar Wright	1820
Arabella Wright	Lawrence Tharpe	1800
	James Tharpe	1803
	Frederick Simpson	1817
	Jane Lloyd	1799
	Nancy Coombe	1810 [mulatto]
Phillis Wright	Sophia Simpson?[3]	

Notes:

[1] Unless otherwise stated, persons listed are, as in the records, "Negro".

[2] Names of fathers are absent from the records.

[3] No surname was given for Phillis but there is a Phillis Wright in the list as mother of Sophia Simpson. We assume that Phillis and Phillis Wright are one and the same. No age is stated for Sophia who dies shortly after anyhow.

Source: Derived from the Return of Registration of Slaves, 1817, 1820, 1823 and 1826

who carried the surnames of men living on the Palmetto Grove estate. The tendency, it appears, was to, like Jane, mate exogamously. The American-born women clearly had intimate relationships with non-American men and men who lived outside of their plantation precincts. With time, intimacy involving white men occurred as well, for we find mulattoes, quadroons and a sambo among the women's descendants.

The names of the Americans' children who survived in Palmetto Grove until 1832 are listed below by year of birth, colour being mentioned in this list only when an individual is not "negro".

Grandchildren of Americans

Nancy, daughter of the American Arabella Wright, produces *Bellora Gillies*. Bellora was born in 1831 and was a sambo.

Susannah Thomas, daughter of the American Sophy Collinridge, produced a child in 1817; however, she died shortly thereafter.

American Lucy Germaine's daughter Peggy Germaine produces *Frank Davis*. He was born in 1825.

Susan Edwards produced *Selina Lee*, born 1813; *Amelia Pollack*, born 1818; *Robert Markland*, born 1820; *Robert Green* [Quadroon], born 1822; *Mary Ann Markland*, born 1826; *Rosey Williams*, born 1829; and *Jane Deans*, born 1830. These latter are all grandchildren of the American Jane Roberts.

Louisa, who is Dorothy's daughter and Old Judy's granddaughter, produced *Mary*, born 1816. Mary is a quadroon. The name "Mary" sits on the list of enslaved persons without a surname. Could this Mary, granddaughter of Old Judy and child of the mulatto Louisa, be Mary Clarke, the only quadroon on the Palmetto Grove estate and listed as one baptized in the Anglican faith between 1818 and 1831?

There is a set of "Lees" whose matriline is contentious. Charles and Henry Lee are brothers born in 1785 and 1796 to a Susannah Thomas. The name "Susannah Thomas" appears in the list of those enslaved for 1817 and 1820, and there is no evidence up until 1832 that she had died. There is another mention of Susannah Thomas; this time she is the daughter of the American Sophy Collinridge, but this Susannah is nine years old in 1817. How can this be explained? A Jacob Lee is born to Jenny Wright in January of 1820. Jenny's name does not appear on the list of those enslaved; it appears only as the mother of Jacob. Who is Jenny's mother? Are Jenny and Jacob descendants of one of the Wrights brought from America after the War of American Independence? Perhaps there are errors in the list. But what other sources have we?

With these creole descendants of the Americans brought from Georgia–South Carolina and enslaved in Palmetto Grove, St Mary, Jamaica, this work continues in its quest to throw light on the enslaved loyalists as per the request of Wallace Brown and in the quest to note a "moment" of incorporation of one set of Africans of the diaspora into the space of another. I do this by following the descendants of these Americans into the present day. I look at the names on the relevant polling division lists to see what surnames survive and interview the people so named. On this short list are Campbell, Edwards, Johnson, Lee,

Thomas, Walker, Wilson and Wright. The most accessible genealogies are those of the Wrights, and the offspring of Jane Roberts, the Edwardses and the Lees, derived through informal interviews with people having this surname. These will be the focus of our attention.

The Palmetto Grove plantation declared itself a bankrupt sugar estate in 1832, but it was not totally out of business, for we find upwards of fifty-five of its acres being cleared by the management of nearby Petersfield in 1837, one year before emancipation. By 1840, though, it had changed hands. It was then with M.J. Purrier, possibly of the firm of Hibbert, Fuhr and Purrier, to whom the Wrights had mortgaged it in the pre-1817 days. By 1842, it was selling out bits of its backlands. Sales continued through to 1882, as we see in figure 7, where it is noted that the estate's 1,140 acres had been reduced to 810 and were then the property of Reverend Henry Scott. By 1938, Palmetto Grove had been reduced to 745.5 acres. A William Wright, a Bob Thomas and a Jane Campbell were among the purchasers. Alexander Lee was among those paying taxes in 1869 and 1882 for the bits of Palmetto Grove.[33] We will look more closely at such people who carry a surname associated with the descendants of the Americans while appearing on the voters' list for 2007.

There are areas of Wright's Palmetto Grove where only stumps remain to indicate that they were once populated. "Cottage" and "Farm" are among these. The spaces with the highest population density today are Kilancholy, Dean Pen and a part of what was once Cottage but which is now spoken of as the original Palmetto Grove. In Kilancholy, there are still Wrights. In Cottage/Palmetto Grove, we find Edwardses and Lees in significant numbers.

THE BLACK WRIGHTS OF PALMETTO GROVE

If Mary Bennet came to Jamaica in the 1782 evacuation of Savannah-Charleston, she would have done so in someone's arms, for this lady listed in the 1817 slave returns of Alexander Wright of Palmetto Grove was registered as thirty-seven years old and therefore born about 1780. By 1820, at age forty, she was registered as the mother of two male children – George Hibbert, then seventeen years old, born about 1803, and Alexander Wright, then eleven years old, born about 1809. Mary was twenty-three years old when she gave her first child to Palmetto Grove's labour force, and twenty-nine when she gave the second, to whom she also gave the name of the recently deceased master, Alexander Wright. Did Mary Bennett expect her last son to be a memorial to the past existence of the white Wrights of Georgia–South Carolina? She could, of course, have simply named him after his father, for there was an Alexander Wright on the estate, aged fifty-seven, in 1817, seventeen years older than her forty years, who could have fathered her child. This Alexander Wright was, like her, an American-born slave.

When emancipation came in 1838, young black Alexander Wright would have been twenty-nine years old. Like the others of his class and colour throughout Jamaica, he would have been qualified by experience to be a farmer but had no land to farm. Palmetto Grove was no longer a viable estate, but to the extent that there was work there, he would have been able to exchange his labour for cash. He might have farmed on squatted land and sold the produce, or he might have found work on the estates around Nonsuch, Tremolesworth, Hopewell or Crawle. By whichever of these paths he chose, Alexander Wright was able to obtain land in a part of Palmetto Grove called Martin Gully.[34] The yam, cane and potatoes which he planted were able to support his several children, one of whom was Eustace. This Eustace stayed at home while others travelled to and stayed in foreign lands. Eustace produced three girls and two boys. He too farmed, but in addition, he worked in "drogeridge", pulling bananas with his dray and mules to the buying station five miles away. By this time, the early decades of the twentieth century, the banana was king in St Mary, and though Eustace did not have the patronage of the estates, there were enough small farmers to support his business.

Eustace's daughters did well: they were able to buy land. One of their brothers, Leopold, owed the spot on which his one-roomed house was built to the generosity of a sister. Another provided this brother, sightless until very recently, with meals. Nieces and nephews and cousins had taken advantage of the democratized education system in Jamaica to access secondary- and tertiary-level education and to be teachers, owners/drivers of taxis, security guards and storekeepers.

THE LEE FAMILY

If Jane Roberts did come to Jamaica and Palmetto Grove with Nathaniel Hall in 1782, she would have done so in her late twenties. She was already a

mother to Sophy Collinridge and produced several children in Jamaica to live
as enslaved workers on the Palmetto Grove estate. Among these was Susan
Edwards, twenty-three years old in 1820 and therefore born about 1797. Susan,
like her mother, added considerably to Palmetto Grove's labour force. Among
her seven children is her first-born, Selina Lee. Monica Lee, born around about
1944, claims Selina as her great-grand-aunt, making Selina sister to Robert Lee,
Monica's great-grandfather, and to Zander Lee (Alexander Lee), claimed by
Monica as her great-grand-uncle. Zander Lee had the reputation of being able
to dance with a glass of water on his head. Mrs Edwards, a child in the 1930s,
recalls mouthing rhymes in her childhood which told of Zander Lee's dancing
feats.[35] But Alexander Lee was not only a dancer: he was one of the small number
of ex-slaves who managed to own, by 1880, some of Palmetto Grove's lands. He
owned one acre for which he paid taxes in 1868 and in 1881. His acre of land was
in ground provisions at that time, but within twenty years, he would be putting
in bananas as well, this being the most lucrative cash crop of the late nineteenth
and early twentieth centuries in St Mary and other farming parishes.

Zander Lee's nephew, Monica's grandfather, John Lee, was also a landowner,
purchasing seven pounds sterling worth of land at the border of Palmetto Grove
and Woodside.[36] Additional lands bought allowed him to leave an inheritance
for his son John Lee, named after him, and to his grandchildren, Monica and her
brothers. This offspring of the American-born Jane Roberts has given his name
to a landmark: the Lee bridge was built over water which flows through the Lee
property and into the road linking Palmetto Grove to Woodside. Monica Lee
has descendants who live comfortably in England and in Germany.

THE EDWARDS FAMILY

Markland Edwards, son of the American Jane Roberts, paid no taxes, perhaps
bought no land, and, if he did marry, was baptized or was buried, these ceremonies
were not conducted by the Anglican Church, for there is no record that speaks
of his existence. He lives, though, in the hearts and memories of some of the
people in Palmetto Grove and of people in Springfield and Seafield, villages no
more than four miles from Palmetto Grove estate, where written records left
him in 1817. They, whether looking like mixed breeds or pure black, claim him
as their cousin, and they claim that all the many Edwardses are descended from

one ancestor, Isaac Edwards, a very black-skinned man. In 1817, Markland, son of June Roberts, was the only male Edwards on the Palmetto Grove estate. Could he really have peopled Braehead, Montreal, Seafield, Woodpark, Woodside and Rockspring, areas contiguous to Palmetto Grove, on which he was a slave, and which fall in the political division then called the Bagnolds?[37]

There was one other enslaved male with this surname in the surrounding area. He was James Kelly Edwards, one among the five slaves owned by Mrs Patience Hermit of Carpenter's Hut, a place near to Woodside and in the Bagnolds district.[38] Mrs Hermit's slave returns do not give the age of her slaves, but we find this name in the list of enslaved persons baptized into the Anglican faith between 1818 and 1831.[39] While this baptism could have taken place late in his life, it also could have taken place when he was a child. If this were so, then he would be considerably younger than Markland, who was born in 1801. The search for a definitely older male as the father of Markland takes us to Seafield. All respondents, in whatever area we have found them or of whatever skin colour, claim that Markland moved between Palmetto Grove and Seafield, and truly it is in Seafield where most people with this surname claim him as a cousin. This Seafield was in the nineteenth century called Top Hill; it was the property of Hugh Edwards, already mentioned, and there is knowledge today of a person called Dr Hugh Edwards. He is claimed as the first ancestor, and deep in a forested area, there is a revered tomb said to contain his remains. If Markland was, as some Palmetto Grove Edwardses say he was, the coachman of the Palmetto Grove "massa", he is indeed likely to have been travelling frequently from his home estate to surrounding areas and to have been in a position to produce children far and wide in that surrounding area.

The dominant estate in this area now called Seafield was Top Hill. This plantation, along with Dove Hall and Ragsville, was owned by and was the home of the Edwards family – Hugh, Bryan, Zachary Bayley and Mrs E.J., the latter of whom had only one slave, while Zachary Bayley had 216. Politically, the area in which the Edwardses' Top Hill, Dove Hall and Ragville plantations were located is St Thomas in the Vale, a parish which shares a border with St Mary, both parishes sharing the area called the Bagnolds. If Markland was indeed the coachman to the master of Palmetto Grove plantation, he would have been required to drive his master to the Edwardses' plantations for social reasons, if for no other. In any case, Palmetto Grove is in fairly easy walking distance of the Edwardses' plantations. There could be another reason why Markland would have been moving between Palmetto Grove and Top Hill, apart from being the coachman of the master of Palmetto Grove.

In the British West Indies, as in Britain, a significant person's employees were often referred to by his or her name. It was normal that slaves would take the surnames of their masters after emancipation in 1838, if they had not had one before. On Dr Hugh Edwards's Top Hill plantation, there was in 1823 a man named Adam, who, like all the other slaves on the estate, was registered without a surname and was likely to take the master's name after emancipation.[40] He was fifty-five years old then and would have been thirty-three years old when Markland was born. If Adam was the father of Markland and his sisters – Susan born in 1789 and Janette born in 1799 – and also the child of Jane Roberts, then there would have been a relationship, which lasted at least twelve years, between a slave on the Top Hill estate and one of the Palmetto Grove estate, between an enslaved woman born in America and an African, for Adam was an African. He had been bought by his master, Hugh Edwards, the only such one, and the oldest male among his slaves, for Dr Hugh Edwards's male slaves were mostly the children of Rose and Becky, women whom he had bought years before. All these males were under twenty-five years old in 1823. Adam would not have been satisfied with the company of these young creoles and is likely to have walked down to Palmetto Grove, where there were older people and people not born in Jamaica. It is easy to imagine that he could have found a mate there in the American-born Jane Roberts, with whom he could have made Markland Edwards, who as their child and a male would have been likely to move between the two areas. The young creole men in Hugh Edwards's Top Hill were about the same age as Markland and therefore unlikely to have sired him. It would be very reasonable for Markland Edwards to be remembered so passionately as kin in Palmetto Grove, as well as Seafield, if he was indeed a coachman travelling through the area and the child of a man enslaved at Top Hill and a woman enslaved at Palmetto Grove. The oral sources claim that Markland had seven sons scattered throughout the Bagnolds district. It is his son, Isaac, these reports claim, a very black-skinned man who mated with the Watsons and Moores, people who claim genetic attachment to late European arrivals in the Palmetto Grove area. It is this Isaac who, it is said, gave the surname of Edwards to the present brown-skinned Edwards of Palmetto Grove.[41] And there is indeed scribal evidence of such a union, if not "the union": William Edwards of St Thomas in the Vale, the parish which abuts Palmetto Grove and contains Top Hill, made Elizabeth Moore his wife in 1852.[42]

The word is that Markland was a community-oriented person, pointing out the unused areas in which the needy could safely squat, lands abandoned by Palmetto Grove's succession of absentee owners. Markland Edwards laid down a way of treating one's neighbours which could be a model for others. According to Frank Mattie, a young man when universal suffrage came in 1944, young men like himself did not know what getting the franchise was about and instead of going to political meetings would meet in the yard of an older man, there to understand life by searching the Bible for answers while smoking ganja.[43] It was in this setting that Frank heard of Markland Edwards as a man who championed the cause of the less exposed, a position for which men were now vying among themselves by way of the ballot box.

A particular style of basket making is popular and peculiar to this area of St Mary in which the Americans had settled. Though this style resembles that of the South Carolina–Georgia area, neither the people who practise this craft nor anyone else knows this craft to have been passed on by Americans, nor indeed do they recall any old attachment to America. The claim is that the craft was taught formally at the social work centre at Guy's Hill nearby, learned there and taken by one of the Wright line to the village, where it became an industry. All agree that the palmetto trees which provide the raw material for this craft were around in the lifetimes of their grandparents. There are some who claim that Markland brought the plant from the Top Hill area to Palmetto Grove. It could be that the craft was easily learned by those in this area because the old Americans had used the palmetto to do this work before. The same reasoning could go for Zander Lee's ability to dance with water on his head, and for the Africa-inspired funeral rite, dinki mini, to be peculiar to this area. African Americans, possibly originating from the same parts of Africa as the African Jamaicans, might have reinforced these behaviours in the area in which the South Carolina–Georgia Wrights settled at the end of the War of American Independence.

{CHAPTER 2}

The African American in Jamaica in the Mid-Nineteenth Century

IN AFRICAN JAMAICAN SPIRITUAL PRACTICE, IT IS POSSIBLE FOR one to direct an evil spell towards another, but it is equally possible for this same spell to ricochet on the sender; so it has been with Euro-America's transportation and enslavement of Africa's children, whom they called "Negroes". This evil act by the nineteenth century had turned back on Euro-America and forced it to expend a great deal of energy on what was called the "Negro Question". Euro-American thought and action struggled to find an answer to this question. The transported Africans in the Caribbean and North America approached the question in terms of freeing themselves, but this action was successful only in Haiti. British thought and action opted for abolition of slavery de jure in 1834 and de facto in 1838, and gained the love and respect of abolitionists in the United States. David Walker took time out in his diatribe against "white America" to mention Britain positively: "The English are the best friends the colored people have upon the earth ... there is no intelligent *black man* who knows anything but esteems a real Englishman," he declared.[1]

Since British anti-slavery thought interested itself not only in the abolition of slavery but in the condition of the formerly enslaved, Britain became even more attractive to the African American freemen and freedmen, found in comparatively large numbers in the United States. In 1830, there were 319,599 of them, and in 1840, 386,303.[2] In Jamaica in 1834, there were 42,000 – that is, 31,000 plus some 11,000 persons – and in 1844, six years after all people of African descent were legally free, there were 68,529 plus 293,128, totalling 361,657 in Jamaica.[3] The United States considered such American people, whom they variously called freedmen, freemen, free Negroes, free coloureds and free people of colour, to be a national problem, and did so from the late seventeenth century. From as early as 1691, Virginia felt the need to pass a law that there should be no manumission of slaves unless their owners arranged for their transportation out of the state.[4] But in spite of the resistance to their existence, the numbers of these people increased in several states and particularly in the northern states and the upper South. In Delaware, the proportion of the free among the black population moved from 74.1 per cent in 1820 to 86.7 per cent in 1840, and in Maryland from 29.0 per cent to 40.9 per cent.[5] Most state legislatures took steps to staunch this increase. Virginia in the "upper South" was in the forefront again. In 1793, it prohibited the immigration of free Negroes into the state, and one of its favourite sons, Jefferson, as president of the United States, began talks about the establishment of a colony outside of the United States to house "removed" African Americans.[6] Colonization of free African Americans outside of the United States became a solution to the Negro Question favoured by white-controlled state governments throughout the nineteenth century.

It was at this stage of the development of the Negro Question in the United States that Alexander Barclay was sent by the Jamaican Assembly to encourage African Americans to migrate to Jamaica to help to solve its labour problem. Had it been left to Jefferson, the West Indies – Jamaica included, it must be presumed – would have been the place of removal, for at the turn of the nineteenth century, as he pondered the end point of the removal of the descendants of Africans from the shores of the United States to which they had come unwillingly, he said in exchanges with Governor Monroe, "Nature seemed to have formed these islands to become a receptacle of the blacks transported into this hemisphere."[7] Such a "removal" as imagined by President Jefferson and planned by the Jamaican legislature would involve face-to-face interaction and relationship between these two branches of the African diaspora. How could, or did, this interaction affect Jamaican society?

A British West Indian connection was nothing new to America and African Americans. So enamoured were African Americans in the early post-emancipation years with the concept of abolition of slavery and its manifestation in the British West Indies that they celebrated the first of August, the day which marked the emancipation of slaves in the British West Indies.[8] They discussed the issue of emigration to Jamaica and the West Indies in their newspapers and in their conventions. But even before this, they had had historical connections to Jamaica and the other British West Indian colonies which some might have remembered. As "the thirteen colonies in British America", white Americans had owned and run properties in Jamaica and had moved between this island and the mainland with their enslaved workers.[9] This was still so in 1840, though their black companions would not have been slaves, since slavery was outlawed in the British territories. Among the white Americans in post-emancipation Jamaica was Theodore Calkins Fitch, formerly of New York, who in 1841 was petitioning the House of Assemblies to lay acceptance of his right to a machine he had built for his manufacture of jalousies. Another manager was Samuel Whitmarsh, formerly of North Hampton in the United States, who, since 1839, had been trying to set up and manage a silk factory in St Ann, Jamaica. Early in the 1840s, he landed on the beach there with machines, silk culture and houses for his workers and workers from Boston.[10] Black boat men had travelled between the two areas singing songs about each other.[11] It was not difficult to enter Jamaica – the many bays on the north coast made this easy[12] – and by 1840, diplomatic relations between the United States and Jamaica had been established, and the United States had nine consulates around the island. These were in Kingston, Montego Bay, Falmouth, Lucea, St Ann's Bay, Port Maria, Annotto Bay, Morant Bay and Port Morant, which means that there was an official American presence for every thirty miles of the Jamaican coastline and that American vessels with their crews would be often in the eyes of the Jamaican natives and vice versa.[13] Some of these people on both sides would be of African descent. Jamaica and Jamaicans would not have been strange to the coloured population of the United States. Barclay and colleagues can be excused for feeling that coloured Americans might be willing to migrate to Jamaica.

One of the states to which Barclay went in his emigration drive was Maryland. This state considered itself one of the major sufferers from the free Negro presence. It had in 1810 the largest free Negro population in the United States, and this was growing. Between 1755 and 1790, the free Negro population there grew by 300 per cent.[14] By 1810, a quarter of all Negroes in the state were freemen, and there were thirty-four thousand of them. By 1831, a national organization, the American Colonization Society, had established Liberia as the removal point for free African Americans, and slaveholders were on paper and in fact willing to manumit their slaves on the condition that they would settle there. Many of the white Maryland elite were understandably active in the Negro removal schemes and the emigration of free Negroes. Throughout the states and certainly in Maryland, there were emigration chapters helping with funding and with popularizing the programme of Negro removal. Maryland emigration societies early on managed to get the state legislature to vote a sum of one thousand dollars per year for "the establishment on the African coast of free people of colour who had been resident in Maryland during the preceding twelve months before embarkation".[15] Maryland had further streamlined its Negro removal programme by establishing a board of managers. The legislature ordered that all manumissions should be reported to this board, which would then instruct the state-supported colonization society to remove the emancipated slave to Africa or wherever else the society deemed suitable. Newly freed black people who wished to remain in the state could either chose re-enslavement or appeal to a county's orphans' court to remain. Those who rejected both re-enslavement and emigration but were unable to obtain court permission to stay might be forcibly deported.

So strong were those supporting Negro removal in Maryland in their faith that white people and free Africa-descended people could not live comfortably together, and so invested were they in the notion that the solution lay in the removal of the latter to the West Coast of Africa, that they were upset by the slow pace of the national emigration movement and actually acquired a property, which they called Cape Palmas, on which to build their own colony of free Negroes. The emigrants were offered transportation and support in West Africa for six months, along with land in the built-up area and farmlands in the rural area. There were services in part or whole of a medical doctor and eventually a governor. It was in 1831 that Maryland sent its first set of emigrants to West Africa, and in that same year was Sam Sharp's determination to show Britain and Jamaica that African-descended people were tired of being unpaid for their labour, that there was the conflagration in western Jamaica which encouraged Britain to take emancipation seriously. Three years later, there was an emancipation proclamation, and by 1838, when slavery ended in Jamaica, some of these ex-slaves were unwilling to work for their ex-masters even for pay. Britain had chosen emancipation as her solution to the Negro Question, Jamaican slaves had chosen strike, and the US government and individual states had chosen Negro removal.

The discussion about slavery and emancipation did not end in Britain with emancipation. The planters in its West Indian colonies were complaining about their lack of labour. There were those who sympathized with them and their loss of ready and continuous sources of labour and raised the issue of immigration of labour; there were those who felt that the planters were responsible for their shortage of labour, for they offered the ex-slaves no financial incentive for returning to work for them. The issue of importation of labour fell neatly into these two old factions – Sturge and the Society of Friends versus the others. Those who were sympathetic to the planters supported their cry for imported labour, and those who were not feared that imported labour would be made into slaves. When W.A. Mackinnon rose to sell the notion of the necessity for the labour question in the West Indies to be given serious attention, he formulated his speech in terms of this "pro" and "con": "Mr Sturge of Birmingham, and the Society of Friends all oppose such a measure, they assert that you will begin slavery again."[16]

The governors sent to Jamaica in the early post-slavery years appeared unsympathetic to the planters and their vaunted distress concerning lack of ready labour: they felt that the planters were short of labour because they continued to treat the ex-slaves, who they hoped would labour in their plantations, in an inhumane way. Governor Elgin early in the 1840s chose to take a more sociological approach to the development of Jamaica. The future lay not just in imported labour for the planters' estate but in decent prisons for adults as well as youths; in a lunatic asylum, in which the recalcitrant could be redeemed; in a railway, which would allow for the transportation of agricultural products; in education for the children of the former slaves; and in the diversification of the economy.[17] It was clear to him that the ex-slaves were not waiting for their ex-masters to reform themselves so that they could go back to their employment. Elgin's travel around the island had told him that a new class of black people was being born: the small settler. Sufficient labour to support the plantation sector of the economy had to come from elsewhere. He was willing to support immigration of labour. Thirty thousand pounds was to be put aside for the immigration of free Africans, and an Order in Council of 1838 was to be reworked to make immigration of "free coloured" people from the continent of North America more attractive. They were to have citizenship, no military service, no duties on the furniture they would take with them and no contracts to be prewritten, for "they are competent to protect their own interest".[18]

Elgin was here continuing his predecessor's work, for Governor Metcalfe, seeing small settlers as well as planters as necessary to the health of Jamaica, had turned his thoughts to the immigration of labourers, who would work in the way and at the times that planters' businesses required. The Jamaica Assembly passed in 1840 and several years after the acts to encourage immigration.[19] Barclay, knowing of such insults to the coloured population in the United States as not being able to give evidence in court against whites, no matter how well-read they were, while there, emphasized in his *Remarks on Emigration to Jamaica: Address to the Coloured Class of the United States* the absence of discrimination in Jamaica. In trying to coax African Americans to migrate to Jamaica, he made heavy weather of the fact that Trinidad and British Guiana, Jamaica's competition for labour, had come into the British empire as Crown Colonies, mentioning that the "free constitution of Jamaica [which] is more in unison with the liberal form of government which they have, in their native land, [and to which they] anxiously, but in vain, sought participation" would be available in Jamaica more than in Trinidad or British Guiana.[20] The Jamaican and British governments were at pains to insist that emigrants from North America not be asked to make contracts before getting to Jamaica and not be indentured. They had somehow learned that African Americans entertained "extreme repugnance . . . to enter into any apprenticeship whatsoever" and wanted to appease and entice them.[21] But by the end of 1840, Barclay, writing home from New York, as he moved on to find richer and deeper veins of labour, admitted: "I regret to add that the conclusion at which I have arrived, upon the fullest inquiry, is, that although some labourers of color of an eligible description may be obtained from this country, there is no chance whatsoever of obtaining them in sufficient numbers to meet the needs of Jamaica and avert the ruin which is impending, over its agricultural property from a deficiency of labour."[22]

This slow response existed, according to Barclay, despite the fact that Europeans were streaming into the United States and providing competition for what vacancies in the labour market existed. He blamed the paucity of the emigrants going to Jamaica on the free coloured's preference for going to Trinidad (a matter he could not explain), on emigration to Africa but mainly on the work of the abolitionists who were "a powerful bugbear".[23]

Black abolitionist thought in the United States had several streams. There were those who supported emigration because they saw no hope for blacks being treated as citizens in America and because it would consequently suit them to build a state for themselves. Among those who were against emigration was the editor of the *Colored American*, who heard from Brother Wright the story of an African American male, Thomas C. Brown, who, writing from Jamaica in 1837 to his mother, spoke of the "sweetness of the liberty" he had found "in a strange land". The editor responded to Brother Wright:

> One thing Brother Brown lackest: he should not count his life dear unto himself, but stay in our midst, that his noble soul, with so many holy traits of character, might unite with other kindred spirits, and burn out the impurities of our nation. Here is the spot. On this rock should we build, and if need be, die martyrs to principle. No colored man, possessing the talent of Thomas C. Brown should leave the country at such a crisis as this. We would not be willing to go to paradise with every free colored American in this land, and leave the millions of our brethren who are in bondage, behind. Nor would we go slaves and all, if we must leave the body of our white fellow citizens with slaveholding hearts and involved in the enormous guilt of prejudice against color – the sin of hating God's image, because he has dyed it a darker hue. No Brother Wright, nothing short of the purification of the church of Jesus Christ from these foulest – blackest stains, which have been found on her character in any age of her existence, will satisfy our ambition, or make us willing exiles from our OWN, our NATIVE land. [24]

Popular opinion makers and newspapermen like Samuel Cornish and Frederick Douglass held these opinions, hoping and praying, as Martin Luther King would do centuries later, that the whole American society would see the need for inclusion of all in the "blessed community" and approach the Negro Question in terms of inclusion rather than "removal".[25] They worked for this; their readers were inspired to forcibly prevent entry to and to take passengers out of ships in the harbour there to take potential emigrants out of the country. The editor of the *Colored American* wrote in 1840 in his report on an Anti-Trinidad meeting, congratulating himself thus: "The truth is public sentiment among our people in this city, settled down long since in opposition to that scheme, and the matter rendered about dead among us, and we trust our humble efforts have added some to put a stop to it. We have labored for it, believing it to be wrong in principle, and hazardous to the peace and interest of all directly or indirectly concerned."[26]

The people of African descent in Jamaica, despite the fears of elite whites, were not a discrete group. Those called "coloureds" were distinguished from the others. Skin colour, level of education, wealth and of course the distance in time from the state of slavery were markers. When in 1865 the governor of Jamaica, in response to the disturbance in Morant Bay, chose to disband the elected legislature and install a nominated one, Samuel Constantine Burke, a coloured parliamentarian, remarked:

> Why should the class to which I belong, be deprived of their right of free expression? What have they done that they should be disenfranchised? Is it because of the wicked insurrection of the negroes of St Thomas in the East that a class of men who have ever been most loyal and conservative – who have done good service to the State – who have by their honest industry acquired property equal in proportion to their white fellow subjects … who have educated their children so as to fit them to be good and useful citizens – and who have the greatest possible interest in maintaining peace and good order in the community, should be deprived of the right of electing their representatives?[27]

Burke's comment underlines the distance which the "coloureds" put between themselves and the newly freed people of African descent who had genuine and unattended issue with governance. It also underlines the conservative, uncreative and imitative approach of the elite people of African descent in Jamaica's post-slavery existence. There were exceptions, such as George William Gordon, but not enough of them to match the care of the free coloured in the United States for their enslaved brethren.[28]

The British government, by recognizing these coloureds as a group and upgrading their status legally, helped the free coloureds by the 1840s to be a substantial sector in the Jamaican polity, some of whom were reported to have been more abusive of slaves than whites and just as invested in the maintenance of slavery.[29] The elite white Americans, on the contrary, were just as harsh if not harsher towards free Negroes and coloureds than they were even of their enslaved Negroes. Except in some lower southern states such as Louisiana, white Americans, in contrast to white and brown Jamaicans, made no distinction between people of African descent. Without Jamaica's stratification by shade, the way was therefore clear in the United States for the bonds of fellowship to develop between all these people of African descent. The gut-wrenching appeal of David Walker, a learned man and perhaps fairly economically comfortable – certainly comfortable enough to print his book – makes no distinction between people of African descent in terms of colour and treats all coloureds as one, even when he is quarrelling with a black woman who obstructed the escape of her fellow slaves.[30] It was probably such a bonding which resulted in the limited success of "Negro removal" and emigration. African Americans, apart from actively preventing their fellow men from boarding the ships to take them out of the United States, wrote letters to the press, and, more importantly, had regular conventions in which people of African descent in several states could meet to debate issues, clarify positions and express hope. They supported each other's activities: the newspapers – the *Colored American*, the *Liberator*, the *North Star* and the *African Repository* – published news of schools this one or that one had established for blacks, a coloured asylum for orphans and a home for coloured seamen. They raised funds for charities. They carried letters from British West Indian people describing as lies statements that the emancipation of slaves in the British West Indies had ruined these societies. These stay-at-home African Americans were really involved in building a nation: in a later time, they would have been called "race-men". There are those who were super-nationalistic and saw with anger the British attempt to secure labour by emigration as an anti-American action. They noted Britain's influence over African Americans who had fled to Canada and could become part of a British force that could attack the United States, as well as the proximity of the British West Indies to the United States and how African Americans invited to emigrate thither could form a phalanx against their native land.

How many African Americans braved the comments in the newspapers and the anger of their fellow African Americans to accept Barclay's offer and emigrate to Jamaica cannot be conclusively stated. One nebulous quoted figure is "less than 200".[31] Barclay, the agent general of this project, reports that "a few coloured Americans came from Baltimore in 1840 and some came in from Philadelphia in a group of mostly Europeans".[32] For Ewart, the officer immediately below him and functioning in Jamaica while he travelled in search of willing emigrants, the word was that a "few colored people arrived here at various times from Baltimore".[33] A contemporary, George Davison, gave "ten colored from Philadelphia and fourteen from Baltimore".[34] Nancy Prince quotes the American consul as saying that many succumbed to illness.[35] This suggests a larger collection than the twenty-four (ten plus fourteen) people of Davison's estimate. Since Baltimore is mentioned by more than one authority as the place from which the coloureds came, I have chosen to use those who are officially said to have come from Baltimore as the true African American migrants to Jamaica in the 1840s.

Arriving thus on the *Isabella* were Jash Hallius Brown, aged sixty; Absolom Parraway, aged forty-five; Maria, aged thirty-eight, who seems to be Absolom Parraway's wife; and children who could be theirs – Maria, aged sixteen; Miriam, aged fourteen; John, aged twelve; Caroline, aged eight; Mary E., aged six; William E., aged three; and Charles, aged four months. The next year, the *Isabella* brought Caroline Williams, aged seventeen; John Wefe, aged sixty; his wife, aged sixty; and some young people in their twenties: Richard Henderson, aged twenty-two; John Schafflen, aged twenty-eight; his wife, aged twenty-six; Alexander Bell, aged thirty; and his wife, aged twenty-four. On 25 April of that year, the *Northumberland* brought from Baltimore John Franklin, aged twenty-six; Ellen Franklin, aged twenty-eight; Juliana, aged five; John, aged three (both Julian and John were apparently Franklins as well); and the Lloyd family: George, aged twenty-five; Elizabeth, aged twenty; James, aged twenty-three; and Jahnett, aged sixteen. There was, too, William McCulloch, aged eighteen. Coming from Baltimore in June on the *Northumberland* were Washington Hooker, aged twenty-two; Mary Hooker, aged twenty; Nathaniel Cole, aged twenty-three; Elizabeth Laws, aged seven; William Creek, aged twenty-eight; Samuel Wood, aged twenty-four; James Bell, aged thirty; and William Jones, aged twenty-six – the last three came via the *Orb* on 18 August. All apparently came in through Kingston. Ewart adds that a small number of African Americans came in from Philadelphia among a larger number of Germans, Irish and Scottish who had recently immigrated to the United States.[36] Disaggregation of these emigrants according to race is not possible. Those we have identified as African Americans, who answered Barclay's call to labour in Jamaica, tended to come as nuclear families. Their ages ranged from four months to sixty years. Only three of the women were defined in terms of occupation: Annie Parraway, aged sixteen, was listed as a domestic, and Maria, aged thirty-eight, likely to be her mother, was listed as a washerwoman, as was John Wefe's wife, aged sixty. Of the men were four labourers, two bricklayers, two servants, one barber, one shoemaker, one shopkeeper, one carpenter, one boatmaker, one blacksmith and one storeman.

In the society to which they came, people of their colour and economic status were the majority, but they were mostly at the bottom rung of the stratification system. They had only experienced two years of freedom and were struggling to establish their independence from the plantation system. Their lifestyle was under threat, and their response did not consist of letters and discussions in the press; it was, instead, physical confrontation. In Christmas 1840, a few weeks after their arrival, the mayor of Kingston banned the festival which the former slaves had enjoyed annually. He considered their drums and noise, regular features of the festival, to be improper. In the process of the riot, a Roman Catholic church was burned down. The elites and the government had also taken aim at their religious observances: they were congratulating themselves that Myalism, an African religious retention, was on the decrease.

But these African Jamaicans whom the small number of African Americans might have encountered were desperately trying to move from the base of the society. By the mid-1840s, many of them had bought small portions of land and were making themselves into "small settlers" or "peasants", introducing these other status-related terms to the political lexicon. Their land room was likely to have three or four cottages, one with a man and his wife and children, another with brothers and sisters, and another with the mother and father of the man and his wife.[37] They would be cultivating their small portion of land and feeding themselves from this labour. These settlements were more often than not near to the plantation on which they had worked as slaves and where they now worked usually on a job basis. In the immediate year or two post-slavery, they had been in contention with their ex-masters over issues such as accommodation. Now that they were no longer available when the estate wanted their labour but rather when they themselves needed the cash, these ex-masters had been playing fast and loose with the huts in which they used to live during slavery, attaching enormous charges to them.

Special magistracies had been instituted to mediate between ex-master and ex-slave on matters such as this. The reports of these magistrates to the governor and through him to the Colonial Office indicate that much of this animosity had passed by 1840, when the African Americans entered Jamaica – that the masters and servant acts of the post-emancipation period helped to create a more peaceful climate. African Americans coming in as labourers would benefit from this changed situation. The special magistrates seemed all to agree that the problems that planters faced after emancipation were not really due to the reluctance of ex-slaves to work for them but rather due to the lack of capital available to planters and the fear of the loss of a protected market for their sugar; they agreed that although the black people were building their own account businesses, they were still available to the planters, from whom they expected to get money to build their houses and buy luxury items such as horses.

The Africans of the diaspora settled in the United States would find in Jamaica people who looked like them and who were building communities. One stipendiary magistrate expressed his faith in the African Jamaican thus: "I unhesitatingly affirm that the general happiness and prosperity have been accelerated, promoted and consolidated upon a just rational and durable basis."[38] They would find government-aided villages in which Europeans lived. Unsuited to the climate, these Europeans were having difficulties settling in as field labourers. The African Americans would find free Africans who were coming in by the hundreds from Africa's west coast to answer the planters' call for steady and continuous labour.

What could these African Americans coming in from Baltimore in 1840 and 1841 add to the Jamaican society? What did it have to offer them? Barclay had offered them free passage to Jamaica, "comfort" while at sea and protection on arrival until they had found employment. They had also been exempted from military service, and to pander to what the Colonial Office thought was their fear of making a contract or arriving as indentured servants to employers, they had been left to make whatever work arrangements they chose on their arrival in Jamaica. Ewart, the agent general of immigration in Jamaica, said they worked well, and he was sorry that more had not come. Lord Stanley, in the parliamentary debate of 1842, included them in his praise song: "whether from the United States or the coast of Africa, people of African descent had done well".[39] This was, he added, in contrast to the Europeans. Lord Stanley's comments, written from his home in England, were based on the stipendiary magistrates' reports. But Nancy Prince, the African American who arrived on the island in December of 1840 and stayed for some parts of 1841, declared that the American consul in Kingston had told her that "it was folly for the Americans to come to the island to better their condition; he said they came to him every day praying him to send them home".[40] And her personal experience was as follows: "I called on many Americans and found them poor and discontented – ruing the day they left their country, where notwithstanding many obstacles, their parents lived and died, a country they helped to conquer with their toil and blood."[41] She also mentioned that they had left their home under the impression that passage to Jamaica was free and that they were to be taken care of until they could take care of themselves, but they found that they were indebted for the cost of their passage. Some mistake must have been made indeed, as Nancy Prince had gone on to say, for Barclay's *Remarks on Emigration to Jamaica* surely had made these promises. This was an unfortunate way to enter Jamaica. How could they have been so unhappy and still have done such a good job as Ewart and Lord Stanley, depending on stipendiary magistrates' reports boldly maintained?

It was the planters who complained of the dire need for labour. Their major crop was sugar. This required labourers to clean and plough the land, to plant the cane seeds, to water them, to clean the young shoots and to put salt at their roots to keep away snails and other insects, rats and mongoose. Then there is the harvesting of the mature canes. This was a very delicate phase: the canes had to be reaped at the right time. To do otherwise would be to affect the sucrose content of the canes and thus affect the quality of the sugar. All these processes had to be done by hand, requiring many hands, and hands at the time in the process when the canes needed the particular kind of attention. The cut cane had to be quickly put through the mill and its juice boiled, clarified and panned. This, the manufacturing phase of the process, was the only part which required a professional scientist. A chemist was needed to test and assure the quality of the sugar and the molasses. If labour was really the major need of the plantations, a cohort of fewer than two hundred persons would be of little use in an economy in which one sugar estate could be of as many as a thousand acres, and there were many of these.

The African Americans arriving in 1840 and 1841 would be a mere drop in the bucket. None described himself as an "agricultural labourer". Africa-descended people might work better than others in the tropics, as was the going theory, but Baltimore/Maryland was not the tropics. If Nancy Prince quoted the American consul at Kingston truthfully, the mortality rate among the African Americans was high, indicating a difficulty in transference from one climate to the other and a difficulty in managing high-energy tasks such as agricultural fieldwork under a tropical sun. Moreover, these people, left in Kingston to find their own employment and employers, would hardly be able to find their way to rural Jamaica to agricultural labour. The fewer than two hundred African

Americans could make little dent on the labour question, if it really did exist, but a blacksmith, a bricklayer, a carpenter, a boatman, a shopkeeper, a storeman, some common labourers, some washerwomen, servants, domestics, barbers and shoemakers could fit anywhere in an economy in which horses were the main means of transportation; where people wore shoes and needed to have their hair cut and their clothes laundered; where commerce was advancing, with freedmen now having cash, willing and able to buy articles; and where people were accustomed to having household helpers. George Davison, the African American writing from Kingston in 1841 who claimed that emigration from the United States had failed, with only about ten coloured people from Philadelphia and fourteen from Baltimore having come, also opined that the common labourer could not live here, the remuneration of fifty cents per day being too little; but servants, butlers and housekeepers could get plenty of employment and were in great demand, as "the *great* folks here prefer American *servants* to their own, knowing that they are *more industrious*".[42] Davison's observation seemed to be acute, for Hall Pringle, the special magistrate of Clarendon and Vere, indicates that good domestic servants were difficult to get: "the most observable difference between the state of things in Jamaica and other countries is to be found in the difficulty of domestic servants, the exorbitant wages paid them and the consequent unsteadiness in their conduct and engagement". He blames this behaviour on the existence of an alternative source of gainful employment – fieldwork, which allows the worker more freedom: "This, no doubt, has risen from their affluence (in other countries so unusual) from the means they have of acquiring money by field labour, a species of employment they generally prefer as giving them more freedom from the restraint of domestic occupation."[43] The stipendiary magistrate from Savanna de la Mar saw domestics as "disappointing". According to H. Moresby, the special magistrate for Kingston, butlers got fifteen shillings per week, grooms got ten shillings, cooks eight to ten shillings, and maids eight shillings.[44] Douglas Hall's research gives higher values than Moresby's on-the-spot report. According to Hall, in 1841, blacksmiths earned six shillings per day, which would be about thirty shillings per week, and butlers earned more than this. The general labourer, according to Hall, earned one and a half shillings per day for a five-and-a-half-day week, which would translate to about eight shillings per week.[45] The pay for butlering and smithery, which African Americans were likely to get jobs in, given their place in the occupational structure that seemed open to them, was thus indeed an "exorbitant" wage compared to that earned by a field labourer. Household work like butlering and housekeeping, likely to be found in Kingston, seems to be the part of economy and society in which the African Americans accepting Barclay's invitation in 1840 and 1841 would find themselves.

It was part and parcel of the pro-slavery thinking that Africans, whether at home or abroad, were uncivilized savages, saved only by their association with white people of the Euro-American brand. It was even argued that kidnapping, transportation and enslavement in the New World was God's design to make them worthwhile. If it could be proven that the abolition of slavery had brought social mayhem, and that the Africans had deteriorated, this would be a positive for slavery. The British West Indian islands and Jamaica in particular were close to the United States and had easy access to each other. The governor of Jamaica in his 1842 speech to the House of Assembly had noted:

> The British West Indian colonies seemed destined to exercise an influence very disproportionate to their territorial extent upon the general interest of humanity. The recent history furnishes the example of the most generous sacrifice to principle and duty which the annals of the world record. They are still regarded by other nations as the theatre of the great experiment which may affect the doom of thousands now in bondage, of millions yet unborn.[46]

Several on both sides of the abolition argument came to Jamaica to look and, having looked, to remount their arguments for or against emancipation and the capacity of the Africa-descended to relapse into barbarity. Anti-emigration as they generally were, the African American newspapers published news that showed the British West Indian islands as progressing better after emancipation than they were before. The *Colored American* published on 2 March 1839 a letter signed by Amos Townsend and written from New Haven on 21 February 1839, in which this gentleman shares comments from a Mr Hayes from "Barbadoes [*sic*]", Mr Jackson of St Vincent and Mr Nelson of Trinidad, stating that "the emancipation of slaves . . . works very well" and that the plantation "produces more and yields a larger profit than it has before. The emancipated slaves now do in eight hours what was before considered a two day task."[47] These men had come to the United States to confer with the architects for the "removal" of free Africans from the United States – Mr Calhoun and Mr Clay – in the hope that their islands could be the removal destinations. People with no involvement with the motion wrote in and were published. Vide once more the testimony of George Davison: his letter, written in Kingston on 15 January 1841, when some of the African American emigrants would have just reached Jamaica, and published on 6 March 1841, when another group was about to set off from Baltimore, reads:

> You may perhaps want to hear the state of the island. There has been no great change, except for the better; *commerce has increased double this year* – agriculture has improved – the people are becoming settled – the planters begin to see where their interest lies, viz: in the treating people more liberally which a few of them are beginning to do: very few of them will give more than 25 or 37 cents per day, for labourers; if they would give 37 and a half, they would get plenty of labourers; many labourers are idle in different parts of the country, because they cannot get good wages. [48]

George Davison could have been reading from any stipendiary magistrate's report. Even Nancy Prince, who claimed to have been treated deceitfully by her co-religionists in Jamaica, and who reported on the ill treatment of African Americans, had good words for the ex-slaves. She had been to the market and had counted the different stalls – ninety-six for vegetable and poultry, all under cover; nineteen for fresh fish; eighteen for pork; thirty for beef; and eighteen for turtle – all "regular built markets" and run by coloured men and women. And this was not the only market. She was forced to conclude: "Thus it may be hoped they are not the stupid set of beings they have been called; here *surely we see industry*; they are enterprising and quick in their perception, determined to possess themselves, and to possess property besides and quite able to take care of themselves."[49] She had stated these truths in her book, which got ringing endorsement from the *Liberator*: "we should like to have a copy of the book". Harrison, the US consul in Kingston who described Jamaicans as "idle worthless vagabonds", however, sent negative articles to his office in Washington. He sent newspaper clippings of the 1841 riot in Kingston,[50] he sent letters of disgruntled Jamaicans, and he sent his own opinions of the ex-slaves: "Emancipation has instilled in the people a haughty behavior which results in various affronts. Jamaican blacks refuse to pull their hats off when coming into a gentleman's home. They always make a white man give way to them when walking in the streets and habitually insulted whites."[51] He complained too that there was no justice in Jamaica for the white man, as the stipendiary magistrates were always taking the side of the ex-slave.

African Americans would have been happy to hear the complaint of the US consul in Kingston that African Jamaicans were not subservient to whites, and they would have been very happy to hear of their industry as reported by Nancy Prince, for they understood that Euro-Americans thought of behaviour in racial terms and people of African descent as universally and genetically stupid and lazy. It was one of the goals of the African American elite to prove this to be false, as is reflected in the comment from the editor of the *Colored American*: "We cannot remove the slander that are now heaped upon us, only by a long course of unceasing activity and persevering industry in those pursuits which lead to intelligence and respectability."[52] African America could handle the calumny about the capacity of the black man by referencing contrary reports concerning the freed people of the British West Indies through their newspapers, but they wanted more: to show the world that the Negroes were industrious, intelligent and respectable. They would achieve this through education. Thus, they established in America several schools for African Americans and set up temperance societies. It was not enough to do this at home: African and Africa-descended people, wherever they were, had to be shown to be "intelligent", "respectable" and "industrious". It is this thrust for a spotless character that began to take anti-emigrationists closer to emigrationists and gave us a new African American branch of thought and action: "civilization". Civilizationists had to take the message of intelligence, respectability and industriousness and temperance to whatever points those who looked like them could be found. Jamaica caught their eye. Although they had seen men of their colour sitting on the bench in courts in Jamaica (a thing unheard of at home), had seen them in the assembly and knew of Wolmer's school, in which children of all colours sat and where one of the brightest boys was very black-skinned,[53] they knew that not all Jamaicans could attain such heights: they came to help the Jamaican freedman to stretch further and to reach such heights. Like Alexander DeGrasse, graduate of Newark college with a master's degree, known for his interest in black education, and who had travelled on the same boat to Jamaica as Nancy Prince and performed the divine service to her delight,[54] they came to offer education to the freedman and his children who by all accounts were eager for it; they came as Lisle and Baker had decades before to see to it that their brethren be helped to a seat in Heaven by exposure to Christianity.[55] Nancy Prince herself had set off for Jamaica for similar reasons: to change the "moral condition of the emancipated, to raise up and encourage the emancipated inhabitants, and teach the young children to read and work, to fear God and put their trust in the Saviour".[56] She had been recruited by white missionaries who had been in Jamaica since 1837, convinced, as Gale Kenny tells us, that as abolitionists they should not just look to the British West Indies as a model for emancipation in America, their own country; they should move to Jamaica to "enact the world they could not yet have in their own nation".[57]

They came too because of the free produce movement. From as early as the 1820s, Quaker abolitionists in North America and Britain had thought and tried to act on the principle that to consume slave-grown food was detrimental to the anti-slavery cause and had supported a campaign for using free-grown food and fabrics. The far-sighted notion was that if the produce of the slave state was boycotted, the slave states would have to cease using enslaved labour in their industry, and so slavery would dry up and die on the vine.[58] Action supporting that theory would see more creative use of the soil and the companion creation of agriculturalists and agribusinesses. This campaign had never entered fully into the arsenal of the anti-slavery movement, but we find the Reverend Pennington, formerly a non-emigrationist, raising a related issue at a national convention meeting at Liberty Street Presbyterian Church in New York. He would recommend emigration not to Africa, Asia or Europe, "but from the crowded cities and servile employments, to the manly and dignified labours of agricultural life, to promote the principles of temperance, frugality".[59] Civilization and emigration were moving closer together, as was racial bonding across political and geographic borders. Pennington's hopes for the African Americans fitted well into those of the Colonial Office for the newly freed African Jamaicans. The governor stressed in 1845 the need for ex-slaves' education. There was also the hope that their agricultural skills would be improved, especially as, according to some special magistrates, their approach to farming could lead to the depletion of the soil.[60] What was the Colonial Office's plan for the development of territory? The administrators of Jamaica seemed to be moving towards a new approach to agriculture. The existence of a division in the Colonial Office called Land and Emigration, which oversaw the immigration of labour in the colonies, suggests a revolutionary approach to land use occasioned by immigration. The problems with the sugar industry and the Sugar Duties Act, which would diminish returns from that fallen "king", encouraged the island's managers to think of other agri-industries. The governor reported happily on the existence of the silk plantation in St Ann;[61] a sample of a kind of hemp made from the plantain and banana leaves at the home of Stipendiary Magistrate Bourne, who even had a school of industry at his home, was sent to the Colonial Office;[62] the governor reported on an attempt to make linen out of a plant called "Pengine";[63] and specimens of sea island cotton were sent as well.[64] The thinking population was on board: there was a proliferation of agricultural societies all over, for the idea that there should be the encouragement of more "scientific ways of farming" was gaining ground. They wrote to the *Falmouth Post* suggesting new sources of commercial use for plants such as calabash as utensils (I suppose), mango for starch, coconut for fibre, and breadfruit and naseberry for their "milky substance".[65] There was much talk in this local newspaper about the introduction of the plough and even of efforts to create one to suit the Jamaican terrain. There was news of the great efforts of the agricultural societies to popularize scientific farming by the organization of ploughing matches and contests for the best arrowroot, cotton, ginger and indigo.

It seems that the central government was not just interested in the recovery of the sugar plantations and agricultural labourers to do this, but also had in mind the restructuring of the economic base of the society. Barclay, in his search for labour, had from 1840 written to Higginson that "agricultural labourers are most required but mechanics and domestics are also needed".[66] And very positive words were said about the skills and the intelligence of African Americans and African Canadians. A more catholic approach to development of the island and of agriculture would fit well with those of the African American immigrants. American missionaries, here since 1837, had, according to William Wenyss Anderson, "settled in the mountains of Jamaica", places that were "now little centers of civilization, industry and piety".[67] The area in which these "radical abolitionists" settled was between Kingston and Annotto Bay. They had come "not just look to the British West Indies for a model of emancipation; some moved there to enact the world they could not yet have in their own nation", as Gale Kenny has opined.[68] The chief of these missionaries was Reverend Ingraham, very likely the same with whom Nancy Prince came to work. With him were Amos Dresser, Julius Beardsill, Stewart Renshaw, Ralph Tyler and

George Harvey. Their vision, intending to replicate the Oneida Institute system of education, which many of them had experienced in New York, was of self-supporting churches. They encouraged good farming techniques and offered hands-on experience in industrial arts. These were white American missionaries and abolitionists, but their work was sanctioned by black abolitionists such as the Reverend Pennington.

In January of 1840, Reverend Pennington, a black abolitionist, called a meeting about the condition of the people of colour on "this island" to discuss the condition of Jamaica, to where a small number of his compatriots were migrating and would migrate.[69] Pennington was the quintessential African American elite of the 1840s. He had begun life as an illiterate slave and ended it with the award of an honorary doctor of divinity from the Faculty of Theology at the University of Heidelberg, Germany. In between these events, he had run away from his master and earned his living at twenty years old as a blacksmith in Long Island, New York. He found a way of educating himself and was offered a position as a teacher at an all-black school. Changing the educational status of his black brethren became one of his life's goals, whether this eventuated in the building of schools, the founding of temperance societies or writing books such as *A Textbook of the Origins and History of the Colored People*; his autobiography, *The Fugitive Blacksmith or, the Events in the History of James W.C. Pennington*; and a colleague's biography, *A Narrative of Events of the Life of J.H. Banks*.[70] His passionate support of education for black people was so well known that during his 1846 visit to Jamaica, Governor Elgin asked him to make a tour of the island to encourage an interest among the ex-slaves in education.[71] It must have been on this tour that he visited the white American missionaries in the parish of St Mary and wrote on 20 February of 1846 from "Annatta [*sic*] Bay" to his fellow abolitionist Brother Tappan, speaking highly of the work being done by these white missionaries.[72] He must have approved of a curriculum which made farm produce a central part of its programme, for should this succeed, another hope of his could materialize: the resurrection of the free produce movement. The foundational thought behind this movement, which began in England, was that there was a connection between the price of a slave and the demand for slave produce. The argument was that by purchasing slave-produced goods, one employed a slave, thus maintaining the institution of slavery. Black abolitionists and their white allies asked their audience to boycott "slave-produced rice, sugar, cotton on the understanding that such action would lower the price of slaves and dry up slavery's profits".[73] The corollary was that collectives of black farmers could thus also gain economic freedom and, in this instance, that the kind of education brought by the white missionaries in St Mary, Jamaica, could prove to be an economic weapon in the charge against slavery wherever it was practised. An approach to the economy which favoured the introduction of a wider variety of crops would be attractive to abolitionists such as Pennington interested in self-employment at farming by African Americans.

Pennington, like most men of his status, was an avid abolitionist and travelled to Europe frequently to make his point and to help to set up abolition societies. Like most men of his status, he was against the efforts of the American Colonization Society to "remove" African Americans to Africa. In praising the work of the white missionaries in St Mary, Pennington approved the kind of education offered by them, for such an education could lead to self-employment and independence, and the industry and piety that William Wenyss Anderson would describe in the early 1850s as existing in the mountains of St Mary, where these white abolitionists served.[74] In this same year, Pennington was in conversation with the agent general of immigration in Jamaica and, through him, the Colonial Office in Britain about a plan to allow African American fugitives from the US South into Jamaica as settlers.[75]

Elite African Americans, mostly religionists, six years before, in 1840, had given no support to, and in some cases passionately opposed, Barclay's emigration scheme. He called them "a powerful bugbear".[76] Pennington among them, they had also opposed violently the emigration programme of the American Colonization Society. Under this latter programme, African Americans who emigrated to Liberia got house spots in the urban area and farmlands in the rural area free of charge. Their transportation costs were met, and they were given support in West Africa for six months. This was more than Barclay and Jamaica had offered. It was also a chance to be a self-employed farmer. How is it that Pennington in 1846 was negotiating with the Jamaican government for African Americans to go to Jamaica as settlers? He had clearly modified his approach to emigration, now recommending to an African American audience "emigration not to Africa, Asia or Europe but from crowded cities and servile employments to the manly and dignified labour of agricultural life, to promote the principles of Temperance, Frugality . . . ready and willing to fight in the glorious cause of freedom".[77]

There must have been something that made the Jamaican situation different from the Liberian situation. "Manliness" and "freedom" must have seemed to Pennington more possible in Jamaica than in Liberia. Emigration to Liberia had emerged out of the white American desire to cleanse American society of the people of African descent; emigration to Jamaica would be the brainchild of African Americans and would be motivated by oneself rather than by those who wished for one to be "removed". Pennington would have had little association with the white governing classes of his country, but we find him in 1846 bringing a proposition to Jamaican authorities who were white. This must mean that he saw himself as able to communicate as an equal with the white people and even officials in Jamaica and that he was comfortable in the Jamaican society with its whites, browns and blacks.

There were other African Americans who were forthright in their approval of the nature of Jamaican society. Thomas Brown wrote from Jamaica on 17 February 1837 to say that in that society, he felt like "a man among men".[78] Robert Douglas wrote from Kingston in 1848, his letter introduced by editorial comment, that he was "an artist of skill and promise, who in this country was unable to gain a livelihood by his profession . . . and has therefore emigrated to a country where he hopes the colors he uses, and the way he uses them will be the test of his merit, rather than that upon his body which he can neither put on nor rub off".[79] This Robert Douglas was comfortable in Jamaica. His letter is full of the beauty of the island, though he did find the costs exorbitant, and he found several rogues among the people. Douglas was a trained Daguerreotypist. He found many others of this profession in Jamaica principally American. Finding men in one's line of business in a country would have made that country even more attractive. George Davison, writing in the year that a group of Americans answered Barclay's call for labourers, speaks as if he is breathing new fresh air: "I am now in a free country where there is no distinction on account of color, the only distinction known here is loyalty and disloyalty, vice and virtue. In America how different! There every man is judged according to his color."[80] He writes about the easy mixing of whites and coloureds; of the existence of black magistrates, earning what seems to him a very decent living; of learned black men, such as Robert Hill, holding significant positions such as secretary

to the governor; and of the many black men being in the governing council –
he personally knew some of these. George Davison was clearly moving in the
upper middle class and was obviously surprised at and approving of a state of
affairs which allowed him to rub shoulders with this class.

African Jamaicans were at the same time finding merit in an African
American–African Jamaican relationship. On 28 April 1846, a group of high-
powered Jamaican coloureds – Edward Vicars, Peter Constantine, George Ennis,
Peter Jellep, James Millington, George Reilly and Robert Duaney, among others –
convened at a meeting at which they launched the Jamaica Hamic Association.
The point of this association was to encourage commerce between African
Americans and African Jamaicans: "In whose hands, whether in America or on
this island, is this important department [commerce] of national prosperity?
In the hand of friends or foe, of the advancement of the African race?", they
asked themselves. And they concluded,

> We fear that with few exceptions these interrogations must be answered in the
> negative. This state of things ought no longer to continue. Did we possess a body of
> merchants in America, and a corresponding body in Jamaica, impressed with that
> indelible type which is the peculiar characteristic of the African race, we cannot
> mistake the vast amount of good that would be accomplished on all sides. White
> Americans visiting our parts, and having to transact business, for the most part,
> with men of our hue, would be found ere long to have acquired more humane and
> rational views of our race. They would stand rebuked as regards the prejudice and
> oppression which evil minded men are ever disposed to invoke against us and to
> inflict upon us. – They would return from our shores with more favorable impres-
> sions, and the re-action upon North American slavery would be irresistibly great.[81]

These men believed in the therapeutic powers of commerce – it could,
and would, "unite the most repulsive of mankind in enlightened commercial
intercourse, and their antagonism will be found to lose its edge, and the feelings
of civility and politeness succeed to its place". These African Jamaicans felt,
their document continued, that "with the means which Commerce supplies,
enlightenment can be carried forward, religious and philanthropic institutions
sustained, and the natural resources which God caused to be buried in the
bosom of the soil, may be successfully developed, and made to contribute . . .
to universal happiness, which is calculated to bind all mankind in one common
brotherhood".[82] They agreed to solicit the cooperation of their white anti-slavery

friends, whom they apparently thought had yet to see commerce as a binding factor. They invited the Reverend Pennington to this meeting because they wanted him to try to get African Americans on board. Formal cooperation between two parts of the African diaspora was envisioned here, as would be greatly expanded in the thought and action of Marcus Garvey. Agriculture and commerce were here seen as the activity which this pre-Garvey effort to link people within the "wide range of our dispersion" into a therapeutic bond would proceed. The African Americans in turn proposed to establish a committee of thirteen to more seriously respond to the suggestions of the Jamaica Hamic Association.

Alexander Barclay had a far sight. In the light of his dismal failure to get African Americans to Jamaica as labourers, he commented: "They will eventually find their way."[83] The records do not say whether the Pennington plan worked, but we certainly know that men like Highland Garnet and Samuel Ward, black abolitionists like Pennington, served in Jamaica. Highland Garnet came to Jamaica as the first black missionary to Jamaica for the United Presbyterian Church and pastored a church in Westmoreland where he kept a school for about two hundred students.[84] If the black Jamaican needed a character recommendation, H. Highland Garnet could give it to them. In October 1854, he wrote to the British and Foreign Anti-Slavery Society: "it is becoming more, and more apparent that the emancipated people, use their liberty with more moderation, and propriety, than their former masters exercise government over them. It is also a fact which ought by no means to be forgotten, that if the former slave holders are sinking, the emancipated are rising daily."[85]

Samuel Ringgold Ward, also a black abolitionist, was, like Pennington, associated with the produce movement. If the complaint that he had acquired land in Jamaica and was now a planter is true, then Ward, now a producer, would have had the basics for realizing the goal of producing saleable goods with free labour. Jamaica was in the 1850s no longer a place trying to attract African American labour, or even one with the help of which one could imagine what freedom in the United States would be like. It had become a place of refuge, where the old and wise black abolitionist, very literate, well-read and philosophical, stopped in what seemed to be a residential life, lived in different states in the north of the United States, in Canada, and in Britain and in Jamaica. They had the ear of the most highly placed and apparently felt at home here. Those who not only administered school but actually taught would be in face-to-face contact with ordinary Jamaicans as well. It would be so too for those who pastored churches. One such as John Willis Menard felt very much at home, still operating within the notion of "civilizing" people who looked like him; he founded a literary society, and was so openly involved with radical politics, that is, supporting the rise of a peasantry over the enrichment of the planter class, that he was charged with association with the Morant Bay rebellion and deported.[86]

Our historical excursion in the preceding pages shows that few if any African Americans in the 1840s ploughed alongside African Jamaicans, sharing their grouses and their pleasures as agricultural labourers. They did not swap songs or stories or share grandchildren. The connection implicit in the behaviour and hopes of the African Americans was with the middle-class people of African descent, African Jamaicans who called themselves "coloureds". These were the aspiring men of commerce, the professionals, lawyers, assemblymen, journalists, members of literary societies – people who had already proven themselves to be "industrious", "respectable" and "intelligent", the marks of the civilized for Pennington. If there were others like Reverend Richard Warren willing to share a pulpit with the likes of Paul Bogle, the peasant preacher who would, in the next decade, be accused of creating a riot and summarily hanged, my search has not unearthed them. The African American attitude to the newly freed seemed principally an inferior/superior notion of people needing to be civilized, a state which required education and an economic base comfortable enough to allow the enjoyment of the vote. In African Americans like Pennington and the African Jamaicans of the Jamaica Hamic Association was a glimmer of the pan-Africanism that would be clearly outlined in later nineteenth-century thinkers such as Alexander Crummell; but the actual path for these early nineteenth-century thinkers lay through the development of an international black middle class, it seems.

{CHAPTER 3}

Marcus Garvey and the
African Americans

JOSEPH B. EARNEST WRITING OF THE AFRICAN AMERICAN of Virginia in the late nineteenth century calls him or her a "joiner".[1] The church, he says gave the African American the opportunity to "jine", there being in it many societies such as the temperance committees, the Sunday School committees, the home mission and the foreign mission, plus societies such as the Sisters of Charity, the Young Sons of Liberty, the Loving Sisters of Worship and the Zion Travelers. To this list one could add, from newspaper advertisements for the twentieth century,[2] the many lodges: the Invisible Lodge of the Odd Fellows, the Knights of Pythia, the ancient and accepted Scottish Rite masons, the National Grand Tabernacle of the Galilean Fishermen, the independent Order of Good Samaritans, the Daughters of Samaria and the Elks. This comment could be applied as well to the other states. It seems that blocked out of the national society, except for the few Reconstruction years, then blocked again since the Tilden-Hayes compromise, the African American society divided itself into internal church groups and lodges.

These churches and lodges stretched across several states. To keep in touch with each other, members had to and did travel far out of their states. In August of 1915, the newspaper called the *Commonwealth* advised its readership that a big group of people left Virginia for the annual meeting of the ancient and accepted Scottish Rite masons in Los Angeles, California. People journeyed from other states as well. We are informed, too, that the Elks had a big meeting in Philadelphia, which opened with a street parade. Lodges from Richmond, Virginia, were well-represented there. Several of these African American lodges carried names with a Christian Euro-American resonance. They were associated with "Samaria", "Galilea" and "Zion" – terms from the Christian Euro-American sensibility. Then there was "Elk", a Scandinavian dog according to *Webster's Dictionary*, and Pythia, a Greek oracle. And the descriptor "Scottish" appears as well. When the fraternities and sororities with their Greek letters of the alphabet are added, one sees African American points of reference as European.

No collection of Africans of the diaspora in enslavement had a history of central authority being located within the family. Orlando Patterson recounts a tale told by someone who had experienced slavery in the United States. It is worth retelling, for it aptly demonstrates this ex-family location of authority with respect to the enslaved people of the African diaspora:

> I had a sister, my older sister, she was fooling with the clock and broke it, and my old master taken her and tied a rope around her neck – just enough to keep it from choking her – and tied her in the back yard and whipped her I don't know how long. There stood mother, there stood father, and there stood all the children and none could come to her rescue.[3]

Authority, as in the case above, resided outside of the family. All social beings recognize an authority figure and are likely to seek one if there is none such to recognize. The African American, as with all other Africans of the diaspora, would be looking in the post-emancipation period for one which replaced the "master" – an authority figure who brings order to social life and in whom are the laws by which individuals are conjoined. Seeking and joining others who have found this figure would be part of the post-emancipation culture. "Joining", as Earnest described, would be part of post-emancipation activity. When Marcus Garvey came to the United States in 1916, he would have met an African American collection of individuals eager to join something which was larger than themselves and which would have authority over them, to interpret and define aspects of a new life for them.

In the first decades of the twentieth century, the African American was a rural person,[4] not yet wedded to seeing a physician annually and a dentist semi-annually. Of course, like anybody else, they were aware that the human body was susceptible to ill health and that the dead needed to be buried and in fine styles, as in Africa and other places of the diaspora. Lodges like that of the Sons and Daughters of Esdras came to the rescue; they offered benefits for sickness and death. To keep themselves healthy, African Americans turned to home medicines and, those who could afford it, to patent medicines. As in Jamaica, Linda Pinkham's medicine was offered as a cure for women's problems.[5] Then there was, at the turn of the century, Mrs Dennison, who was advertised as being able to cure diseases – fits, silica, poison of all kinds – all within nine days; and James P. Kerr, with his magnificent beard, told the African Americans about the old Indian herb cures. Add to this advertisements for Dr Williams's pink pills, which helped a seventy-three-year-old woman to regain the strength of her youth, and, as in Jamaica, the promotion of the sarsaparilla as a good bush medicine. It seemed from the advertisements that the population suffered and needed healing from rheumatism, lumbago, neuralgia and dyspepsia, as well as needing laxatives, kidney cures and chill cures. Given their racial situation and lack of funds, African Americans might not have been comfortable waiting in a medical doctor's office, and there were then only two black medical schools graduating black doctors – clearly not enough for the population.[6] Patent medicines, which allowed self-medication, would have to do.

If the early twentieth-century African American newspapers and their advertisements tell us of the concerns of the African American of the time, we certainly have to recognize a concern not just with health of the body but with a reconstruction of it so that it approximates the Euro-American somatic norm. There were advertisements for "high brown" face powders and several ointments to "brighten" the skin, to make "kinky hair soft and luxuriant", and the large advertisements of a woman with hair so long she was sitting on it, hair that the reader could have if she used the right pomade. Indicated here is a feeling that the physical features with which a black-skinned, kinky-haired person had been born were not good enough. Advertisements like "Don't have kinky hair, make your hair straight, soft, flossy, glossy", makes "kinky hair", natural to most people of African descent, seem more like an illness to be cured. These advertisements appeared in all the newspapers of the first two decades of the twentieth century, suggesting that people of African descent saw their natural physical endowments as illnesses which could be cured by ointments.

Bishop Henry Turner died in 1915, in the same year as the influential black principal of Tuskegee, Booker T. Washington. For most of his public life, Bishop Turner had seen the African American's hope for advancement in life by emigration to Africa.[7] He had found ships and actually taken people to Africa;

he was not alone in his efforts. In the year after his death, on 5 December 1916, there was a scathing comment on emigration to Africa: we are told of Sam, normally mentioned as "chief", here called "king" and "emperor", who had "lured" coloured folks to the African coast with his injection of "mysticism and formality" into his advertisement, making "folks" now "victims scattered on the African coast". This appears in the *National News* of November 1916 copied from New York. There was no plenitude of advertisement inviting people to emigrate to Africa, but there was one on 26 June 1920 in the *Richmond Planet*:

> A SHIP TO GO TO AFRICA OUR FATHERLAND. To go to Liberia now, one must travel nine days to England then wait as long as the ship owner there wishes you to and then travel fourteen days before you reach Monrovia. By our ship, you go from New York to Charleston, South Carolina direct to Monrovia in twelve to fourteen days for half the present rate and half the time. Don't dream, get in our drive, take stock now and help the most glorious thing negroes ever did. Make all money orders, drafts and checks payable to the Africa Steamship and Sawmill Company. For further information, write the company 2643 South Street Philadelphia, PA or L.G. Jordan DD, Campaign manager.[8]

Garvey's *Black Star Line* was clearly not the only ship about to make its way from the United States to Africa, nor was immigration of African Americans to Africa an original Garvey idea. Apparently, the links with Africa through migration existed and continued to exist before Garvey entered the United States and while he was there. In the *National News* of 16 August 1917, we get a report of a group of African Americans going off to Africa which is associated with a very negative notion. The report of this visit to Africa appears under the headline "In Our Stead and in His Name to Bury Themselves in Africa".

But all is not negative about Africa nor about emigration in the thinking of the African American of the first decades of the twentieth century, for we find news of a Dr Johnson honoured by being made a knight of the order of African redemption for his good work on the colonization scheme. We find, too, in the *Commonwealth* of 1915 a Lott Carey convention being mentioned. The object of this convention was "the prosecution of the work to which Lott Carey gave his life". This was building churches in Africa and sustaining missionaries there. And there are editorials in the *Commonwealth* of 1915 on the matter of colonization. The newspaper of 5 December 1916 shows the Abbysinian delegation being welcomed by Dr W.W. Brown of the Metropolitan Baptist Church. Africa was in the thinking of the African American of the first two decades of the twentieth century, but it was not a place to migrate gladly to; it was a place with which to make a religious connection.

It does appear that late nineteenth-century fissures in African American thought concerning colonization and civilization, between migration to Africa and the struggle for civil rights at home, still existed in the early twentieth century when Garvey entered the United States.[9] We are left with the understanding that for some vocal African Americans, Africa and Africans were welcome in their lives as continentals, a set of people related but distinct from they who were of the African diaspora, who were ex-Africans turned into Americans. Marcus Garvey entering the United States in 1916 would have met a people for whom Africa did have some meaning but who were not in solidarity concerning what this meaning was. There was no such conflict over the functional meaning of "race". African Americans definitely involved themselves with issues of race, but this meant race in the United States. As such, they advertised meetings held or to be held by coloured people; they continued as in the early nineteenth century to consider the issue of "racial uplift". Byron Gunner, president of National Equal Rights League, asked on 15 July 1916 for a national race congress on citizenship rights, it is reported in the *New York Age*, and such a congress is indeed called for 14–16 September in Washington, DC, at Mount Carmel; this three-day congress was "great", the *National News* trumpeted. It was helped to be so by the coloured press, which was duly congratulated. Such meetings discussed ways and means of getting the white-controlled sociopolitical order to recognize coloured people as their equals. One article of 28 February 1920 by Lieutenant William Clifford in the *Richmond Planet*, entitled "A Ringing Appeal to the Negro Race", reflects well the African American hope and case for inclusion, pointing out as it does that the Civil War had caused the abolition of slavery and that the First World War had been instrumental in opening wider doors of opportunity to the coloured race: "time has arrived", the writer opined, when "self-determination should be applied to the Negro race in America". He was addressing a group of coloured men, many of whom had fought in the First World War and were meeting in Washington to discuss the issues he raised.

Empowered by the bonding and the support with sickness and death which the lodges and churches offered in the second decade of the twentieth century, African Americans faced the white power structure and the resurrection of the

Ku Klux Klan in nine states, as stated by the *Richmond Planet* of 16 October 1920, with cartoons meant to inspire shame in this white power structure. One such cartoon pictured a large white man with a rope and a fire stick; it is captioned "American Outlaw". A message coming out of the man's mouth says: "I am not a savage, a Wildman not a heathen. I am AMERICAN, A THUG, A RED FLAG, A BOLSHEVIST, A LYNCHER"; another showed a little white man with a gun, with President Lincoln telling him: "Take em back Sonny, that's a dangerous toy. Next time tell your Uncle Sammy all about them first." Cartoons posted in the *National News* were also intended to arouse the African American to action. A black man is pictured with something in his hand marked "ballot". Enter a wiry old black man, who says: "Don't wine, cry, crawl nor petition but STAND on your FOOT like a MAN. THAT AND ALL TEMPORAL THINGS WILL BE crowded UPON YOU." It seems from the newspapers that African Americans felt they knew how to achieve parity with whites: if they changed their colour to "high brown", straightened their "knotty kinky" hair, used skin whitener, attended college and used the ballot, the door of the polity would be opened to them.

The race situation was on the general mind, but rarely in association with other international black suffers. One of the coloured newspapers does mention, in 1919, that a pan-African congress had been called and that W.E.B. Du Bois had gone on behalf of the National Association for the Advancement of Colored People (NAACP). The news is, as the editor of the *National News* relays it to the reader, of Du Bois's action and that of the NAACP, for the report gives no further information on pan-Africanism or what Du Bois did at the congress. The reader is only told that the NAACP feels that "civilized negroes should have the same rights as other people". The content of the news indicated an interest in the state of being "civilized".

With this notion of civilization came class prejudice in the African American ranks, and this is not a twentieth-century phenomenon. Earnest, in discussing the Negro church in Virginia, references a report of 28 August 1904, in which coloured Sunday School workers of the Virginia Baptist State Convention (Negro) read a paper on caste in their church: he reports that some of these coloured Sunday school workers felt that a class line should be drawn separating those who had drawn themselves above the ordinary level and those who remained low.[10] An article on the "British West Indian Negro" in the *Southern Workman* manages to put a positive spin on classism as it makes a case for British

West Indian exceptionalism: "Unlike the American who is only now trying to differentiate his colored fellow citizens into classes, the West Indian colonists recognized classes among them nearly two hundred years ago."[11] Marcus Garvey would have found in 1916 a desire among the African Americans to distinguish themselves in terms of class and would have found that one of the distinguishing features of class and social mobility was the respect shown to one by white people. Sometime in 1916, while on professional business, Mitchell, the editor of the *Richmond Planet*, had a run-in with the police. White men came out to support him. Someone commented in his newspaper on 22 April, "We need more such men as John Mitchell who at a moment can command respect and support of the best white people in the South. When that day comes, the race problem will be solved." In other words, the race problem which exorcized African Americans would be settled when they had people whom the white man had to respect.

One of the ways to have a white man's respect is to not respond in kind to his aggravation. On the matter of the editor's run-in with the police, another contributor writes: "Some white folks aggravate us, but may also please us, so continue to cultivate a friendly relationship with all of them. It will pay in the long run." Another in the same newspaper in 1920 offers an axiom of a similar kind: "Colored folks, continue to be polite and obliging to everyone. It will win friends for you among the white folk and admiration from your own people." The wife and brother of Moton, the head of Tuskegee, sat in the wrong place on a train and were duly booted out by the train's officials. Many contributors to newspapers had been upset that they were booted, and others that they put themselves in a position to be thus treated. Moton is quoted as having said that he had warned his wife and her brother to keep to their place. This statement angered some; the editor of the *Richmond Planet*, for instance, said he refused to believe that Moton could have said that, and added that "if there is discrimination let it be of the 'low down' of either race".[12]

When he came to the United States, Marcus Garvey would have found among the African Americans a desire for the respectful attention of white people. He would have found among them too an acceptance of class prejudice. This state of affairs would have left a segment of the African American population in need of a sympathetic ear. He also would have found a notion of the West Indian/Jamaican as exceptional – "exceptional", yes, but also as problematic, a position which encouraged debate over West Indian–African American relations. Carter G. Woodson, the famous African American historian, found time to write a paper in the *Negro World* on this matter, concluding that the "West Indian Negro is free" and attributing this to the nature of the programme of education in Jamaica.

At the beginning of the twentieth century, white Americans thought to demonize African Americans, whom they had, after 1877 and the Tilden-Hayes compromise, continually stripped of civil rights. To justify these actions, they published so-called scientific and other works to show that the Negro was by nature inferior to whites. Some of these books were Charles Caroll's *The Negro, a Beast*, published in 1900, and his *The Tempter of Eve*, published in 1902.[13] Then there was William Calhoun's *The Caucasian and the Negro in the United States*, published in 1902. This was followed in 1905 by William B. Smith's *The Color Line: A Brief on Behalf of the Unborn*. In 1907 came Robert Shufeldt's *The Negro a Menace to American Civilization*. There were also popular novels from the pen of Thomas Dixon Jr: *The Leopard's Spots* (1902), *The Klansman* (1905) and *The Traitor* (1907).

Whether stimulated by these calumnious works to reply or not, the early twentieth century saw advertisements for books on and by black people in the African American newspapers. In 1915, the *Commonwealth* carried an advertisement for a book on Maryland entitled *A History of the Colored People of Maryland*. Neither the author's name nor the publisher's name was attached. There was another on Maryland: this was *Men of Maryland*, written by Rev George S. Bragg, rector of St James Church in Baltimore. The *National News* announced Bishop Walters's forthcoming book, *Great Men of the Race*. There is also mention of a book that M.R. Delany was either writing or had written for a southern publishing house. It was entitled *A Complete History of the African Race in America*, its presence announced by the *Missionary Record*. In January 1916 came news of John E. Bruce's novel called *An Awakening of Hezikiah Jones*. The editor of the *New York Age* had received a copy, and he declared that no book better served its purpose in these critical times. *An Awakening of Hezikiah Jones* tells the story of an ex-slave who went with his master to the war and, when he became ill, nursed him back to health. He refuses emancipation and comes back from war ready to work with his master's family as a slave. At his death, he is carried on the shoulders of the family's sons to be buried in the family burial plot. Why does this book "better serve its purpose than any other in these critical times"? These times are critical, it can be assumed, because whites are treating blacks so badly. This novel seems to be inviting the reader into the understanding that a kind and selfless black person can be loved by white people and accepted as part of the family. The editor seems to want us to see this work as a model of what race relations could be.

On 4 November of that year, the *National News* tells us of Sutton Griggs's book entitled *Life's Demands, or, According to the Law*. With this book, Griggs became the first Negro to have a book approved for use in public schools by the Southern Board of Education. A book by Professor Miller of Howard University was also announced. It was about black soldiers and sailors in the war. Neither the book's title nor the publisher's name is shared with us. Sweeney also wrote a book mentioned in the same issue; his is the *History of the American Negro in the Great World War*, and he had given the editor a copy.

The *Richmond Planet* carries two poems by Lucian B. Walker. The one for 28 February 1920 reads:

Hail to thee our fatherland
Here Mary brought her little Lord
Who, safe from Herod's scarlet hand
Wrote high in heaven thy rich reward,
Here gentle Jesus on the Nile
Hallowed thy ages with his smile

Hail, Hail to thee, our other – soul –
More dreamful than the dark of night
The night that is the mystic [whole/whale(?)]
The sleeping beauty of the light!
Out of the night the morning wakes
Out of the night God's glory breaks!

The one on 21 February reads:

My god is Black
My god is black. He made me so
His image, breathing as I go
He is my soul's lone vision, though
The best of all I dare and O

The hopes I have; my faith's glad glow
The spirit urge I feel; each blow
Me facing towards my foe;
There are the signs unfailing, true,
My god is black

My Dear Christ when thou hast fallen low
Beneath the cross, the world of woe
My brother Simon bore for you –
Up Calvery's Hill, towards Heaven's bright blue –
Our mutual burden. This I know
My god is black.

African Americans were fighting the printed word with the printed word. Africa's contribution to Christianity, the Ethiopianist view of history that we glimpse in the poems, the editor must have felt could be used as artillery in this struggle; thus, he printed these pieces of romance in his newspaper.

It seems that the newspapers of the early twentieth century did not think African Americans were interested in other areas of the African diaspora. Of the non-American countries of the African diaspora, it was Haiti that was most often represented in the newspapers, which is hardly surprising, since the United States began its occupation at about this time, and it had been a point to which popular African Americans had chosen to migrate in preference to Liberia.[14] There was news of Haiti in the *Black Republican* of 1905 and an editorial in the *Commonwealth* in 1915. This latter claimed that Haiti has been "spanked" because it was little and weak. It figures, too, in the slate of cartoons possibly meant for the easy absorption of key aspects of the news. In the *Richmond Planet* of 15 February 1919, there was a tribute to Touisaint L'Ouverture. In the same issue, among pictures of ex-European royalty, is a picture of a black warrior; at its base is the statement, "Tribute to Zerah fought ASA 815 BC with 500 chariots and 1,000,000 black soldiers". Still in this issue is a large picture of a Negro man captioned "the Black Builder". In capitals at the base is "HOMAGE TO SECROPPS, AN ETHIOPIAN [WHO] FOUNDED ATHENS IN 1500 YEARS BC". It seems that the African Americans felt a need at this point in their history to prop up their egos by leaning on past conquests by people whose skin was as black as theirs. Marcus Garvey would find here, when he came in 1916, ancient black history used as a defence mechanism of an ego battered by official discrimination and by unkind fictional portraits. Before long, African Americans would have to contend with other people of the African diaspora who were real, present and in their physical space.

The *Richmond Planet* of 3 January 1920 announced to the world what the editor called a rumour that Britain was about to give up her West Indian territories to America for the help the United States gave her (in the First World War). But he opines, "this could not happen for blacks of the West Indies would revolt against being in America where lynchings of blacks take place". The implication here is that West Indian blacks are aggressive and assertive when compared with African Americans, who are submissive – that they would find a way of beating off lynch mobs. This interest in the West Indies and West Indians continued to indicate that Britain was monitoring America's approach to the race problem before finalizing any transfer. These comments by P.W. Wilson, said to have been a former member of the British Parliament and later a representative of the *London Daily News* as parliamentary reporter and then that paper's American correspondent, are reprinted from the *New York World* from an article dated 11 April 1920, and are followed by the comment that "colored men are drifting here from the West Indies" and that "this is a compliment to this country and the educational achievements of Hampton and Tuskegee". These two colleges are African American, and the writer is pleased that they are providing material for the improvement of "English children", in that they are "associating the hand and the head in the development of the personality". The comment ends with the statement that "the colour line is drawn here more strictly than in England and for this very reason, with us, the colored man is too rare to make a difference". The editor of the *Richmond Planet* probably agreed with the sentiments aired in the *New York World*, which he reprinted in his newspaper; he certainly thought it was "news" that would interest his readers.

The statement about "coloured men drifting in from the British West Indies" carries a feeling of awe towards West Indians and the notion that the West Indian is different from "us" – that unlike "us", he is defiant, warlike and willing to fight when disturbed. He is exotic. She or he is not the slave of the late eighteenth century going with Mrs Burrowes from St Mary, Jamaica, to Georgia, United States, and having to fraternize with slaves there, nor with slaves leaving Georgia–South Carolina with their masters to live in St Mary.[15] It seems that by the early twentieth century, the easy movement between African Americans and

Jamaicans/West Indians of the days of slavery, when they each travelled with their masters from one colony to the other, were over. Word of the Morant Bay Rebellion, the War of 1865 and the killing of white people who prevented blacks from using Crown lands must have filtered down to this brother of the African diaspora; knowledge of African Americans' equally rich history of aggressive struggles, such as Nat Turner's rebellion, must have been kept from the African American.

So exceptional was the British West Indian Negro thought to be in African America that Samuel B. Jones, MD, resident physician at the Agricultural and Mechanical College, Greensboro, NC, felt in 1911, years before Woodson's piece, the need to write a paper on him, in which race relations in the area are praised:

> The Southerner in the United States may view with increasing concern the widening chasm between his son and the son of the black man with whom he played in childhood. He knows that where sympathy and affection are wanting and race instinct strong, cruelty and might become dominant and that these two hurt the oppressor as much as the oppressed. The West Indian white man has no such fear. He has his prejudices; equally strong are those of the black man. For this reason the one race respects the other's prejudices, both feeling that on a broad field of industry, of education, of good citizenship, and of manhood, there is room for both black and white.[16]

The Jamaica in 1911 that African Jamaicans knew was not the one above, where whites and blacks cared for each other. Nor did the British West Indian/ Jamaican have a history as stated in the article – of planters encouraging stable relationships between their male and female slaves, thus producing stable families. The true history was one in which career choice in the early twentieth century was stymied by colour, encouraging black Jamaicans to migrate to Cuba and elsewhere.[17] According to the Jamaica League, a quasi-political organization operating in Jamaica and New York, times were so difficult for black people in Jamaica in the first decades of the twentieth century that the "brains" went off to America and the "brawn" to Cuba.[18] Winston James reminds us that emigration of Caribbean people increased from 411 in 1899 to 12,247 in 1924, the greater part of this number consistently going to New York, and especially New York City, where in 1913–19 they comprised 47.1 per cent of immigrants.[19] Jamaicans were the principal Caribbean immigrants. They went to earn, and they went for educational certification in the colleges of the United States, which were far more accessible physically and financially than those of Great Britain and appeared to offer a wider choice of study areas.

Dr J.D. Harris was one of the brains that went off to America. He would have been one of the 13.3 per cent of black immigrant aliens who, according to James's data, went neither to New York, Florida nor Massachusetts. He settled in Hampton in the state of Virginia. His life history demonstrates the courage which the African American commentators perceived to be African Jamaican, for Harris had made himself significant enough in the state of Virginia to be invited to a place on the republican ticket shortly after the Civil War as lieutenant governor, with H.H. Wells as governor for the state of Virginia. He was attacked throughout the campaign for being a native of Jamaica and being a man with a white wife. The brave Jamaican Dr Harris, as the author of *Reconstruction in South Carolina* relates, was offered a job by the regents of the lunatic hospital in South Carolina as an assistant physician. His appointment was met with complaints that the hospital was being "negroized", and questions were being asked not about the validity of Dr Harris's medical degree but about the nature of the resistance of the general public to Harris, a black man who in this job would have to work in a setting in which there were two hundred patients, only thirty of whom were black. Harris, whose great strides in Virginia and South Carolina epitomize the confidence of the Jamaican imagined by the African Americans and perhaps real, found the courage to resign.[20]

Jamaicans continued to come to the United States, particularly to Hampton. The *Southern Workman* of 4 February 1904 mentions the visit of Dr Murray, a prominent Wesleyan clergyman in Jamaica, to give a talk at the school; twelve years later, the visit was the other way around. Dr Moton and his wife, the *Southern Workman* for April 1916 reports, travelled to Jamaica in that month. Dr Washington, his predecessor, had thought that an examination of Jamaica's education system would be good for his institution. At a large meeting at Mico Training College, the principal of the college and the mayor of the town greeted them. They also visited the Farm School, where Percival Mussing, a Hampton graduate of the class of 1903 was in charge of the agricultural department, and they visited too Dr James S. Myers, a Hampton graduate of 1905 who was in charge of the Kingston asylum. Moton was happy with what he saw at Mico and felt that the coloured people were getting a good education there. It was in this same year that Marcus Garvey found his way to the United States, primarily to consult with Booker T. Washington with respect to replicating his Tuskegee experiment in Jamaica – a meeting which was called off given the death of Washington.[21] West Indians and particularly Jamaicans were known in African America, but the knowledge seemed to begin and end with the elite of both areas. What existed in the public mind was a stereotype which painted Jamaicans/ West Indians as different from African Americans in their social fearlessness and their aggressiveness and determination to succeed. The Caribbean people were aware of this: Hubert Harrison, one of the outspoken Caribbean intellectuals, an erstwhile colleague of Garvey, remarked, in discussing African America's perception of the Caribbean people living among them: "It was taken for granted that every West Indian immigrant was a paragon of intelligence and a man of birth and breeding."[22]

The United States in the first decades of the twentieth century called itself a "melting pot", and it surely was, especially in New York City. There were migrants from Ireland, from Italy and, especially with the end of the First World War, from Eastern Europe. This pot was slow in melting: the several nationalities tended to bond together, making the United States sociologically into a collection of mini nationalities. The African Americans took note of this sociological fact and seemed to view African Jamaicans as another one of the culturally distinct, if respected, nationalities. This was the United States that Marcus Garvey entered in 1916, a place where the Jamaican was seen by others of his colour as rebellious and defiant, unwilling to accept lynching – a people who historically related well with whites who had conducted a compassionate slavery system. They were a people who not only valued education, as they themselves did, but made their way to the colleges in greater numbers than they did; they were a people who were part of the British colonial system and did not need to fear the larger American system, for they had recourse to a place where racial conflict was mild, and referral for support from the British High Commission was possible. But Harold Cruse and Wilson Jeremiah Moses are quite right in maintaining that Marcus Garvey did not, even given his West Indian traits of fearlessness and aggressiveness, create the success with which his organization was associated – that he had found on his arrival in the United States a firm foundation on which he built the largest movement of black people that the world had seen and has yet seen.[23]

According to Cruse, "every Pan-Africanist trend of the twentieth century, including Garvey's has its roots in the American Negro trend".[24] To claim a direct link between Garvey's mind and action and "American Negro trends" may not be easy to establish. To copy something, as seems to be the charge here against Garvey's activities, one has to be aware of it. Were Garvey and the folks he attracted aware of the history of ideas said to have predated him? What is without doubt true is that African America produced several pan-Africanist thinkers, but were they around in the first two decades of the twentieth century?[25] A review of the coloured newspapers of the period shows far more interest in the local race issue than in links between Africa and its diaspora and within the diaspora itself. Moses comments: "Whatever may be said of Garvey and his movement, favorable or unfavorable, the idea that he introduced radically new ideas is debatable."[26] To both Cruse and Moses, a counter-comment can be made to the effect that though thought is action, action does have a more activist aspect to it. Moses goes on to quite rightly claim that the "pseudomilitarianism [of the Garvey movement] already existed in the uniforms and drill practices of the Hampton-Tuskegee traditions and in the fraternal institutions".[27] There is ample evidence from the newspapers of the tendency to mass and march in the streets, an activity also common to the Ku Klux Klan. But what about the numbers and the variety of people that filled the streets for the Universal Negro Improvement Association's (UNIA) International Convention of Negro People of the World? Numbers must be part of the truth. And they are right: Garvey did not introduce an interest in commerce to the African Americans. The newspapers are indeed full of advertisements from saving banks and, in particular, the Mechanics Saving Bank.

In the concept of "the civilized" travelling down from the 1840s, thrift was allied to temperance, so it is not unusual that Bishop Walters, at a luncheon where a visiting cleric from South America was a guest, should have talked of matters pertaining to the church as well as the "commercial uplift of the race".[28] Moses holds that "the entrepreneurial spirit of the National Business League encouraged the same spirit of economic independence and energetic self-sufficiency as Garveyism".[29] Indeed, such an entrepreneurial spirit had to exist to support the purchase of shares in Garvey's commercial enterprises. And Garvey was aware of its prior existence and paid obeisance to it. Acknowledging the entrepreneurial spirit of the African American, he said: "The acme of American Negro enterprise is not yet reached. You have still a far way to go. You want more stores, more banks and bigger enterprises."[30] What Cruse and Moses have told us is that the African American was ready for Garvey, and Garvey was ready for the African American. How else could he in two years have encouraged into being a newspaper, mass meetings, a shipping line, a business corporation – the African Communities League – and an International Convention of Negro People of the World, at which Negro people from all over the world were actually in attendance? Added to all that Garvey might have inherited from other thinkers, as Cruse and Moses have reminded us, is his singular gift for organizing people.

"Who will lead us?" was an issue among African Americans when Garvey was settling himself in the United States. A cartoon of 7 June 1919 in the *Richmond Planet* illustrates this concern. It shows a big muscular black man, behind whom are people lined up with placards saying, "Our leader" and "Follow the leader". But how does a leader emerge? The preaching of sermons in the church was so much a part of African American tradition that the newspaper took note. The religious leaders had traditionally been thought to be race leaders so that their sermons became remarkable. The Reverend Henderson, pastor of the First Baptist Church of Newport News, delivered a sermon, and the *National News* carried word of it. Lodge leaders were likewise seen as significant: the *Richmond Planet* reports on 22 April 1916 that Pythians and Calanthians celebrated their anniversary throughout the Commonwealth with elaborate programmes and "fine sermons", sermons often described as "lectures". The editor of the *Planet*, the Honourable John Mitchell, Jr, also on the board of a bank and the grand chancellor of a lodge, was often invited to lecture, as on 30 May 1916, when he did the Memorial Day lecture for the Court of Calanthe mentioned above. Having given a sermon or a lecture, the reputation of the speaker becomes enhanced, his fame spreads, and he might be a respected voice on African American affairs and become a leader. It was after such a speech at the Atlanta Exposition in 1895 that Dr Booker T. Washington found himself the leader of the Negro people. He recalled that after that speech, his office was bombarded with letters and telegrams "demanding that I take the place of 'leader of the Negro people' left vacant by Frederick Douglass's death or assuming that I had already taken this place".[31] He subsequently discovered what was expected of him as a leader and what made him the natural successor to Douglass: like Douglass, it was his concern about the importance and value of industrial education for the Negro.

Whatever the reason, Washington was without doubt the leader of the African Americans until his death in 1915, the year before Garvey began his sojourn in the United States.

It was the intelligentsia among the African Americans who gave sermons and lectures, and they used these sermons and lectures to battle with each other. Du Bois was another sought-after lecturer. In his 11 November 1916 speech at Virginia Union University, reported by the *National News*, he was introduced as "the most finished product of the Negro race", and he naturally "charmed the large Richmond audience". Such talks were not available to the ears of all kinds of African Americans, given the technology of the day. To hear this speech, the only face-to-face possibility available, one had to pay twenty-five cents for a reserved seat or fifteen cents at the door. Several would have to hear of Du Bois's great ideas, though well-articulated, through a third party. Until his death in 1915, Du Bois was Washington's main and worthwhile rival for the title of leader of the African American people. Garvey himself seemed to consider him so. According to Tony Martin, in 1920, two weeks before the start of what was to be an electrifying international convention, Garvey wrote Du Bois thus:

> Dear Dr. DuBois:
>
> At the International Convention of Negroes to be held in New York during the month of August, the Negro people of America will elect a leader by popular vote of the delegates from the forty-eight States of the Union. This leader as elected, will be the accredited spokesman of the American Negro people. You are hereby asked to be good enough to allow us to place your name in nomination for the post.[32]

Du Bois declined, as he had a 25 April 1916 invitation from Garvey to chair the first meeting of his UNIA. Garvey's courting of Du Bois as the African American race leader subsided with this snub.

Du Bois said of himself, "In 1905 I was still a teacher . . . and was in my imagination a scientist and neither a leader nor an agitator."[33] He never gave up this sense of himself, though he realized that "Negro civil rights called for organized and aggressive defence".[34] He was not willing to take up the mantle of leader and see to this "organized and aggressive defence". Du Bois's colour prejudice was very close to the surface. He describes someone whom Booker T. Washington's "Tuskegee machine" cruelly hurt as "a young colored man, one of the most beautiful human beings I have ever seen".[35] The reader expects, in the context of discussion of professionals, some reference to intellectual capacity and willingness to work hard, but the thought and sentence continues to describe the young man in terms of his physical features: "with smooth brown skin, velvet eyes of intelligence, and raven hair". Only after presenting this physical image does Du Bois tell us that this young man was educated and well-to-do, and he needed capital to build a Negro town as an independent economic unit in the South. Philanthropists and capitalists were fascinated by his project, but it needed the assent of Washington, who remained silent, saying not a word in favour of what so many thought was a worthwhile project.

This unfortunate measure of a human being appears again in Du Bois's comment in a ten-page article attacking Garvey. This sociologist, university lecturer, writer and Harvard scholar described a political and philosophical opponent in terms of his physical features: "a little fat black man, ugly, but with intelligent eyes and big head".[36] More African Americans in the 1920s, when this remark was written and published, looked like Garvey than they did Du Bois. How could a person who sees the majority of African Americans as "ugly" lead them? Garvey's main opposition among African Americans were those who called themselves "integrationists". Another one of them followed Du Bois in assessing political opposition in terms of somatic profile. In objecting to Garvey's pro-nationalist stance, Pickens, too, focused on Garvey's physical features: Garvey was "a Jamaican Negro of unmixed stock, squat, stocky, fat and sleek with protruding jaws, and heavy jowls, small bright pig-like eyes and a rather bulldog-like face".[37]

Not only did Garvey's opposition see him and the majority of African Americans as physically odd and unpleasant; they saw themselves – and they made this clear – to be intellectually superior to the mass of African Americans. Owens, one of them, declared in 1920, "we educated scientific-minded and higher minded Negroes do not want a Negro nation. It would forever kill our dream of world equality."[38] African America needed at this time, as Du Bois himself had said, "organized and aggressive defence".[39] This would require the organization of all tendencies, including the unlettered and especially the "Negro of unmixed stock" – the fat, black and ugly, as most of African America was – into a united force. Such an initiative could hardly come from people who saw African Americans as ugly.

The African American social structure had evolved into discrete groups whose raison d'être lay in their distinctiveness. Even the Christian churches fell into style. We find word from the *Commonwealth* in 1919 of the effort of the Methodist church to bring its various branches together, and we hear the cry in the *Richmond Planet* of 1916 for a meeting called by the Negro Welfare and Civic League to discuss troubles in the African Methodist Episcopal Church. A contributor confounded by these splits makes the point in the same issue that blacks are not coming together and that "selfishness and self-aggrandisement seems to be the watch word of colored leaders everywhere". Dissension was even within the same locale in the same denomination. The *Richmond Planet* of 21 February 1920 notes the contretemps between the Reverend Morris and the Reverend Dr Lewis, both of the Second Baptist Church. The *National News* notes in its 14 October 1916 issue that two clergymen had recourse to the court: Reverend S.P. Harris had filed a suit against R.H. Boyd for ten thousand dollars for defamation of character. They were both of the Baptist union, in which there are other wranglings involving the same Reverend R.H. Boyd. It is this time with the Reverend W.H. Moses, leaving the commentator to conclude: "While the clergy fight the sinners are finding their way to hell."

Organization of the African Americans required the existence of an entity which could envelope the small groups into which the African American had formed themselves, but the intelligentsia who thought they were the ruling class were similarly fissured. Martin's research shows that the coalition of voices in the "Garvey Must Go" chorus, which contributed to his arrest and deportation, "had previously crossed swords with one another in their competition for leadership of the Afro-American mass, and many were to cross swords after the removal of Garvey". Lenox Street in Harlem was home to several soapboxes manned by speakers of several shades of political philisophy. In any case, pulling the people together was not part of the intelligentsia's programme – the programme for the socialists and communists relied on action defined by thought emanating outside of the African American intellectual creation. Du Bois, the Harvard graduate needing no hair straightener nor "high brown powder" to make him feel presentable, was acknowledged as a source of correct thought within African America when Garvey arrived in the United States and remained so for most of his time there. He was the most "educated scientific mind" and he felt himself to be so.

Of himself, Du Bois says: "From 1910 to 1920, I followed sociology as the path to social reform and social uplift as a result of scientific investigation."[40] Much of this scientific investigation was done while he was a professor at Atlanta University with a very small budget, which did not allow for the collection of data applicable to the wide United States. Nevertheless, he did have material on mortality among Negroes in cities, the social and physical conditions of Negroes in cities, some efforts of Negroes for social betterment, the Negro in business, the college-bred Negro, the Negro common school, the Negro artisan, the Negro church, notes on Negro crime and a select bibliography of the American Negroes.[41] Du Bois had produced a databank which was used by others interested in the uplift of the Negro. His sociology was statistical and had a narrow social and geographic base; the rural African American who was about to move into the cities and those who remained at home would be absent from this database. Moreover, this "scientific study" – this sociology, a discipline in its infancy trying to be seen as science – looked at human beings as objects; it was unable to plumb values and feelings so essential to creating linkages between disparate groups.

Out of his sociological ruminations, Du Bois developed a praxis: "In practice, I had conceived an inter-racial culture superseding our goal of a purely American culture." He continues: "Before I had conceived a program for this path, and after throes of bitter racial strife, I had emerged with a program of Pan-Africanism, as organized protection of the Negro World led by American Negroes. But American Negroes were not interested."[42] Had his sociological method allowed him to examine "values", he might have found that American Negroes were indeed "interested".[43] And if his definition of "American Negro" had not been narrowed by his own prejudices, he might have found that the thousands of African Americans who lined the streets and attended the session of the UNIA's 1920 Convention of the Negro Peoples of the World were interested in pan-Africanism. So Du Bois did not canvass this idea, this generalization to which his sociological inquires led him, for he had an epiphany:

> Abruptly, I had a beam of new light . . . Karl Marx was scarcely mentioned at Harvard and entirely unknown at Fisk. At Berlin, he was a living influence, but chiefly in the modification of his theories then dominant in the Social Democratic party. I was attracted to the rise of the party and attended its meetings. I began to consider myself a socialist. . . followed some of my white colleagues into the socialist party.[44]

But he did not stay. He looked in at Communism and accepted an invitation to Russia but saw that it could not solve Negro problems. He also went to Africa. While others spoke of the European causes of the world war about to burst forth, Du Bois spoke as lovingly of Africa as Edward Blyden did and as his hero Alexander Crummell would have:

> Most men assume that Africa lies far afield from the centers of our burning social problems, and especially from our present problem of World War.
>
> Yet in a very real sense Africa is the prime cause of this overturning of civilization which we have lived to see. . . . Always Africa is giving us something new and some metempsychosis of a world-old thing. On its black bosom arose one of the earliest, if not the earliest of self-protecting civilizations and grew so mightily that it still furnishes superlatives to thinking and speaking men. Out of its darker and most remote forest fastnesses came if we may credit recent scientists the first welding of iron and we know that agriculture and trade flourished there when Europe was a wilderness.[45]

He went on in this speech, which was published in the *Atlantic Monthly* in May of 1915, to trace the history of European dependency on Africa and its exploitation of it, finally stating that "the ownership of materials and men in the darker world is the real prize that is setting the nations of Europe at each other's throat today".[46]

Du Bois outlines strategies that blacks could use to end the exploitation and the resulting wars. This was Du Bois before Garvey entered his space, but he felt pinned to the NAACP, an agency with few coloured people at the helm. His newspaper *Crisis*, which he had nursed from its birth, he felt too to belong to them, but the NAACP could not see the connection that he saw between the condition of the African American and the condition of Africa. Du Bois gave in and continued to work with the NAACP within the conceptual framework of making Negroes into American citizens, though the position he wanted to state to the American Negro was as follows: "work together in unison; you must evolve and support your own social institutions; you must transform your attack from foray of self-assertive individuals to the massed might of an organized body; you must put behind your demands not simply American Negroes, but West Indian and African and all the colored races of the world".[47]

Du Bois, the "most finished product of the Negro race", did not have the courage of his convictions and was late in arriving at them. It was not until the 1950s, thirty or so years later, that Du Bois felt free to walk his thought and to project himself as a pan-Africanist relating with others from the African continent and the West Indies, eventually drawing his last breath on that continent of Africa.

In the 1950s, in later life, Du Bois came in conflict with the law. The result of this misfortune was that "negro newspapers were warned not to carry my writings"; "Negro colleges no longer asked for my lectures or my presence at commencement exercises"; and, he concludes, "I lost my leadership of the race."[48] For Du Bois, it was his association with academia that gave him "leadership of the race". He also admitted in his autobiography that his "experience of practical politics had been small". He blamed this on his upbringing: "I had been reared in the New England tradition of regarding politics as no fit career for a man of serious aims, and particularly unsuitable for a college bred man." He was also, in his own words, "no natural leader of men".[49] With such a mindset, he could not help African America to the "organized and aggressive defence" which he said it needed.

On the contrary, by the time he came to the United States in 1916, Garvey already knew what his convictions were and had already reached, in 1915, the philosophical position that Du Bois had in his heart at that time but around which he had been hesitant to organize his fellow men. After Garvey's sojourn in Latin and Central America and in Europe, where he saw the conditions of black people, of which he knew himself to be one, his epiphany came: "my doom ... of being a race leader dawned upon me".[50] Then he asked himself these questions: "Where is the blackman's government? Where is his king and his kingdom? Where is his President, his country and his ambassador, his army, his navy, his big men of affairs? I could not find them and then I declared, 'I will help to make them.' "[51]

That he was destined for leadership of black people, and that he would have to gather them into a nation and a state, was clear to Garvey. Jamaica was to have been his starting point and education his first point of attack. He had been impressed by the work of Booker T. Washington and had contacted him in the hope of getting support for this endeavour, but by the time he was ready to accept the offer to visit, Washington had died. He was in touch with Moton, Washington's successor, but waited until a year after Washington's death, in 1916, to visit. In America, Garvey met people working for the black cause, some due to their ideas being published in the *Africa Times and Orient Review,* on which he had worked while in England. He had come as a lecturer hoping to operate as such in the southern states and to be rewarded with enough money to develop his school in Jamaica. He met other intellectuals and was invited by some to share their platforms in New York, speaking on request about conditions in Jamaica. But as he had done in the other parts of the world that he had visited, Garvey quickly understood the sociology of the surroundings and felt confident enough to speak not only of conditions in Jamaica but also of local conditions. He intended to establish a branch of his organization, the UNIA, in New York, but was invited to make this unit not just a subsidiary to the parent body in Jamaica but its headquarters. Garvey had never intended his universe to be Jamaica alone. He had visited most countries in which there were black people and had noted that their condition was the same everywhere. As such, it did not matter where he let down his net: African America was as good as anywhere else.

Garvey, like any other aspiring leader, was attuned to the socio-psychology of those he intended to lead. Du Bois used sociological methodology to know his people. Garvey everywhere used the participant observation techniques associated with anthropology: he moved among the people and so could capture more than the statistics. He knew the feelings and the hopes and the immediate needs of the people. In his journeys in Latin and Central America, he took on the role of ambassador of the West Indian workers, harassing the British consuls into caring for the people from the British colonies.[52] He used his journalistic skills everywhere as an organizational tool. In his first year in the United States, Garvey visited thirty-eight states, meeting black people of all kinds and hearing their concerns. He was very aware of their bad treatment. He could make such concerns his, having pledged to serve the Negro wherever he was. His oratorical skills had been honed during his travels throughout the black world, and so he was able to attract crowds, drawing them away from his competitors, and he could link local problems with those in the wider international world. Garvey was a West Indian/Jamaican and known to be such. He inherited the image of exceptionalism that resided in the African American mind and, like the migrant that he was, could dare to go and was expected to dare where natives feared to tread.

He understood the African American culture and social structure; he therefore knew what lodges and churches provided and was careful to give the impression that his organization was open to all, and that they needn't discard their allegiances in order to be a part of the UNIA. Thus, all the tightly bonded groups that constituted the African American social structure could find a place in the UNIA, and new units were created for those who were not so bonded but wanted to "jine" something bigger than themselves, to find some place where authority was grounded or to change their affiliations. The culture of the groups – their marching, their thrift clubs – became part of the UNIA's culture. The UNIA was home; it was the umbrella under which the several groups could live together.

Garvey knew from his observations, and from the knowledge he could induce from his travels in the black world, that what linked all Negroes together was the state of what Orlando Patterson calls "social death", which living in a white space had conferred upon them.[53] This is clear in the following statement: "For the last ten years I have given my time to the study of the condition of the Negro here there and everywhere, and I have come to realise that he is still the object of degradation and pity the world over, in the sense that he has no status socially, nationally or commercially (with a modicum of exception is the United States of America)."[54]

Garvey early realized that if the Negro were to have a place in the melting pot that the United States was said to be, a place where people saw themselves in a collective of mini nations displaced by war or by other disastrous conditions, the Negro would have to organize himself into a nation. The same applied to the world: if the Negro were to stop being the downtrodden of the world, he would have to join the world as a nation. As Cruse and Moses have pointed out, there was a long history of race consciousness and racial uplift among African Americans. Garvey, even if he did not know of this history, was able to feed into this latent stream of African American knowledge and use it to link the African American into a wider pan-African group as Du Bois had seen to be necessary. In Garvey's theory and praxis, this consciousness was not to reside only in the middle-class intelligentsia but among the masses who were in the direct gaze of the lynch mobs and discrimination everywhere.

Cruse and Moses have rightly said that pan-Africanism was in the African American mind from as early as the eighteenth century, but while Du Bois and other black intellectuals met in 1919, 1921 and 1923 with a small band who frequently used the term "pan-Africanism", Garvey mounted conventions in which black people from all over the world sat with each other and discussed their particular issues, knowing without having to call the word that they were a part of a larger pan-African family, which they were actually working at melding into a functioning unit. Garvey's greatest coup was the establishment of UNIA units throughout the world: this was the nation. Separated by bodies of water, the nation had to have a shipping line and a centralized geographic space in a place which held romance for all, a place in Africa, from which all of this oppressed race had initially descended, and which was being divided and grabbed by the same Europeans who were insulting them in the places to which their forefathers had been unwillingly brought by these same European nations.[55] The *Black Star Line* and the effort to link with Liberia were not just a rehash of earlier emigrationist impetus. Under Garvey, they were the black man's efforts at nation-building and self-reliance, and they were the efforts of the ugliest and most illiterate to transform himself or herself from an unhappy, slighted individual into a patriot, buying share in this nation's business.

C.L.R. James, a premier black intellectual, pan-Africanist and Marxist, expresses well the change which Garvey wrought:

> Up to 1918 blacks, as a whole, played no particular role in world politics. The world was not conscious of them except as objects. Blacks were not conscious of themselves. A spirit of frustration, humiliation, rebellion is not political consciousness. The man who made both blacks conscious of themselves and the world conscious of blacks as a force to be reckoned with in world politics was a Jamaican, Marcus Garvey. By 1925/26 Garveyism as a force was finished, but the political problem represented by black people had been placed before the world once and for all. Henceforth it had to be taken into consideration in all calculations on a national as well as international scale.[56]

Marcus Garvey, an African Jamaican, used his stay among African Americans to make the world conscious of the Negro and his aspirations. But first he had to gather them into an organization. He seems to have done this by setting himself to respond to key issues in the African American psyche as demonstrated by the news and the advertisements in their newspapers: he gave them something to "jine", something with the authority of a parent; he entered fully into the discourse concerning the place that Africa should have in their minds, clarifying issues for those conflicted; he was very clear on what black beauty ought to look like, even encouraging the building of a factory to produce black dolls to early socialize the African Americans into accepting their dark skin and kinky hair as natural and normal; the Black Cross Nurses possibly helped with health issues of which the poor were aware but could not financially address; he even, in meeting with the Ku Klux Klan, made this unit of which blacks were afraid seem less of a bogey; in lashing out as he so often did at his political contemporaries, he spoke to classism. He joined fully in the literary culture and, with comments in the organization's newspapers and its study groups, drew the unexposed into the literary circle, formerly the preserve of what Owens dubbed the "scientific" minds. His dramatic offerings not only provided entertainment for the less scientific minds but helped them to participate in the ego defence mechanism of leaning on black ancient history to which newspapers alluded: they too were the kin of Toussaint L'Ouverture and "Secropps".

{CHAPTER 4}

African Jamaican and African American Religious Cooperation and Incorporation: A Case Study

Joy to the savage realms, O Africa;
A sign is on thee, that the great I am
Shall work new wonders in the land of Ham;
And while He tarries for the glorious day
To bring again His people, there shall be
A remnant left from Cushan to the sea.
And though the Ethiop cannot change his skin
Or bleach the outward stain, yet he shall roll
The darkness off that overshades the soul,
And wash away the deeper dyes of sin.
Princes submissive to the gospel's sway
Shall come from Egypt; and the Morian's land,
In holy transport, stretch to God its hand;
Joy to thy savage realm, O Africa.[1]

SLAVERY ENCOURAGED A DEFINITION OF THE African enslaved in the Western world as "supernational": the one born in Dahomey, as the one born in Angola, was defined by some people resident in the slave societies of the New World, and especially by clerics, as "African", and not only African but "Ethiopian", the extended version of the term "Ethiop". This Ethiop, this African, the thinking continued, was destined to "stretch forth his hands to God". The evidence for this was Psalm 68:31 of the Holy Bible, and the "God" was the Christian god. Did the defined accept this sense of himself? Edward Blyden, the late nineteenth-century African Caribbean philosopher, agreed with R. Williams, the rector of the Church of Advent who authored the poem above. In his 1880 discourse delivered before the American Colonization Society, Blyden says:

> The lot of Africa resembles also His who made Himself of no reputation, but took upon Himself the form of a servant, and having been made perfect through suffering, became the "Captain of our salvation". And if the principle laid down by Christ is that by which things are decided above, viz., that he who would be chief must become the servant of all, then we see the position that Africa and Africans must ultimately occupy.[2]

This sense of self as a supernational entity that is specially regarded by the god of the Christians was accepted among many Africans enslaved in the New World and their descendants. The historian Wilson Jeremiah Moses attests to this, calling this approach to self-definition the "Ethiopian view". He says it inspired the action of black people "from the Congo basin to the mountains of Jamaica to the sidewalks of New York", and this, his research showed him, existed from 1797 with the success of the Haitian Revolution.[3] Did this view arise from physical contact between Africans of the diaspora, or was it the commonality of treatment meted out to them in the New World, each group arriving at this sense of self independently? This chapter looks at the kinds of interaction between Africans of the diaspora from two parts of the New World – Jamaica and the United States – to see which of these alternatives facilitated the spread of this notion. The chapter looks at this issue through the religious organization called the Church of God and Saints of Christ which spread from Oklahoma in the United States to Jamaica.

In 1741, a plot to burn New York, kill the whites and take their women as wives was said to have been hatched by black slaves and a few poor whites. Among the so-called plotters was Thomas Edison's enslaved man named Jamaica, who was hoping to play the fiddle for the city's whites "while they were roasting in the flames . . . he had been a slave long enough".[4] Other slaves in the New York area had names such as Congo and deAngola, and some in the 1741 plot were Scotland, Windsor, Sterling, Worcester, Hereford, London, York, Galloway, Cambridge, Warwick, Sussex and Dundee – place names in Great Britain. At that time, Jamaica supplied 30 per cent of New York's slaves. It is quite likely then that the man called Jamaica was indeed from the island of Jamaica, and the historian of the planned attack on New York does support this conclusion. She says that "Jamaica and Barbados were points to which New York merchants exported grain and lumber in exchange for sugar and sometimes slaves, the Caribbean dumping notoriously rebellious, sick or old slaves on New York", adding that "these places too became names. In the 1730's and 40's black men named Jamaica and Barbados walked the streets of New York."[5] This is evidence of contact between enslaved Africans from a wide variety of places, but did the substance of their contact carry an Ethiopian view of history? It is clear from the account and the reported action of the New York slaves that the commonality of experience made all, like the man called Jamaica, angry at the treatment they had received from their masters in slavery, and they were ready to cooperate in retaliation. Although there is a class angle to this action or proposed action, poor whites being engaged in it, that there was cooperation between blacks of the diaspora from several parts of the world remains. These plotters – who, as their names suggest, had been in several parts of Great Britain and Jamaica and were now meeting in New York – wanted power to change their status from enslaved people to something else. Jamaica did say he had been a slave too long.

Orlando Patterson, the Jamaican-born sociologist, describes slavery as "one of the most extreme forms of the relation of domination approaching the limits of total power from the viewpoint of the master and total powerlessness from the viewpoint of the slave".[6] It is this sense of powerlessness – the converse of which would be Jamaica playing his fiddle while the whites, the master class, roasted – that he would have felt as a slave. Patterson continues by positing power to have three facets: the use of violence to control another person, the capacity to persuade a person to act outside of his or her interest and, along with these, a culture which makes the powerless feel that their condition is justified by a higher power. Religious ideas are obviously a part of the culture that can provide justification for such a power skew. Patterson gives a graphic example of powerlessness. This is from the United States, though examples of this event related by a Mr Reed in 1930 could be found anywhere in the countries in which Africans were taken as slaves.

> The most barbarous thing I saw with these eyes. . . I had a sister, my older sister, she was fooling around with the clock and broke it, and my old master taken her

and tied a rope around her neck – just enough to keep it from choking her – and tied her up in the back yard and whipped her I don't know how long. There stood mother, there stood father, and there stood all the children and none could come to her rescue.[7]

Revolutionaries among the enslaved African population understood that their condition was due to their powerlessness, wanted power and knew that their powerlessness was in great part due to the religious ideas embedded in the culture in which they lived with their masters. As early as 1791, Boukman had tried to and succeeded in inspiring his followers by drawing a distinction between the god of the whites and the god of the blacks:

> The god who created the sun which gives us light, who rouses the waves and rules the storm though hidden in the cloud, he watches us. The god of the white man inspires him to crime but our god calls upon us to do good works.... Throw away the symbols of the god of the whites who has so often caused all us to weep, and listen to the voice of liberty, which speaks in the heart of us all.[8]

Gayward Wilmore has aptly called Gabriel Prosser, Nat Turner and Denmark Vesey "the three generals in the army of the Lord".[9] They did not point their followers to a god distinguishable from that of the whites as Boukman did. They appropriated the Bible, the word of God according to their masters, and found in it dicta that they used to empower themselves, arise and free themselves. The Jamaican Sam Sharp learned that same lesson from the same Bible, the sacred book of his masters. It told him that he should not serve two masters, and he choose to listen to his god rather than to his slave master. His Christian priest, William Knibb, with whom he had a close relationship, was given to calling his enslaved listeners "Ethiopians".[10] As an Ethiopian, Sharp chose to stretch forth his hand unto God rather than to his slave master. Nat Turner, the Bible-reading African American slave, empowered himself to attack the Virginia slaveholders in the same year of Sam Sharp's uprising and through the inspiration of the same book. Does this coincidence spring out of the fact that conditions in the slave states of the United States were much the same for the enslaved African Americans as they were for the African Jamaicans, or were the principals able to infect each other through personal contact?

Significant physical relationships between African Americans and African Jamaicans came about in the late nineteenth century. Between July of 1782 and

January of 1783, twenty boats with seven thousand blacks made their way from
Georgia and South Carolina to Port Royal, Jamaica.[11] On arrival, the African
American blacks laboured as slaves among creole and New Africans in the
island and spread their version of Christianity. Among them was George Lisle,
a freedman who laboured in the South, in Kingston and St Catherine; Moses
Baker, in the far west parish of St James; George Gibb, in the northern parishes
of St Mary and St Thomas in the Vale; and George Lewis, in the southwestern
parishes of Manchester and St Elizabeth. Between them, they covered most
of Jamaica.[12] There is, however, no evidence that the Americans convinced the
Jamaicans to see themselves as the chief servants of the Christian God and,
by his design, more deserving than any other set of people, as is implicit in the
"Ethiopian view". What they did do was encourage them to see themselves as
capable of being visited and empowered by the pantheon of Christian spirits,
grounding the hegemony of the spirit, which already existed in Myal and other
African forms of religious expression among the Jamaicans. If the spirit, ancestral,
African or any other, can give one commands that one has to obey, as was the case
with Myal and the version of Christianity brought by the African Americans,
the masters' claim to authority and the notions on which it is built were likely
to be undermined.[13]

But even if the intellectual foundations of the skew of power are breached,
there is still violence and the ability to persuade the other to act outside of one's
own best interests. The uprisings of the "three generals in the army of the Lord"
and Sam Sharp's rebellion were put down violently: their fellow slaves had
reported them to the authorities. So, with superior force, and with people among
them who felt that the enemy's interest was theirs, powerlessness remained
among the Africans enslaved in the New World and with it the facets of power
that Patterson isolates – though the balance between powerlessness and total
power would be compromised if, as happened, the enslaved continued to believe
that there was a higher authority than their masters', and one which they had
to heed. Hangings, whippings and amputations did not eradicate this faith.

Jacob S. Dorman, in his essay "I Saw You Disappear with My Own Eyes",
says of the decade of the 1920s in the United States, known as the "Harlem
Renaissance": "rather than being simply the decade of the novels, politics
and rent parties, [it] was a period of profound religious creativity".[14] One of
the manifestations of this religious creativity, as seen by Dorman, is Rabbi

Matthews's organization called, in the literature, the "Black Jews of Harlem", though Matthews and his followers referred to themselves "from the name of their lodge, the Royal Order of Ethiopian Hebrews, the Sons and Daughters of Culture Inc."[15] But this creation was not only in New York, nor was it the only aggregation to be called "Black Jews", as Dorman admits. In any case, Rabbi Matthews's people did call themselves "the Commandment Keepers" as well, emphasizing that they were not Jews who happened to be black-skinned but people who wished to keep the Commandments, which the God of the Old Testament had required of his chosen people. One of the aims of the Commandment Keepers was to alert Africans of the diaspora to the fact that to be defined as "Negroes" as whites defined them was erroneous: they were in reality the true Israelites, the Hebrews, the people with whom God had made his covenant, the descendants of Jacob, smooth as only black men are, of Solomon, who himself said he was black, and of the Ethiopian Hebrews made from the connection between the Queen of Sheba and Solomon.

It was the task of these blacks who had now found their true identities to observe the Commandments of God as laid out in the Holy Bible, such that they would become the light of the world that God had intended them to be. This was not a new theory or strategy: nineteenth-century Europeans had made the same claim for Europe.[16] Nor was it new to African Americans. It had been propounded by others, including the Prophet Crowdy, who did so in the last decades of the nineteenth century. It is Prophet Crowdy's intellectual creation, his version of Ethiopianism, that we examine now. Called the Church of God and Saints of Christ, Crowdy's religio-intellectual creation had spread its roots to Jamaica by the 1930s. Was this by coincidence, the existence of two peoples of similar problems fashioning consequent similar solutions, or was one the heir of the other, fathered by contact?

The post-Reconstruction years in the US South were terrible for the African Americans. After sitting as representatives of the people in the highest institutions of the states, the Tilden-Hayes compromise had stripped them of federal support and exposed them to angry whites who were intent on returning to their states the nature of the relationship between blacks and whites that had held sway during slavery. Prophet Crowdy experienced the perfidy of Reconstruction. Like several other blacks, he took the federal government's offer of land in Oklahoma, moving there from his birthplace in Maryland. He was one of the seven thousand who entered the territory in the first year of settlement, and by September 1891, he had laid claim to 160 acres under the federal homestead law. A settled family man making a living from farming, he became an ardent mason of the Prince Hall variety, a Baptist deacon and a captain of a black militia.

Although blacks, following the breach between the northern and southern states which had led to the Civil War, had been moving out of the established Christian churches, organizing their own versions of these churches and faithfully attending them, there were those African Americans who felt that their creations were not linking the spiritual and the mundane well enough for the betterment of blacks and that the race was accordingly in a moral bind, still powerless, perhaps because it was out of sync with God. Crowdy was one of those who felt like this. On 13 September 1892, he, like the prophets of the Old Testament and Africans in various parts of the diaspora, thought he heard the voice of God calling him to be his messenger to the children of Israel and all nations on earth who had not been obeying God's Commandments.[17] Like Jonah, he was so overcome at being thus selected that he pretended that the order had not been given.

More startling communication came the year later, in which he was shown the name of the organization he was to lead and where in the Bible to find the seven keys that would be its theological base. Still hesitant, he bargained with God: if you give me a good harvest, I will go. He got a good harvest that year and the following, and though he did go out and preach, it was only in the town near to him, though he knew that God expected more of him. Finally, a poor harvest and ill health convinced him to keep his side of the bargain, and in 1895, he set out to proselytize far and wide. He went to farther parts of Kansas, to Arkansas, to Chicago and even to Canada. His notion was that all church organizations had failed to keep the statutes of God; they had left the real church. His major task was to re-establish this church; he would reawaken the true children of Abraham, and he would help them to behave themselves as the Lord had hoped Abraham's children would. One of the things they would do was respect and observe all rites decreed by the God of the Holy Bible, such as the Passover. Taunts, arrests, even denunciation by fellow African American preachers followed, but they did not deter him.

Crowdy was as troubled as Marcus Garvey would be by the social and economic conditions of black people, and in his mid-career, 1901, he opened in

Philadelphia a restaurant and a dry goods store called Noah's Ark for the people of his church; but though he did care about the conditions, spiritual and otherwise, of people of his race, neither the historian of the organization, Elly M. Wynia, nor the history published by the organization explicitly states that Crowdy saw the children of Abraham as African Americans only, or that he entertained only blacks. In fact, it was an Irish man who, hearing him preach on State Street in Chicago in 1896 and convinced of the righteousness of his message, advised him to "go back and get some of your people to ordain you a bishop, and organize yourself, then you won't be arrested so much".[18] He did accordingly, organizing a unit in Kansas, appointing an elder and, as he travelled, setting up tabernacles in the towns he visited. In 1898, he was able to call a state-wide assembly in Kansas. At this assembly, Crowdy appointed J.M. Groves as an acting bishop and appointed, as well, the first Board of Presbytery of the church. According to Elder Locke, local pastor at the International Headquarters at Beth-El, in Suffolk, Virginia, with whom I spoke in 2008, Bishop Grove was white, and his photograph displayed on a wall confirms this. At this assembly, Crowdy was consecrated to the office of bishop. Acting Bishop Grove, the white man, was one of those who officiated at the consecration. It is also written that most of those subsequently baptized into the church on Crowdy's post-consecration travel to Upstate New York were white.[19] The board of the Presbytery, recently formed, then installed Crowdy as the organization's executive head and gave him papers permitting him to preach. Crowdy and the Church of God and Saints of Christ, a name revealed to him by God and mentioned in 1 Corinthians 1:1–2, now had an institutional base. Before the assembly closed, an administrative structure of secretaries, pastors, travelling evangelists and a state Sabbath school superintendent were added to the administrative tree; bodies were found to fill these slots; and a women's unit was formed. A constitution governing all these roles was also drawn up. Crowdy now pressed on more confidently on his proselytizing missions, baptizing whites as well as blacks. He travelled to several cities, New York being one of them. Here a tabernacle was officially organized on 6 May 1899, twenty-one years before the Harlem Renaissance and the rise of black Jewry as discussed by Dorman.

It is not surprising that it was blacks, the children of the powerless slaves, who, no doubt realizing that part of their continued powerlessness lay in the definition of themselves inherited from the children of the slave masters, were thus more eager to define themselves as children of Abraham, as Israel; to be called "saints" as per the passage in Corinthians; and to join in the re-establishment movement.[20] The movement grew, and so did the messages from God, many of them dictating miniature orders, such as the colours to be worn to certain services, the importance of a fine choir, the seating placement of church officials in public worship and the positions which people should assume in their private prayers. Crowdy passed away in 1908. He left a tried administrative system, a liturgy, a theological base and tabernacles in most northern US cities, in which there were significant aggregations of blacks. He also left for his people a place of refuge. The Spirit of God in another verbal encounter led him to the spontaneous purchase of forty acres of land in Virginia, which he called Canaan. The voice told him that he needed this as a refuge for his people. The Church of God was re-established, Canaan was re-established in the New World, Abraham was reseated in physical bodies in the church and so were the several daughters of Jerusalem. He left, in order of succession, Joseph William Crowdy, a very young man, William H. Plummer, next in age, and Calvin S. Skinner, the eldest. They died in this same order, the youngest going first, evidence of special foresight, lauded by the church today.

Prophet Crowdy, by what has to be called divine intervention, also left a church unit in Africa. In the style of Old Testament prophets and African religionists, Albert Christian, a missionary worker, in a dream saw Crowdy beckoning him towards a specific task. With only the outline of a face to guide him, he left his country and eventually found the man in his dream on Fitzwater Street in Philadelphia in 1902. Crowdy subsequently ordained him an elder, and in 1903, he was elevated to the position of evangelist, then consecrated as a bishop and sent back to Africa to the work of re-establishing God's church there and raising up the saints into the Church of God and Saints of Christ, the name under which the church was incorporated in 1896. Crowdy was not just a preacher and an avid reader of the Bible; he wrote hymns and published the *Weekly Prophet* as the organ of mass communication for the saints and whoever wished to read it. He also wrote his experiences in a publication called *The Bible Story Revealed*. In this kind of intellectual activity, activity which attacked the religious base of the black powerlessness, Crowdy joined a number of African Americans, among them David Walker, who understood that the facet of powerlessness by which the enslaved are convinced that their condition is so decreed by a higher power must be eradicated from their minds if they are to feel powerful. They must place an alternative "authority" within the culture.[21]

There were many revolts by the enslaved Africans in Jamaica; there was a consciousness that a racial and cultural distinction was made in the thinking of the definers and that this described blacks as inferior, but the African Jamaicans' consciousness of this did not lead to the kind of intellectual activity we see in David Walker or the late nineteenth-century works of Crummell, such as "The Destined Superiority of the Negro".[22] The post-emancipation late nineteenth-century African Jamaican, such as Festus the schoolteacher, brother of Claude McKay, read, but the works they read were written by Englishmen. They wrote, too, and owned newspapers, as Robert Love did, but their focus tended to be on civil rights, on the rights of blacks who had qualified themselves to share in the running of the country, rather than on natural rights, the rights of everyone to be treated equally simply by being a human being. Black intellectuals like Love, with access to the printing press, were quite aware of the powerlessness of the African Jamaican: they looked to structural change of the government for an end to this condition.[23]

There were those – the many – who looked to changes in their sense of self: they looked to spiritual power, to the de Laurence publications' prescriptions for approaching the power that Moses and Solomon were able to wield.[24] These were people who, unlike Love, were from families that had seen little change since emancipation in 1838. Some of this class, still hoping for the kind of spiritual power which came from being able to summon ancestral spirits and communicating with the pantheon of African and Christian spirits, had been by the 1930s seduced into the many Christian churches coming in from the United States. As Diane J. Austin-Broos has shown, the native creations Myal and Revival were consequently sanitized into Pentecostalism.[25] By the time the Harlem Renaissance was in full swing in the United States, Pentecostalism, that American import, had seated itself comfortably in African Jamaica. The Seventh-Day Adventists had come too, and so had the Roman Catholics, both from the United States as well. It was not just church attendance in which black Jamaican peasants were involved; it was discourse on the rightness or otherwise of theological positions and the benefits to be derived from each.[26] Into this fray came the salvationist/city mission, a healing mission, bringing some respectability to the healing activities of Myal and Revival.[27]

There was a plethora of organizations in the years preceding the Wall Street Crash. African Jamaicans, mostly peasant and rural, had to consider how trade unions battling with the sugar cane factories beneath whose shadow they lived could help them out of powerlessness. How should they feel towards the Chinese, progressively the shopkeepers in all their villages? This discourse was shaped in racial terms at a time when Marcus Garvey was advising blacks throughout the world that the path from powerlessness lay in unity among them. His return to Jamaica in 1927, with his meetings at Edelweiss Park, his concerts and his marches, aroused the African Jamaicans into self-evaluation; so did the many organizations, petitions and meetings from other political groups to discuss the relationship between Jamaica and Britain – black Jamaica and white Britain – and the benefits to be gained from ending the colonial attachment. A new voice was that of the Rastafarians, encouraging a poor and tax-ridden African Jamaican population not to pay taxes on the grounds that King George of England was not their king; theirs, given their race and ethnicity, had to be an African.[28]

The poem which begins this chapter as well as the Psalm on which it is based mentions not only Ethiopia but Egypt: "Princes and princesses shall come out of Egypt" is the way the verse begins.[29] It is more than likely that R. Williams, the English clergyman said to have written this poem, and the many other clergymen, black and otherwise, would have offered the whole verse to their audience. In any case, with literacy, and especially Bible literacy, blacks are likely to have read the whole verse for themselves and understood the prophecy to mean that they would be or could be royalty here on earth. This thought might have been difficult for their white patrons to believe, but hardly so for West Africans, who prior to their journey to the New World were likely to have seen a durbar and the displays of elegance and gold on the persons of the kings and the queen mothers who shared their phenotype. They were likely to pass on descriptions of the events to their descendants, so that traces of the knowledge of the wealth and dignity of black people might be in their consciousness.[30] Being royalty indeed is not far in the imagination from being God's chief servant. The slaves and the ex-slaves would not only have access to the hand of God as they stretched out theirs to him; they also would have had the status of princes and princesses.

The Church of God and Saints of Christ under Bishop William H.J. Plummer got positive mention from the African American middle class. Of Canaan, which

Prophet Crowdy had been led to purchase as a refuge for his people, the saints, Carter G. Woodson's assistant Lorenzo Greene wrote in his diary:

> What a place! Virtually self-sustaining. These people have their own saw mill, laundry, barber and tailoring shops, general store and studio. Also have their own mechanics, carpenters, brick layers, engineers, electricians etc. A guide pointed out the new Tabernacle which was in course of construction. Its architecture defies description – a combination embracing ancient Assyrian, Babylonian, and Egyptian styles. There is also an industrial building, a two story frame affair; the old tabernacle, a long narrow yellow frame structure about 200 feet long and 50 feet wide; and a primary school, presided over by one Professor Coleman of New Jersey.[31]

The middle-class academic Lorenzo Greene and perhaps Carter G. Woodson, to whom he reported, were also intrigued that Bishop Plummer, formerly a lowly storekeeper in Roxbury, Massachusetts, had been raised up to headship of the organization by Prophet Crowdy and given the title of Grandfather Abraham – that Crowdy had thought so well of him as to pass up his own son for the headship and given it to Plummer. The diarist, Greene, remarked that a wise decision had been made, for when Plummer succeeded Crowdy, there had been but five cents in the treasury, and later the church owned 810 acres of land, the original 40 acres expanded by judicious purchases. The property was now valued at $250,000, with only a $13,500 mortgage left to be paid off.

The diary continued to describe the bishop's home, a description which makes it clear that the bishop was attracted to the culture of Africa, and especially of Ethiopia, and wanted to maintain a connection with it – though the church makes no claim to a connection to an African high culture, brought to the United States by their enslaved ancestors: "We were escorted through the bishop's home [by his son]. It was palatial. Everything reminiscent of Africa, the walls, the ceiling, curtains and some of the fittings all suggestive of Ethiopia. The bishop's son informed us that his father is making an effort to recreate the lost Ethiopian art."[32]

At this time, there were four sister churches in South Africa, one in Cuba and two in other parts of the United States.[33] It was in 1922 that Bishop Plummer gave Evangelist-at-Large Chase, appointed to this position in 1917, permission to establish the work in Cuba, and it was there that Chase met the Jamaican Hugh Henry Levy. They became friends, and Hugh Levy and his wife, Rose, joined the organization, the latter even being appointed as district secretary. The church in Cuba faded, and the Levys, now back at home, invited Evangelist Chase to Jamaica, where in 1931 they established the church at the corner of North and Regent streets. Under Chase and the new head of the whole organization, Howard A. Plummer, Grandfather Abraham, the Jamaican church grew and was moved to 18 Johns Lane. By 1933 there were about 120 members, and an ordained minister was sent to Barclays Town in St Mary and another to Spanish Town.[34]

The Church of God and Saints of Christ in Jamaica followed the style of the original church of Crowdy. Crowdy had been very particular about forms in the church, from seating arrangements to style of dress and form of worship. Theologically, this was the church of the God of Israel, which had lost its way over the ages and was now being re-established. Understandably, the saints of the old days would be returned and were, for all members of the church were seen and addressed as saints. Returned of course was Abraham, the administrative head of the church, his wife Sarah, chief females and other figures such as Ruth and Martha. African Jamaicans had talked with saints of old and had even been possessed by their spirits, but to be the returned saint was relatively new. It is true that Garvey and Bedward had been seen not just as people possessed by the spirits of Moses and Aaron, but as the physical embodiments of these two Hebrew icons; but for a whole church of people to be seen as the physical representative of the biblical Hebrews was new and revolutionary.[35]

Though Garvey and the UNIA had uniformed marchers, these uniforms – of nurses and soldiers – were familiar. The men of the Church of God and Saints of Christ wore suits, all of the same make and colour, and they wore bow ties and sashes across their chests. The female saints wore satin bows in their hair, all in the same position. All wore many-coloured rosettes. They were a new sight on the streets of downtown Kingston, and they were followed, mocked, harassed and taunted on their way to and from church, so much that Evangelist Chase ordered that the men should walk behind the ladies on the streets to protect them from physical abuse. Add to this strangeness the fact that the songs sang in the church were not from the "sankey" of the Pentecostal churches with which most Jamaicans living in the vicinity of the church were familiar,[36] not the hymns "ancient and modern" of the early established Protestant churches which had courted them and their fathers in the post-emancipation days, but were the creations of the members of the parent body. It would seem strange to these onlookers too that there was no spirit possession. Even more strange was the marching. Church ceremonials involved marching within and outside of the church, and this was the marching not of lodges nor of the army to which they were accustomed but movement resembling that of a prancing horse, which the initiates called "the holy prance".[37] As in the American churches, the "stone of truth" on which the church laid was the seven keys, one of which was that the members should wash each other's feet, as John 13:14–17 shows to have been done in the original churches set up by those who had walked with Jesus Christ. Members were to be breathed on and greeted with a holy kiss, as at John 20:22 and Romans 16:16. Sabbath was observed on a Saturday but encompassed the time from Friday evening to Saturday evening. Still more unusual, the church acknowledged and celebrated all the holidays of the Bible – Rosh Hashanah, the Jewish new year; Yom Kippur, the day of atonement marked by fasting from sundown to sundown; Succoth, the harvest festival occurring five days after Yom Kippur; Shavuout, occurring seven weeks after Passover and in honour of the giving of the Ten Commandments; Thanksgiving Day, a time to give thanks to God for all his blessings; and of course Passover, the day when the children of Israel really knew that they were blessed and that God was on their side, for all people except them lost their firstborns.

These festivals were no part of general African Jamaican knowledge. After the First World War, several European Jews migrated to New York. Living close to the African Americans, these latter could see them at worship and at their celebrations and become familiar with their forms, and the Black Jews of New York could be accused, though they denied this, of imitating white Jewry. This was not so in Jamaica, the Jewish community being small and private in their religious activities. The forms of the Church of God and Saints of Christ's celebrations were installed by the evangelists sent to minster to the saints re-established in Jamaica. These forms were themselves the original creations of Bishop Crowdy. These celebrations, many of them colourful and requiring that the saints spend a lot of time going back and forth from their homes to their tabernacle, kept them in Kingston's public eye. A people accustomed to venting as the spirit gave them utterance are unlikely to flock to an organization as disciplined and as exact in its observances as the Church of God and Saints of Christ. They are likely, however, to respect it and to copy externals and even some of its language.

Barry Chevannes, in the preface to his singular work *Rastafari: Roots and Ideology*, in discussing the difficulty of "validation of sources" for researchers using oral testimony, states, with respect to his own work on Rastafari: "I would like to think that there is such a person as the Seven Keys man (chapter 3), even though I have yet to find any written sources."[38] It is in this chapter 3 that he deals most specifically with the roots of Rastafari. These roots, according to this chapter, are located in Revivalism and Garveyism. It troubles Chevannes, though, that some of his informants have mentioned the Seven Keys man and his doctrine of seven keys as a foundation man and thought:

> Several informants, when asked what they knew about Africa, kept referring, in passing, to the "the Seven Keys". I took little notice of this reference until Dixon described the tall, strapping man, him mout' red, big hand, big lip, big nose. He was "from foreign". According to Dixon the man came one day to Oxford Street, stood beneath the piazza of a Chinese shop, and shouted out, "Take seven keys to breathe God's word, Deuteronomy to seal!" A large crowd gathered including children, and with readings from the Bible and hymn singing he began to teach the people about Africa "where the living God is". Soon he formed a religious sect known as the Seven Keys and included children in it.[39]

Chevannes's informant claimed that the man was from "foreign" and was subsequently arrested and, he thinks, deported.[40] Chevannes himself thinks that the Seven Keys man must have been a Revival leader, because his followers were said to have been dressed in white.

The "seven keys" is an often-mentioned concept in the Church of God and Saints of Christ. These are the keys to the church given to Prophet Crowdy by the Lord in a vision, referring to Bible passages found in Corinthians, Leviticus, Matthew, John, Romans and Revelations. The blessings and curses of Deuteronomy 28 are not unknown and are very important to establishing the connection between God and the Africans of the diaspora. From verse 1 to 14 of this chapter in the Bible, we read of the blessings to be given to those who keep the Commandments, and from verse 15 to 68, we read of the curses on those who do not keep the Commandments. Verse 68 is interpreted as a direct reference to Africans enslaved in the New World: "And the Lord shall bring thee again into Egypt with ships, by the way whereof I spoke unto thee, thou shalt see it no more again; and there ye shall be sold unto your enemies for male and female slaves." Deuteronomy 30 deals with restoration, which comes after repentance. Verses 1–4 read:

> And it shall come to pass, when all these things are come upon thee, the blessings and the curse, which I have set before thee and thou shalt call them to mind among all the nations to which the Lord thy God has driven thee, and shall return unto the Lord thy God, and shall obey his voice according to all that I command thee this day, thou and thy children, with all thine heart and with all thy soul, that then the Lord thy God will turn thy captivity, and have compassion upon thee and will return and gather thee from all the nations where the Lord thy God has scattered thee.

The chapter ends compassionately at verses 19–20:

> I call heaven and earth to record this day against you that I have set before you life and death, blessing and cursing; therefore chose life, that both thou and thy seed may live, that thou mayest love the Lord thy God and that thou mayest obey his voice and that thou mayest cleave unto him; for he is thy life, and the length of thy days; that thou mayest dwell in the land which the Lord swore unto thy fathers, to Abraham, to Isaac and to Jacob, to give them.

Though Deuteronomy is not one of the books of the Bible in which we find the seven keys, the selections above as well as most of this chapter are known in the organization to be part of the rationale for the movement's notion that Africans, and Africans of the diaspora, are the Hebrews with whom God made his covenant.[41] Which other people were taken away from their lands by ships? The reference to Deuteronomy which Chevannes's informant Dixon heard could have been coming from someone in the hierarchy of the Church of God and Saints of Christ.

Evangelist-at-large Chase looks from his photograph seen at the headquarters in Virginia to be a big, dark man, big like the Seven Keys man of Chevannes's informant. He is known to have native Indian forebears and could have reddish lips. He is wearing in his photograph a white robe, such as the Seven Keys man was said to have been wearing. Such garb was not unusual among the clerics in this organization, especially in the four summer months, when the colour white is mandated dress. Evangelist Chase is an American, a man from "foreign", as was the Seven Keys man of Chevannes's informant. The church he was helping to establish in Kingston was not far from Oxford Street, where Chevannes's informant heard talk of the seven keys and Deuteronomy; it was on the corner of North and Regent streets then, later on, Johns Lane and East Queen Street. For evangelists to teach on the streets was quite normal. This man, said to have established the Seven Keys sect, could have been Evangelist Chase. Legal proceedings had been brought against the church. The suit was thrown out of court but could have initially been accompanied by an arrest as Chevannes's informant's Seven Keys man experienced. Evangelist Chase left Jamaica in June 1938 but was back before the end of the year. His health deteriorated, and he was therefore not as active as before. Someone not in the heart of the church might not realize that a court case and possible arrest ended with the matter being thrown out of court, and might not know that Evangelist Chase, the Seven Keys man, had not left Jamaica permanently. In fact, he died there in 1948.[42]

Hinds, whom Chevannes calls the most successful of the early Rastafari, had his meeting place at 82 North Street, and later at 6 Laws Street.[43] Whether at the corner of North Street and Regent Street or at 59 East Queen Street, where the church later moved, Hinds was close enough to the Church of God and Saints of Christ and its functioning to have copied its externals. Moreover, given the respect for de Laurence and his books, and the fact that there was one entitled *Seven Keys to Power*, which purported to tell how to remedy conditions known as cross conditions – to be able to show people the key to the power of commanding; how to get rid of fear; how to find the proper hour for all magical undertakings; how to cast out devils, overcome enemies and uncross people; how to pray to remove all evil; and more – an organization which openly spoke of the seven keys as the foundation stones of their theology is likely to have been noticed and very respected, even if ridiculed.[44] The Church of God and Saints of Christ is likely to have been a flagship in Kingston. We hear of Hinds's Rastafarian sect as observing Passover and wearing rosettes.[45] The celebration of Passover was mandated in the Church of God and Saints of Christ; so were the rosettes a part of the dress. Might not this aspect of the church's behaviour be copied by the Hinds sect? The same could be said for their observance of the Ethiopian new year on 1 April. Though not always on 1 April, the Jewish new year, another mandated celebration in the Church of God and Saints of Christ, is held in April, the month of Abib. We are suggesting that Prophet Crowdy's creation brought over to Jamaica by his officer Evangelist Chase may be one of the roots of Rastafari.

After conceding the identity of the Seven Keys man to be Revival, Chevannes says: "The significant thing for us is that, appearing on the scene some time before the Garvey movement, he added another brick to the citadel of ideas that served as a defense against racist ideas."[46] These conclusions of course must apply to the Church of God and Saints of Christ, the organization from which the Seven Keys man could well have come. Before the coming of the Church of God and Saints of Christ, the powerless could be empowered by the understanding that they could be possessed by and converse with the great men and women of Israel, who were no longer on earth. With the coming of the Church of God and Saints of Christ, the powerless could now be those great men and women in the flesh and in the present. Bedward and Garvey, leaders of their sects, might be Moses and Aaron returned, but only they, not their followers, were seen as biblical re-creations – not so with the Church of God and Saints of Christ. The ordinary folk were saints and could be the re-established Sarah, Ruth and Martha. In line with the Ethiopian view, slavery could be clearly understood in terms of the breach of the special relationship that had been between God and black people and which could be repaired quite simply by keeping the Ten Commandments and others given to his people by the God of Israel. How powerful were blacks now, and especially those of the diaspora. They were, from their beginning, in a contract with the Christian God; they had broken this contract, but God had shown them how to reconnect. With this, we are taken past the Ethiopian view of history and into a re-establishment view.

History knows that Marcus Garvey went to the United States and co-opted African Americans into the largest black movement that the world has ever known; it knows that the Bahamas-born Dr Robert Love lived in Jamaica, and from this point was in touch with many of the African American intellectuals such as Blyden; it is beginning to know that other African American intellectuals, such as Du Bois, visited Jamaica and kept in touch with Jamaicans; that W.P. Livingston, the Jamaican intellectual, visited the African American experiment that Hampton College was; that Moton of Tuskegee came to visit Mico College, the educational experiment, in fulfilment of a plan of his predecessor, Booker T. Washington; that Jamaicans studied at Hampton. All of these meetings of African Americans and African Jamaicans in the early twentieth century could have created understanding between the intellectuals in the African diaspora.[47] It needs to be known, and I hope I have helped in this, that a creation by a simple African American farmer – who, supplementing his income by serving as a cook on the railway lines, was brought to Jamaica and could have helped to build the kind of ideas which could puncture one facet of the conceptual system on which white superiority and black inferiority, European superiority and African inferiority, the powerlessness of the children of slaves vis-à-vis the power of the children of enslavers, rested – could lay the foundation for the acceptance of the notion that men and women are the returned saints of the Bible. I have visited three of these congregations in Jamaica, had talks with the elders at their headquarters in Virginia in the United States and seen nothing but black-skinned people there. The Church of God and Saints of Christ has become a black organization. It stands to reason that the new Abraham, Sarah and David the shepherd boy, all black, are people who see themselves as beings who have not only stretched forth their hands unto God but sit with him as his saints and servants.

Was it from face-to-face contact or from similarity of historical and sociological experience that the African of the diaspora in the United States and in the Caribbean welcomed a theosophy which saw blacks as Ethiopian, and, by holy writ, God's particular servants as in the Church of God and Saints of Christ and the Commandment Keepers of the United States and the Rastafarians of Jamaica? We have seen, from 1741, conditions for contact between these two groups of Africans of the diaspora. And there were further contacts. As human beings and as hurting ones, they are likely to have shared their pain with each other and understood themselves to be part of a supernational entity, but did they together develop institutions to deal with this pain? Garvey's UNIA did this, but before the UNIA, the Church of God and Saints of Christ might be the clearest evidence of such cooperation.

{CHAPTER 5}

African American and African Jamaican Encounters Mainly in the Florida Sugar Cane Fields in 1943–1996

THOSE WHO APPLIED TO GO TO THE UNITED STATES as farm workers were men, and mostly from the rural areas. The contexts in which they made their livelihood in Jamaica were, as it had been for ages with rural Jamaican men, multiple.[1] Mr George Campbell, who was not good at the academic subjects taught in elementary school, and who was the second to last of ten children whose father abandoned them while George was still in elementary school, occasionally worked at several low-paying jobs simultaneously. He worked in copra, bundled and sold dye wood, chipped coconuts and, as his father and brother before him had done, worked on the banana boats. He also fished, mainly for lobsters. Added to these multiple tasks was planting crops for the consumption of his family on a small rented acreage. None of these jobs provided a stable income. He was twenty-nine years old when, in 1943, he made his first trip to the United States on the farm work programme,[2] part of the first cadre of men to leave Jamaica on that programme.

Campbell's namesake, Mr Bert Campbell, like George, was from Oracabessa, a village on Jamaica's north coast known for its banana-shipping wharves. Bert was a skilled mechanic, making more money than George Campbell when he did get paid. He took care of the vehicles of a baker/merchant who had a fleet of fourteen vehicles and he was the general fixer for anyone in Oracabessa who had a vehicle, but he had no fixed salary nor scale of payment attached to his labour. He worked with an older mechanic who was his mentor and got the occasional "cut" on a job. This man, Mr Ives, had visited America, and Bert felt that this was an experience to which a bright young man like himself should be exposed. In 1945, he managed to obtain a card, went through his interview and medicals and, at age twenty-seven, set off for the United States through the farm work programme. George Campbell's motive for going on the programme was more economy-based than Bert's. By 1943, George had a family and was having great difficulty in supporting them – so difficult, in fact, that he was often on his knees to his Lord in prayer, asking him to "open the seas" and make a way for him to find a better living.[3]

George Campbell's journey to the United States was fraught with trials: the boat taking him from Kingston to New Orleans was overcrowded; there was just one kitchen, so although passengers were due two meals, they barely had one, for when it was time for the second, the first was still being served; and even when you walked around the boat three times, the line waiting for access to the pipe carrying drinking water was too long to fill one's container. Men chose to drink the salt water from the sea rather than wait. To make things worse, fearing German submarines, the boat travelled without lights. One prospective farm worker was so distressed by these conditions that he threw himself overboard.[4]

George Campbell's five days on land after he reached New Orleans were better. The train taking the workers to the sugar beet farm had five kitchens, and he had time to appreciate the fact that he had a contract with the US government, by which he was to be paid fifty cents per hour. Though he did begin with thirty cents, he was not unhappy. He completed his contract and returned to Jamaica but was back in the United States on another contract within four months. On the first contract, he planted and hoed mint. On the second, he dealt with apple trees, picking the fruit and fertilizing the roots. After this contract, missing his family, he returned to Jamaica, but he kept returning to America, even staying for a run of two and half years.

George Campbell knew himself to be one who had not taken to the academic work in elementary school, but in his thirties, now travelling to the United States, his self-esteem rose a notch, for he knew himself to have become very knowledgeable about farming as a result of his travels to the United States. He learned a lot: for instance, that peach trees are very delicate, and only skilled people can be allowed to work on them. Management was so impressed with George that he was given leadership roles, though he did not receive the matching pay. He made a lot of friends in America, and when he was interviewed in 1990, he was still getting Christmas cards from friends he had made there. Bert, on the other hand, made trouble. His trip on the *Washington* from Kingston to Miami was uneventful. He went from Miami to Lake Harbor in Florida and then to Pickaway, Ohio, but with the tomato and corn burned down by the snow and payment linked to the quantity of work performed, and believing that as a consequence there would be very little pay available to him under the terms of his contract, he thought his stay pointless and wanted to return home. And he showed it.

Moreover, seeing how long it took for a sick mate to get treatment, and having to wait three weeks himself to see a doctor, he refused to work; sure that the management had no lien on his time, for he had come as part of the war project and now the war was over, he told the police when they were called that he was not satisfied with the treatment and would not be going back to work. Bert knew himself to be skilled, and his Jamaican friends told their white American bosses of this; so instead of doing agricultural work, he was made a waterman, and after that was given the task of driving the workers to the "bush". Nevertheless, he set off a mini revolt: being sent to the jail for refusing to labour at farming, eleven of his mates went with him into incarceration. He was shifted to Camp Murphy,[5] where he behaved in the same way and sought to have his case addressed by the state department in Washington, which eventually responded by sending him a "personal cheque", which he collected when he returned home to Jamaica and to his work as a mechanic.

George Campbell and Bert Campbell were African Jamaicans. Rural, low-income Jamaicans needing the farm work programme to experience the United States or to earn there, were normally like them – Jamaicans of African descent. The United States was a racist country: some of the 8,243 other Jamaicans who were in America with George Campbell as farm workers in 1943 and the other 20,995 who were there in 1945 with Bert Campbell faced racist incidents which "became politicized quickly by groups such as the Jamaica Progressive League in New York and Jamaica".[6] What was the nature of their relationship with the people who experienced American racism daily? We will examine this and other issues through the response of a collection of Jamaican men from Woodside, in St Mary, the same parish as Oracabessa, but inland, who participated in this farm work programme between 1954 and 1996 – a period of time when African Americans, Africans of the diaspora like them, through several media outlets, were actively attacking this racism. These men were interviewed in 2013 by two female graduate students from Vanderbilt University.[7]

Bert Campbell was right in associating the farm work programme with the Second World War. Hitler's Germany, intent on world domination, had begun using the waters close to the United States to disturb British shipping with the aim of starving Britain, its main enemy, into submission. At the same time, the social disturbances of the late 1930s in Jamaica and elsewhere in the British Caribbean frightened the Allies into seeing these areas as volatile and a possible chink in their defence in their struggle with the Germans. Continued distressing social conditions, which their researchers reported, and the anti-colonial sentiments manifesting themselves in the call for a new kind of political arrangement with Britain, increased the fear that Jamaica and the other British islands could be infiltrated by German interests. How to quiet the negative forces in Jamaica? The answer was to give in to their colonies' demands for a new constitution and try to ameliorate the social and economic conditions – but the first item that had to be attended to was military defence. The British and US governments shared this thinking and devised the Lend-Lease Act, through which the United States had permission to build naval and military bases in Jamaica and the rest of the British Caribbean, and Britain would secure war machinery to stave off the Germans who threatened her with blockade and intended starvation.[8]

Further thinking and talking led to the establishment of the Anglo-American Caribbean Commission. With the increased presence of German submarines in the Caribbean waters, the US government had to think seriously of war. Its secretary of agriculture projected that ten million men would be in the armed forces by 1943 and that, should America have to enter the war, its farms and factories would be left without the labour to produce and keep the country fed.[9] The 1941 bombing of the US fleet at Pearl Harbour by Japan, Germany's ally, and its attacks on US interests in the Far East propelled the United States into closer alliance with Britain, spurring this alliance into action to protect its resources: it would extend to others its Bracero scheme of 1942 by which, through a government-to-government arrangement with Mexico, its farms would have a sufficient supply of labour to keep US production high enough to meet internal needs.[10] By 1943, a similar agreement was made with the Government of Jamaica, by which thousands of Jamaican males would be recruited to work for short periods on American farms – an arrangement which could at the same time answer the threat to a chink in their defence in the form of angry rioting mobs; some of the potential rioters would be off the island but could then, with paying jobs, support their family so that they need not be so economically distressed that they turn to civil disobedience.

This facilitating programme, known as the War Manpower Commission, is what was in Bert Campbell's mind when he refused to work on the grounds that the war was over. The men chosen for this programme, according to the government-to-government agreement, would be paid a set fee, a portion of which would be sent back to Jamaica to support their families. The agreement that the workers signed stipulated that there would be no strikes. Thus, the programme which took Mr George Campbell and Mr Bert Campbell was a political strategy, a wartime measure to provide the kind of economic sustenance that would stave off instability in the Caribbean and so keep the Germans out while securing sufficiency of food for the American citizenry.

The programme continued until 1947, tweaked now and then to better serve its purpose as a wartime measure for the American economy and as a social stabilizer for the Jamaican government. Trade union interests in the United States were not always happy with it and, especially after 1947, took steps to disband it. Efforts such as these led to a new kind of agreement. Now, instead of the US Department of Agriculture, it was the US farmers requiring agricultural labour who would petition their government for permission to employ Jamaicans. These US farmers would now work with the Jamaican and West Indian governments to secure the short-term help of agricultural labourers. In the wartime programme, Jamaican men served in non-farm areas as well: Mr Sinclair of Oracabessa was selected in 1945.[11] He went to New York via the Hudson River and with five trainloads of mates was taken to Syracuse, where they worked in a factory which made parts for aeroplanes. This factory had a long lane of toilets. Mr Sinclair and his mates, some he found there from Hanover in Jamaica, had the job of cleaning these toilets and sweeping the factory floor. He would also help the native white men to lift the factory-made machinery onto the trains.

The Jamaican workers who came to the United States as a result of the government-to-government arrangement, or the US farmer–to–Jamaican government arrangement, at first lived in camps which seemed to house Jamaicans only, with even their chefs being Jamaican. Understandably, camaraderie existed between these Jamaicans, and they would try to beat the system – for example, they would punch in a friend who happened to be late for whatever reason. But they did interact with people of other geographic areas and with the natives in the factory. And those who worked other jobs, like Mr Sinclair, who sneaked off to work in the kitchen of a hotel during his off times despite the schedule of agreement, which stipulated that the worker should not work for anybody but the person to whom the government had assigned him, would have interacted with locals of whatever colour or race in his second and illegal job.[12]

A much-discussed internal issue was generated, mostly by the unions, by the existence of the West Indian/Jamaican workers on US farms. Were they depressing the labour market by accepting wages and conditions impossible for US citizens to accept? In meetings in 1955–57 between US farm owners, the West Indian governments and the US trade unions, the pro-West Indian farm worker lobby was able to convince the trade unions that the West Indian programme was so structured – with its ratio of one compliance officer to 650 workers as opposed to the US arrangement with Mexico, where there was just one compliance officer to 10,000 workers – that the British West Indian farm work programme could not be accused of setting low standards of protection for workers.[13] The question continued to be asked, however, whether the West Indians were not capturing jobs which could be done by a large body of under- and unemployed Americans – the African Americans. Farm owners responded by pointing out that West Indian labour was superior to African American labour. To hold and possibly express such opinions in the presence of the two peoples of the African diaspora could have brought resentment between them. Did it? The business of this chapter is to discern how these two groups got along. Unfortunately, the answers are from the African Jamaican perspective, as we have not been able to speak with a comparable collection of African Americans.

Woodside is an inland village of about three square miles, with a long history of small farming.[14] Of the fifteen men who went from Woodside to the United States through the farm work programme between 1954 and 1996, none was as skilled as Bert Campbell. Elcot was learning a trade but was getting no money; Sibrant knew the mason trade but was not working in it; Vincent could do some mason work and some plumbing but had no opportunity to work in these fields. All depended for livelihood on farming a small acreage of family or rented land and/or working with more prosperous small farmers as labourers. Hopeton was the only one who had a job which carried a salary: he was a security guard. All were dissatisfied with their economic conditions – their main source of income was farming, but they did not have money with which to buy fertilizer and spray for their plants, nor were there markets which gave them what they considered a fair price for their produce. They had seen others go on the farm work programme and return with clothes and money in their pockets, which some had used to build houses; they wanted to do likewise. "Travelling" is in the Jamaican gene pool.[15] Like Bert Campbell, most wished not just to earn money but to experience another part of the world. They considered themselves lucky to get a ticket with which to begin the application process for travel to the United States as temporary farm workers.

Between 1943 and 1946, the agreement between the US government and Jamaica was annually tabled in the Legislative Council of Jamaica. Apparently with actual action, flaws appeared in the agreement, making it clear that it needed to be modified. For instance, in 1943, the Jamaican workers were described as being "employed in agriculture and ancillary service",[16] but in 1944, it is agreed that "all workers may . . . be employed in any form of work which in the opinion of the government of the USA is calculated to further the orderly transition from war to peace";[17] in 1946, it is agreed that "all recruits would be placed in a single category i.e. agricultural laborers".[18] It was only at this time, too, three years after the first workers reached the American workspace, that instructions were laid out and issued to ticket distributors – namely:

(a) workers should be between the ages of 18–45 and should not weigh less than 130 pounds.
(b) workers should appear to be healthy and of good physique.
(c) repatriated workers with good conduct certificates should be given preference where possible.[19]

Initially, recruitment was in the hands of Sam Zemurray, an American and the head, for many years, of the United Fruit Company, which had for a long time dominated banana production in Jamaica. He and the Jamaican government came to the agreement that the workers would be paid three US dollars per day or at least one US dollar and sixty cents per day with food. It was the Jamaican governor, Richards, still preoccupied with the relationship between poverty and social disturbance, who insisted that some of this money stay in Jamaica to alleviate poverty and discourage rioting. He thus saw to it that a clause was written into the agreement that the sum of one US dollar per day be deducted from the farm workers' pay, a sum which would be sent back to a savings account in Jamaica. Before leaving Jamaica, each person had to declare his dependents and appoint one to administer the money kept in the savings account. The Jamaican government could not now feel obliged to offer poor relief to such dependents. Not only did people like George Campbell now have a salary, but so did the wife and children they left behind. Sam Zemurray must have chosen his sub-distributors in such a way that the centres of recruitment were areas which had a high unemployment profile, for this is the answer that the colonial secretary gave when quizzed by Mr Lowe in the Legislative Council on 8 April 1943.[20] In an earlier session (in March), the colonial secretary asked members of the house to suggest where in the parishes these centres should be and that they suggest names of those who should be the distributors.[21]

The year 1944 had seen a new constitution for Jamaica, one in which there was a house of representatives chosen by universal adult suffrage. The members of this house were very pleased with the behaviour of their countrymen on the farm work programme. One, Mr Coke, spoke of the Jamaican farm workers' service as "war service of the most fundamental nature" and proposed that on their return home these persons be given lands.[22] He was no doubt comparing them to the soldiers who fought in the world wars and were settled on lands on their return home to Jamaica. Another was angry that the workers were debarred from taking back to Jamaica luggage in excess of seventy pounds. The Jamaican labourer, he added, had "broken all records for work on the American agricultural front".[23] Another, Mr McFarlane, gave notice that he would propose a resolution that the Government of Jamaica wave the duties on personal effects and other belongings that farm workers sent to their families.[24] Clearly, the Jamaican farm worker was a highly regarded entity in the imagination of his political representatives.

After 1946, this entity moved out of public discourse and discussions in the House of Representatives and the Legislative Council until 1955. In November of that year, there was a report in the *Daily Gleaner* that Sir Hugh Foot, the governor of Jamaica, visited the United States, where he had talks with the state department concerning the farm labour programme.[25] He seems to have gone in at the tail end of a confrontation between the unions and the employers of farm labour, for with the end of the war, the programme had become a private matter between the American employers and the British West Indian governments acting through a regional labour board. The American unions felt, as before, that the employers of foreign labour, and particularly those operating on the US west coast, were intent on flooding the labour market with cheap labour, thus keeping American citizens, who could not exchange their labour for such low returns, out of the market. They wanted to be quite sure that Jamaican/West Indian labour was not similarly exploited by these independent agricultural businesses to the detriment of local labour. This concern and attendant discourse had been part of an ongoing discussion in diplomatic circles, for the governor mentioned that he had been told there that Mr Glasspole of Jamaica, representing the West Indies Labour Programme, had been having favourable talks with the unions and had convinced them that the arrangement by which Jamaican and West Indian labourers worked on farms in the United States was so organized that it could not be a threat to unionized American labour.

By August of the following year, the public was told the following:

> The United States Congress has been urged by the US section of the Joint United States-Mexico Trade Union Committee to enter into an international bilateral agreement with British West Indian Governments in connection with the US farm labour programme. The committee in a statement submitted to Congress has declared itself in favour of the employment of more workers from the British West Indies rather than workers from the Far East or even from Mexico, because of the superior liaison organization maintained by the BWI [British West Indian] governments in the United States and the fact that BWI workers were better able to cope with problems which may arise in connection with their employment.[26]

The union was further asking that the British West Indian Labour Programme be placed on a bilateral basis under an international agreement. The glad tidings manifested gloriously in a buffet supper given by the Government of Jamaica for the visiting American employers of British West Indian labour and the regional labour board in January of 1961. If the governor of Jamaica, Sir Kenneth Blackbourne, who addressed the gathering at this function, is to be believed, this was the fourth time that the American employers of farm labour were visiting the island on farm labour business. Clearly, the employers of farm labour were eager for Jamaican labourers. Some of these visits and talks might have, in part, been stimulated by the word that there was to be a West Indian federation. In

1943, when the programme began, the British West Indies were mere colonies of Great Britain, and the agreements had been arranged between the American government and the British government. A limited form of self-government had come to Jamaica in 1944, but external affairs remained in the hands of the British, who found it more convenient for the matter of farm labour to be managed as a West Indian issue and through a regional labour board, although Jamaica sent the greatest number of men to the programme. In the late 1940s and throughout the 1950s, there was talk of Britain granting independence to her British West Indian colonies through a federation. How this federation would affect the farm labour programme must have been in the thinking of the American employers, especially since only four weeks before the meeting in Jamaica there had been talks between the US government and the Jamaican government about the future of the bases in the Caribbean, which had been leased to the United States, preliminary to her entry into the Second World War.[27] Governor Blackbourne, in his continuing speech, was paraphrased thus by the *Gleaner* reporter: "This farm labour programme over the years had taken thousands of men up to the United States where they learned something of the American way of life and he hoped that it would continue to progress not merely for the benefit that the West Indies government, but because it was vital that the United States and the West Indies should work together for world peace."[28]

Part of the "American way of life" at this time included the struggle of the African Americans for civil rights accompanied by the bombing of their churches, forcible ejection from lunch counters, prevention from entering white educational institutions and other instances which characterized the US way of life as a white supremacist one. Of how much of this American way of life were the Jamaican farm workers aware, and what was their response to it?

As table 5.1 shows, only one of the men who went from Woodside to do farm labour in the United States between 1954 and 1996 was under twenty years old; ten were in their twenties, and four were in their thirties, capable not only of physical labour but of assessing their lives and comparing it with that of others, as they were asked to do in our interviews with them.

These men served all over the United States, and as table 5.2 shows, most were return workers. Called "repatriated workers" of good conduct, they were the most desired and first to be hired. As we see in the table, the Woodside men were obviously among the most desired, some like Leon going back as many as

Table 5.1. Farm Workers from Woodside Distributed According to Year of Birth, Year of First Visit and Actual Age at First Visit

	Name	Year of Birth	Year of First Visit	Actual Age at First Visit
1.	A.P.	1935	1961	26
2.	Elcott	1944	1966	22
3.	Ellis	1932	1964	32
4.	Ephraim	1938	1969	31
5.	Gus	1957	1976	19
6.	Hopeton	1959	1989	30
7.	James	1947	1970	23
8.	Kenroy	1953	1983	30
9.	Leon	1945	1969	24
10.	Lloyd	1938	1961	23
11.	Raphael	1944	1969	23
12.	Roy	1933	1955	22
13.	Samuel	1967	1973	26
14.	Sibrant	1944	1970	26
15.	Vincent	1933	1955	22

fifteen times. Only one, Ephraim, went only once, staying for less than three months. They served in the northern states of Massachusetts, Connecticut, New York, Vermont, Maine, New Hampshire, Pennsylvania, Illinois, Wisconsin and in the upper southern states of Maryland, Virginia, West Virginia and North Carolina. An agreement had been made that they should not be sent to the deep southern states, though, as we shall later see, Florida became the workplace of most.[29]

The social environment in which the farm workers served varied with the state of the union in which they found themselves. As we see from table 5.2, of the fifteen men from Woodside who went to the United States as farmworkers between 1954 and 1996, seven – Elcot, Hopeton, Raphael, Roy, Samuel, Kenroy and Vincent – had worked in other states besides Florida, but only one – Samuel – had not worked in Florida. Outside of Florida, in New Hampshire for instance, the labour force was relatively small and included other races. Samuel found few blacks on the street, and he worked along with African Americans in picking

Table 5.2. Location and Frequency of Service of Woodside Farm Workers

	Name	Location	Frequency
1.	A.P.	Pelican Lake (Florida)	Three times; first time was for three years
2.	Elcott	Mocha and Ronian (Florida), Winchester (Virginia) and North Carolina	1966–69 and 1985
3.	Ellis	West Road, South Bay, Felles Meare, Okeelanta (Florida)	1954, 1955 and 1956, for nine months each
4.	Ephraim	South Bay (Florida)	Once for six weeks
5.	Gus	Pompino Beach, Payote (Florida)	1974 and 1980, for six months each
6.	Hopeton	Auburn (Connecticut), Florida, Massachusetts	Four times: six months one place, four months another; shifting between Connecticut and Massachusetts on two or three farms at the same time in different states
7.	James	Okeelanta (Florida)	1970 and 1971, for six months each
8.	Kenroy	Connecticut, Florida, Miramax Street (Massachusetts)	Six times; 1983 for one year, all other times (1983–96) for six months
9.	Leon	[H]Okeelanta (Florida)	1969–81 twice per year, staying six months; total fifteen times
10.	Lloyd	Pelican Lake (Florida)	Four times in 1961–66; first time for three seasons
11.	Raphael	New York, Belle Glade (Florida)	1969 and 1980, three months each
12.	Roy	Florida, West Virginia, Maryland, Illinois, Wisconsin	1955 and 1957; was there once for two years and nine months; shifted from camp to camp and state to state
13.	Samuel	New York, Maine, Connecticut, Virginia, Vermont	Six times in 1979–1990
14.	Sibrant	Belle Glade (Florida)	Three times, six months each
15.	Vincent	Florida, Maryland, New Hampshire, Pennsylvania	Six times in 1974, 1979, 1980, 1981, 1982 and 1984; shifted from farm to farm and state to state

apples. On the farm in Massachusetts, Kenroy was one of only three – the others were an Indian and a Vietnamese. In this family setting, he went to work at 7:00 a.m., and at 10:00 a.m., the owner's wife would bring them coffee. The family took him to church with them, and he was so loved by this white congregation of Christians that after his return to Jamaica they sent him three hundred US dollars.

The "bossman" everywhere was white. Vincent's in New Hampshire was so good to him that he described him as being "a father to us".[30] He would take his workers anywhere they wanted to go, help them to organize parties in the camp and even find girls for them – white girls. Hopeton's bossman was so comfortable with him that he went to Jamaica on vacation, and the two had a happy reunion in Montego Bay. Roy had worked in Illinois, where he had weeded beside Mexicans and Puerto Ricans. Here white people were ticket writers and managers and were separated by fences from the workers. Roy had been in Wisconsin, too, where two white children held on to his hand and would not let go, though he tried to shrug them off. They took him to their father, with whom he felt so at home that he offered to help him with continuing to mow his lawn. Roy was subsequently invited into his house, where the man's wife offered to do his laundry whenever he needed help. This man invited Roy and his nineteen mates to a nightclub, where they drank and danced with white women. At another time, while he was in Wisconsin, a woman asked to feel his hair, and having done so, she remarked that she wished her hair was like his. Such incidents made Roy feel equal to and loved by whites. Outside of Florida, the workforce was relatively small, the largest by Hopeton's reckoning being two hundred. It was ethnically diverse, though West Indians did find corners in which to live their lives divided according to island. Here in 1967 on the farms, excluding the ones in Florida, the market for white mates was so open that Samuel, an African Jamaican, dated "only white women".[31]

These northern US experiences were quite unlike those in Florida, the state in which all fifteen men, with the sole exception of Samuel, worked at some time or another. In Florida there were large collectivities. The men list the camps to which they went as Pelican Lake, Big Sugar/Ronian, South Bay, Florida Sugar, Sugar House, Atlantic and Okeelanta. These camps, by their reports, could each hold in excess of five hundred people. James, who arrived in 1970, estimates that there were as many as a thousand men in Okeelanta; Leon, there twice a year between 1969 and 1981, calls it one thousand; and Ellis, there three times between 1954 and 1956, gives an estimate of 950, but according to him, it could be as many as nine thousand in the several camps in the area combined. In each camp, men were housed under one roof; the building was more often than not two-storied, and the men slept in bunks of two tiers. Near one's bunk was a place for his personal items. There were no fewer than two bathrooms per floor. The men bathed in water in which the flow was not always abundant because it was recycled water, and it was not always hot when you needed it to be.

On arrival at the camp, the men were given a week for orientation. They were also given a cutlass, which was heavier than experienced at home in Jamaica. And they were given work clothes, the cost of which eventually came out of their pay. After the week of orientation, the men slipped into the schedule – wake at 3:30 a.m., and be dressed and ready to have breakfast in the mess hall and to leave for the farm by 5:00 a.m. The farm would be as far as ten miles away. One was transported there by bus and assigned his task, which was to cut a mile of cane on both sides of a passage. Lunch came at 10:00 a.m. The lunch truck stopped and parked wherever the driver pleased, so the men might have to run a mile to get what was, on most days, a plate of rice and pork and a bottle of milk. On Thursdays, there was fish, and on Sundays, chicken. In their desire to complete their work, the men often had no time to eat this meal, which was not usually tasty anyhow, and it would be given to the birds. The owners were happy when the food was rejected, for they could then give it to their pigs. The bus collected the workers at 4:30 p.m. for the trip back to the camp, where for the first two weeks they lay on their bunks in pain from the bending, cutting and throwing, which were the basic actions involved in cane-cutting as a farmworker in Florida. This was the programme from Sunday to the next Sunday. Sunday churchgoers only knew that it was Sunday by the fact that orange juice was one of the items at breakfast. There was one day off – "the rest day" – per fortnight, and payday was every fortnight as well.

The inhabitants of the camp here in Florida were strictly West Indian, most by far being Jamaicans. James estimates that where there were about a thousand Jamaicans, there would be about "170 or so" from the other islands put together.[32] The cutting and planting of the canes was a West Indian task, but occasionally one saw an African American woman working in the field. Occasionally, too, one saw a white Cuban, but this would be only a fleeting glimpse, for Cubans worked in the cane-processing/sugar-making factory, which was a building separated from the farm. Black Americans drove the buses and the tractors, taking the farm workers to and from the farm and taking the cut cane to the factory. Their women were sometimes employed with the West Indians in cutting canes, as well as in planting the green cane tops. There was usually a "field boss" and a supervisor who were actually in the field with the West Indian farmworkers, seeing to it that the work was being done well. Occasionally, there was a black supervisor, but the people who occupied supervisor roles were usually white American men. Another white American role was "ticket writer". It was not unknown for a black person, even a West Indian, to occupy this role, since, according to A.P., "promotion was possible", and one as a West Indian "might go up as far as mess hall worker or ticket writer".[33] The mess hall in the Florida camp was the preserve of black American men: they usually did the preparation of the meals.

One had to hug the cane stalk in order to cut it. Having cut it, it was then thrown into a pile. A loader would come along to pick up the canes, but stalks could fall out of the loader. It was usually black American women who picked up the excess, throwing it into carts called "grabbers", which followed the loader. There was a "crew house" in the cane field: if workers felt they could not manage the rain or other elements, they could take shelter here, but if the supervisor or the field boss was not also seeking shelter, one might find himself declared an unsatisfactory worker and sent home. Camaraderie was high, especially among the Jamaican farm workers. As A.P. put it: "They just unite together. And you know what I notice, in Jamaica here, sometimes we black people don't [unite] but from you take the plane, everybody just live loving and nice with one another."[34]

"Live loving" included most West Indians, called "small islanders". The Trinidadians, says Ephraim, who served in South Bay in 1975, were "kind, loving, gentle"; "the St Lucians are kinda helpful people. Once you and them working and they finish the cane before you, they will come down and help you," declared Sibrant, who served in Belle Glades in 1970.[35] They did not "live loving" with the Barbadians, called the Bayjee, who were unpopular because of Jamaican values concerning sanitation: "Don't care how they have the cold, they hock and spit same place there on the floor inside."[36] No one wanted to share a bunk with them.

The Jamaicans felt superior to others in the camps and even in the fields. They were aware of their reputation as hardworking and effective workers, and they felt secure as the ones who shared the nationality of the liaison officers, who were charged by their government to straighten out work issues on behalf of the West Indian workers. Confident that the sugar farming enterprise needed their labour, they took chances. Their contracts stipulated that they could join no union and they could not go on strike, but Mr Ellis, in the 1960s, did as Bert Campbell had done in the 1940s – though both were unorganized one-man shows. Ellis packed his personal items and stood at the gate, refusing to go back to the cane fields. In 1964, he and his fellow workers felt that the remuneration for cutting cane was too low, lower than their contract had agreed, so he withdrew his labour, packed his suitcase and stood at the gate. His action would normally be defined as a breach and he would be sent home the next morning, but before one can be labelled as "in breach", there has to be a conference with the liaison officer. The bossman eventually came to hear his grouse and sent for the liaison officers, Pixley and Forrest, who agreed with Ellis, and they managed to get the farm owners to upgrade the remuneration.

James, in 1970, observed two strikes in Okeelanta – one major, one minor. The major strike involved the burning and destruction of the plant and police with guns. The issue was the same as that of the Jamaican, Ellis: work exceeding that for which the workers felt they had contracted. But this was a strike of natives and included guns and policemen. The Jamaicans knew that the terms of their contract did not allow them to participate, though they sympathized. Here again, it is noted that the Jamaicans had a value system which they thought the "Bajee" breached: James records that instead of keeping a dignified distance from this occurrence, the Barbadians broke into the commissary and stole the food. An obsession with food was thought to be a characteristic of the Bajee.

From the earliest days, the farm owners could request the return of workers who had given good service, so there were always "veterans" among the Jamaicans who could give advice to the new ones. It comforted them that some of those in the camp were people from home, from their own village, with whom they had even gone to elementary school. A sense of security also came from the personality traits they exhibited. Of the Jamaicans, James says they were "terrible"; they were "dark", "ignorant" and "aggressive", while the small islanders were superior in reading and writing.[37] But these qualities – being aggressive and illiterate – served the Jamaicans well, for all others were afraid of them and therefore eager to make friends with them, even to learn and to use Jamaican curse words; the farm owners and the general Floridian public liked the workers to be illiterate. They apparently fulfilled the stereotype of black people, sparing the owners the mental gymnastics of having to deal with people who were not what they thought they should be. This characteristic served the Jamaicans in another way. A.P. gives evidence of times when to be thought illiterate got him in and out of places marked "whites only" without being charged, since the authorities assumed that he had entered because of a literacy defect.[38] Those obviously literate were viewed by their bosses as "uppity" and likely to be troublemakers. They were watched with hostile eyes. None of the men from Woodside was illiterate, but neither did any show himself to be interested in books like the St Lucians. None was given to reading in his spare time. Hard effective workers, unlikely to be wasting time reading books or thinking philosophical thoughts, and having liaison officers of their own nationality ready to help troubleshoot, the Jamaicans were, and knew themselves to be, the most desirable source of farm labour. In the Florida sugar belt, the Jamaicans knew, were other camps overwhelmingly staffed by their fellow nationals. As Ellis put it:

> When we go ah America, [it] stay like you deh a Jamaica. Nobody hurt you. About nine camp there right down eena Belle Glade and if you hear sey anything happen to one man, every man you see ah come een. But anytime you tek a plane and ah come back to Jamaica, everything change. Me gone deh so, you gone deh so, the other one gone deh so, we nuh meet again til we a go back to America.

Jamaicans felt secure: "If you hurt one; you hurt all," Ellis continued.[39]

Apart from the "field boss" – the supervisor and the owner – the people whom the Jamaican farm workers met daily were black Americans. The selection process for gaining a place in the programme began in Jamaica. It was a white man who selected Ephraim for the farm work programme, but in his nearly three months' service in Florida, he had nothing to do with any other white man. His contacts were all black. The African Jamaicans were in a position to learn "something of the American way of life", as Governor Blackbourne had hoped in 1961, but it would be from the African Americans.

Though the Jamaicans recognized a racial similarity with the black Americans, they noted distinctions. "The only thing that is different", says Raphael, was that "they much blacker than we, and maybe not as good looking face as we (chuckles). Different from me a black man. Dark, black. Very black, very black, very black."[40] He had worked before, picking apples in New York, where black-skinned people were called "coloured", and wondered whether it was for this deeper hue of the Florida blacks that they were called "black Americans" down there, and if that was why there was so much segregation in Florida. The Jamaicans, he pointed out, did not use any segregation; they consorted with the African Americans. On their free nights, they would go out drinking with their Jamaican mates as well as with African Americans in the pubs. This activity unearthed another distinction: while a Jamaican would buy a round of drinks for everyone at the table, each taking turns to order and pay, the black Americans were more individualistic, each man buying his own drinks.

Ephraim, in his short three months among the African Americans, noted a difference in the comparative value placed on some material things. African Americans, unlike Jamaicans, he noticed, did not care very much what their houses looked like. Instead, they cared that the car parked at the gate be large and that a large television set be visible from the outside.[41] Others got the impression that African Americans were as poor and hungry as the Jamaicans they had left at home, a position which did not lend to respect, for they felt that this state was self-inflicted. In the eyes of the Jamaicans, the African Americans squandered their money on beer. Some agreed but were more sympathetic, arguing that unlike them, the African American was paid instantly for whatever work they did, and this made saving difficult. Jamaicans could have offered help with this. There is at least one case in the general history of their interaction in which Jamaicans offered corrective help to an African American who had befriended them. They advised his wife to ask the "super" to give them his pay, from which they in turn gave to him what they saw fit and when. The rest they gave to his wife to be saved and to run the house.[42]

Since the African Americans divorced themselves from the cutting of canes, they were not allowed on the cane farms and, as a consequence, had to see the West Indians, of whom the Jamaicans were the largest group, as kings of the cane field – meaning that should they feel like eating a piece of cane, they had to beg it from them. This was definitely a demerit. The African Jamaicans felt that no native anywhere should have to go begging for food grown in their country and area from a foreigner. A further demerit was given when they asked that the piece of cane they were given be peeled for them. This seemed to the Jamaicans, who could peel the cane with their teeth, as less than manly. Others held a strong political stance on this matter: if they refused to cut cane, they should not eat cane, and so they paid no attention to their entreaties.

The amount and cut of meat you have on your plate is a sign of prosperity for Jamaicans. The kind of meat is also important. Rabbit is not a high-status food among poor African Jamaicans, but African Americans begged them to catch the rabbits running wild in the cane field and sell them to them. To eat rabbit and to ask the foreigner to catch it for you meant, to Jamaicans, not having enough money to buy meat. African Americans were also seen at the windows begging for food – breakfast and dinner – from the chefs. Only the lowest of the poor in Jamaica, those who had lost their pride, begged for food in rural communities like Woodside. The food-begging African Americans the Jamaicans saw as parallel to the lowest of the low at home in the Caribbean. They could not understand how people in the land of opportunity which they were visiting in order to taste its fruits of wealth could be as poor as the poorest in their homeland.

There are people who carried anti-black notions and prejudice with them from Jamaica to Florida, although they admitted themselves to be black. Interviewed by a brown-skinned St Lucian female, Gus says: "Some black people still alright you know, but mi nuh like too much black people you know... mi nuh like dem too much. Rather the Indian dem and the white. Dem have more manners you know." So although Jamaicans, Gus among them, acknowledged that they were well liked by African Americans who would come to the camp, lie on his bed, ask about Jamaica and express their love for Jamaicans, he still said several times in his interview, "Mi hardly talk to the black American, you know."[43] The black Americans' patterns of behaviour in the Florida farm work situation supported the negative view of black people that Gus carried with him to the Florida cane field. He found the African Americans no better than the Jamaicans at home whom he despised because they would not work, but would "worry you for money"[44] – they spent their money on beer and would become drunk and disorderly. He had seen an African American shoot another, which he took to mean that they did not love each other. Worse still, he and some of his mates believed that black Americans, whom he called "panya", had entered their quarters and stolen their property. They had sharpened their cutlasses and prepared for war with the panya.

This negative view of African Americans and the desire to keep away from them was not unique to Gus. There are others who say that in African America, where there were fights between intimates, no friend or family would step in to intervene to stop the fight; they merely looked on and called the police, which meant to the African Jamaican that African Americans did not love and treat their family well. In addition, while a Jamaican would stop on the road to assist a driver with car troubles, the African American just passed without stopping. This meant a deficit of human kindness.

James waxed philosophical and universal: "De white and de black dem prejudice, you know. They really don't want black kids to sit down beside them, even on the bus. I don't know the reason, but black people, something wrong with black people, man. Every nation nuh like black people, you know. I don't know why."[45] Troubled by his conclusions, he asks the interviewer, "You can tell me?" It seems these pre-prejudiced men had come to America hoping to see their kind better placed than those at home. Like Marcus Garvey before them, they were learning by their travel outside of Jamaica that the black condition is universal.[46] They clearly were not aware of George Beckford's thesis in his *Persistent Poverty* and paid scant attention to arguments of their own prime minister, Michael Manley.[47]

These negatives were the report of some. Others noted and accepted these characteristics of African Americans with no emotional outrage. They knew that African Americans had difficulty in saving, and they knew that this was because, unlike the African Jamaicans, they were paid immediately for any work they did for a farmer. But there were benefits for African Jamaicans of this condition: those African Americans who did not spend their money on beer often had cash in their pockets, with which, from time to time, they could offer gifts to the Jamaicans and bring them drinks. Lloyd benefited more than this, and in a more structured way, from African American benevolence to African Jamaicans. His friend Julian, the chef, owned three cars. He used two as taxis and gave the third to the African Jamaican Lloyd to run as a taxi in exchange for two-thirds of whatever he earned.

Although the African Americans did not cut cane with the Jamaicans – they only drove the buses which took them to the field and drove the tractors which collected the cane they cut – they knew the Jamaicans by name and sight, and they could and did call out to them and guide them home if they happened to notice that they were lost. It was they too who served as taxi men, taking the Jamaicans to places of pleasure and to the shops. Some of these shops, the African Jamaicans submitted, were owned by the African Americans, and in some pubs frequented by African Jamaicans, African Americans were employed as bar attendants. There were others who came into the camp to sell wares. These were very important middlemen in the lives of a people who did not know the area, had money and wanted to buy wares to take home to impress their neighbours, items the true cost of which they had no idea. And, although James was so scathing about black people, African Americans included, had he wished to breach his contract and stay in the United States, he could have done so, for the African Americans had made the offer to hide him and smuggle him out of the area.

The two African diasporic groups met in the practice of religion. They sang and prayed together and "gave witness" in the meetings which travelling preachers held in the camps and at "Jesus Only", the one church in the camp. The wife of the super, a white woman, would take some of the Jamaicans to church on Sunday nights, but it was the invitation of the black Americans that was most prized. A.P. remembers the nature of the interaction with the black Americans:

> De black American, most of them are Christians. Man when they take you to church and when you go home with them, Lawd have mercy – sometimes what they put on the table, before you start to eat, your belly full. Some of the things, you don't even know the names of them. Oh Lawd have mercy! You just have to eat what you are acquainted with and things like that. They are friendly though. Nice man. They are very good.[48]

Then there were those Jamaicans who had steady girlfriends. Vincent had Ula May, who ran a taxi and would take him back to camp after a night on the town. Roy had Bessie May. He unfortunately heard from his supervisor that his Bessie May had recently been discharged from prison, where she had been sent for castrating a man from Nassau; he dropped her and was afterwards scared to pair with another African American woman. Even aside from this incident, African American women were seen by the African Jamaican men as unusual. They were pretty but bigger than they knew women to be. They called them "Mampee", but when they happened to work in the field at cutting cane, it delighted them to see how efficiently they worked. A female running a taxi was odd to Vincent, but he was proud of having a girlfriend who was a taxi driver.

All the Jamaicans knew that Florida was what they called a "white state", and they knew what this meant in real life, for they had seen the "whites only" and "blacks only" signs, and many had read of the Ku Klux Klan before they left home. Some were there for the Watts riots and the police assault on Rodney King. They thought in abstract and generalized terms that it was wrong to treat people in this inhuman way, and some even had talks with whites pointing out that all blood is the same. Some shared the actual experience of segregation. For instance, Roy was in a bus full of farm workers on their way from Florida to Illinois to another work camp. The bus was being driven by a white man. He knew they were hungry and stopped for food. Roy's experience was: "Dem was playing guitar and having fun before we go in but as the white man step up to get us some food, all those white people walked out of the club. Lord it was terrible in the fifties coming up you know."[49]

More generally speaking, though, in Florida, the Jamaicans were treated as honorary whites. On more than one occasion, groups of Jamaicans went into stores marked "whites only". They selected items for purchase, but no clerk would check them out. The store manager would call the police, who, on discovering that they were farm workers, would advise the clerks to serve them because they were foreigners and would soon be leaving for their own homes. This treatment is in stark contrast to what happened in the North. They reported that at one store in the North, all workers got a beer with their purchase, no matter how many times they went into the store per day. They felt special in a positive way. And even in Florida, the "Arabs" who owned the commodity stores would come out into the street and lead them by hand into their stores. African Jamaican farm workers knew that the descendants of Africans enslaved in the United States would – unlike them, whose ancestors had been enslaved in the West Indies – have been jailed for entering a white space; but when African Americans raised the issue of racial prejudice with them, they did not encourage these discussion because they were warned in their preparation for entry into the programme that they were not to get themselves involved with politics, to strike or to join any organizations – after all, they argued, America was not their country: they were just there to earn some money and go home.

The African Jamaican workers were not even angry at the store clerks for not serving them. They argued that the law is the law and it was one's business to act within its frame. In any case, they had gone into the "whites only" shops more to test the system than to buy goods which they could not get elsewhere.

Back at home and talking to an interviewer, many saw the treatment of African Americans as unjust and as something God does not like and will punish. For some, it was disgraceful that the whites should want the blacks to fear them as they did. Elcot experienced this feeling of fear with the African Americans and added to it respect for the African American who was able to manage his anger and perform the act of penitence. One time, he was helping a black friend to get a broken car to the garage in the night. A policeman stopped them with the words, "Nigger, do you know that it is against the law to drive this old junk without light?" His African American friend answered in a humble manner, taking off his hat, bowing to the policeman, calling him "sir" and gently explaining that his car had suddenly lost its light, and they were now pushing it to the service station for repair. Elcot was so impressed by this performance that he had to congratulate his friend, for he did not think he could have held his temper on being addressed in this way.[50] Roy, like some others, felt that whites did treat the African Americans badly, but they were of the opinion that African Americans treated each other badly and, when they got the opportunity, treated white people badly as well. Already amazed that a woman to whom he was attracted could cruelly castrate a man who was a black foreigner like himself, Roy saw an incident which further convinced him of the hard-heartedness of the African American. He recalls this with the same sense of shock that he felt fifty years ago:

> The white always live in the front and the blacks at the back. In this club in Belle Glade, I see this drunk white man come down into the black club. I see a black girl hit him in the head with a beer bottle, knock him out. And what I experience after, I didn't know could happen. I see every coloured come and spit on him. He is sitting on the ground drunk and I see the coloured come in and spit on him; they going out, they spit on him; they coming in, they spit on him. I say what kind of people this![51]

Another oddity was the African Americans' passion against and reason for not being willing to work in the cane fields. An African American deacon in a black church he attended told A.P. that he had a wife and five children, but he would prefer that they die of starvation than that he should drive a tractor or cut cane. The African Jamaican A.P. concluded from this that this black American, in letting his country be so dependent on another country to send it workers rather than do the work himself, lacked interest in the development of his country. He saw this behaviour in an educated African American as unpatriotic and disloyal.

Despite what they saw as an odd social situation and the very trying work of cutting canes, all but Sibrant would live in America and wanted to. Sibrant was put off by America's drug culture, concluding: "Although here [Jamaica] rough, it worse in the US."[52] Of all the farm workers mentioned here, Sibrant was the one who was most closely moved by the racial condition in the United States. Continuing to respond to the question of whether the United States was a good place for black people to live, and how life in racist America could be managed, he commented: "As black people, you must always know that the white generally will play like they love you. So stick to your colour that you know. You know you are black."[53]

The experience of going to the United States as farm workers showed African Jamaicans differences between themselves and African Americans. Florida was where most went. There, they found that the skin colour of the African American was darker than their own and that their women were pretty but of a frame larger than they were accustomed to in women. They coined phrases for the African Americans: they called the men "panya" and the women "mampee". Like Jamaicans at home, some African Americans were willing to beg and steal rather than work. They found it odd that though they were willing to beg the Jamaican workers for pieces of cane, they refused to work at cutting cane. Their argument that cane-cutting was something that white men refused to do and so they would not do it either, found no favour with the Jamaicans. The African Jamaicans were quite aware of the indignities suffered by African Americans in this racist society in the 1954–96 period. They had heard of these from when they were in Jamaica, and though they were too tired after work to deal with anything more challenging than the wrestling show on television or their own taped music, they did hear of the happenings in Alabama, the conflagrations of Watts and the police brutality towards Rodney King. They knew themselves to be black; they laid claim to kinship with African American icons such as Muhammad Ali, Jesse Owens and Martin Luther King Jr; and they rushed to buy and wear their Malcolm X shirts – but nationality trumped race. They heard African Americans discussing the problem of racism but withdrew from these discussions with the feeling that they were not citizens of the United States; they had come to do a job and would be returning to their own country shortly. In any case, they were actually treated as honorary whites, for usually when caught in "whites only" places, the police would allow that they be served on the grounds that they were not natives but farm workers who would be returning home soon. A subterfuge was to tell themselves that to discuss racism in the United States was to interfere in the politics of the country, which could be defined as a breach of their contract and result in their being sent home early. Moreover, although they thought the treatment of black people was inhumane, that God did not like it and would soon do something about it, they did not think African Americans were blameless innocents, for they had seen them do cruel things to their own people and whites when the opportunity arose.

Some had experienced racism, but in states like Massachusetts, Connecticut and Wisconsin, as was unusual in the racist society that the United States was at the time, they dated white women, the super even finding them white women for their parties, where there was drinking and dancing. They knew that Florida was a white state; they read the colour labels; they knew that sexual intimacy between blacks and whites was outlawed – young white women were aware of this, they knew, yet they would come into the camp and throw themselves in their beds. The African Jamaican farm workers knew that to return these young women's touch could mean the police, jail and finding someone to bail them out, yet they interpreted the actions of these young white women to mean that whites liked them rather than that the white girls reified them.

Friday night saw the arrival of what A.P. calls the "harlot women".[54] These women were white as well as black, brought by their husbands, who regulated the advance of men lined up, as if going into a class at school. It was they who collected the money for their wives' sexual service.[55] With this measure of intimacy with the white race, which they did not court, the Jamaican and West Indian farm workers saw themselves as highly desirable to whites and were not likely to empathize with the black American's fear of white people, since they had experienced intimacy and warmth from them. The super's wife took them to church in her car, and the super invited some to cross the fence which separated the white master class from black workers to wash his car. He would share whatever he was eating without benefit of utensil, breaking the sandwich as one would with an intimate – sharing the same sandwich.

So, the Jamaicans' personal experience was not the apartheid that they read about or heard about. It was easy to deny the anti-black racism of American society, to see it as manageable, to adopt a hands-off attitude and even to hold that the American society would be better if black Americans would behave themselves. Yet African Jamaicans felt loved by African Americans, who, even if they did beg them for sugar cane and money and stole from them, would give them gifts of money, would recognize that they had strayed from the right path and would take them home, for they seemed to make a habit of knowing the Jamaicans and to what camp each belonged. As the African Americans were taxi drivers, African Jamaicans could depend on them to drive them around and take them to the best shopping areas and the right pubs and "rude" houses. They were domino, drinking and gambling pals. Some African Jamaicans wanted to and did "run off" to lose themselves in the crowd of black-skinned people and, after many years and lawyers, get a "green card" and, with that, permission to stay in America permanently and legally. It was the African Americans who facilitated this running off. The process started with the African American's offer to hide the African Jamaican.

{CHAPTER 6}

The Transformation of a Jamaican Healer into a Black Jew by African Americans

IN PREPARING MYSELF FOR WRITING THE NOVEL *MYAL*, WHICH deals with spirit thievery and its antidote, I thought to learn about the working of the spirit with respect to healing from specialists in this field.[1] I was not acquainted with any spiritual healers at the time, and so I asked others to share such people in their network with me. The sole male found was the person in the interview that follows. He was introduced to me as a "black Jew", and he sent his card (see figure 9) preliminary to our meeting. This was serendipitous for me because for another project, I had been interested in meeting black Jews of the West Indies. That project had to do with what I then called "incorporation and cooperation" between Africans of the diaspora and particularly between African Americans and Afro-West Indians.[2] I had read in a very old text that there were black Jews not only in African America but also in the West Indies, and that Rabbi Josiah Ford, a West Indian, had tried to unseat Rabbi Wentworth Davis Matthews as the head of the New York house.[3] How and why would these two groups of Africans of the diaspora meet and come to share ideas and activities, thought and action? My interviewee was the first West Indian that I had heard of who was calling himself a black Jew. I expected help from this man, not only in getting an understanding of the working of the healing spirit but in giving me some clues concerning the historical process of incorporation and the nature of the cooperation between African Americans.

As indicated in the interview, some men heard him preach in a village in a rural parish of Jamaica and congratulated him on his delivery but pointed out to him that he needed more knowledge – knowledge they could arrange for him to

---

YAHVAH LITTLE FLOCK ASSEMBLY LIMITED
(MYSTIC CENTRE)
20 MERRYWOOD AVENUE, PEMBROKE HALL,

KINGSTON 20, JAMAICA, W.I.

Repent of your sins and be baptised in the Name of Yahshua the Messiah. Act 2:38-41. St. Matthew 8.

Holy, Holy Holy *Yahvashua The Messiah, Yahvah, El Shaddai of Host. Heirarchus, Cherubim, et Seraphim, Potestates, et Virtutes, Archangelos, et Angelos, Spirutus, et Animus, Hominum, Michael, Raphael, Gabriel, Ugabi, Seraph, Cherub, Tharsis, Araiel. Hallelu-yah, Hallelu-yah, Hallelu-yah.* Get your genuine birth stone for success.

Are you sick. Are you plagued with unclean demons, Simon the Sorceror had bewitched you? Come now to this Centre for your healing in full faith. Do you fail in every thing that you do, you are not prosperous, you are not successful, you are troubled, you are worried? There is a balm in Gilead. Come in full faith to *Yahvah Mystic Centre* now. Get one of the many great seals, the *Tetragrammaton Seal*, evil spirit flee from the wearer of it, Masuza, Solomon great seal and many more. Don't wear nonsense on your fingers or around your neck, wear something real powerful and good. Be wise to what is going on in your life. Get the best bush medicine, hot bush bath daily.

Buy a seal or a Talisman for spiritual protection by faith now, a curio, only.

Buy a seal or a Talisman for spiritual protection by faith now, a curio only, Doctor fail, the Mystic take over and heal you. Herbs Roots,Barks and Seeds sold here, Oils Perfume, Candles Parchment Paper, etc. Books, Books, Books we sell Rings, Rings, Rings for all purpose. *Kohath*

Moshe Ben Kehath Priest of the second Order.

"The Mystic"

Phone 92-53947 x Studied with the Black Jews

Figure 9. Moshe ben Kohath's card

get by taking him to the United States to study among men who could lead him to more depth of knowledge. My interviewee left Jamaica as Bishop Muir and returned as Moshe ben Kohath, priest of the second order, "The Mystic", and set up Yahvah Little Flock Assembly Limited (Mystic Centre). In the interview that follows, we follow the process of change wrought in this African Jamaican as a result of his cooperation with and incorporation in an African American group.

We spoke in what was clearly a well-used study, and as he spoke he pulled books from the shelves to make a point.

INTERVIEW WITH MOSHE BEN KOHATH

Q. I am going to ask you a little about your career as a healer. Let us go back to the first time you ever healed anybody. Can you remember that?

A. Well, yes. The first time I performed healing. . . . I was then in Westmoreland. I was passing through a district in Grange Hill and I saw a large crowd. They weren't hostile, so I walked up and asked what is wrong and they said, "See them hold that man there, he is mad." About five to six people held on to him. And I said, "Alright, I am sorry to know he is mad but if you people will give me a few minutes with him I think I will be able to do something for him." And they said, "Alright," not knowing me, not questioning me. In a plight like that, they would welcome any offer of help. So I said, "Alright, get me some water from a well or from a spring," and I told them to get me three quarts of water. And they got me the three quarts of water, and I send them to get me a vial of olive oil. I asked if there was anyone could give me a washtub or washpan or basin or something, and a lady took me into her house and said she have an enamel bath in her house so I can use it. I asked her to wash the basin afresh and she did so, and I poured the three quarts of water they had given to me into the bathtub, and I poured in the vial of olive oil in the name of the patient into the water. And I took out my Bible and I read a Psalm nine times using one of the sacred and holy name for that special purpose.

When I reach to about the seventh time, the demons that were into the man spoke and said, "We are gone." "We are gone." The man spoke you know, but his demon spoke, said, "We are gone." And then I bathe the man with the consecrated water and he was normal, and I hand him back to his people. It was a great astonishment because they had never seen a healing done like that before. I was in America and there was a woman whose doctor was about to amputate one of her legs, about the Wednesday, and the Sunday she heard of me from Jamaica came to Los Angeles and was preaching and as a healer. She send for me, and I went in their car to her home.

Q. This is Los Angeles.

A. This is Los Angeles. And when I went I saw the woman lying down in her
    bed with one of her leg cocked up on the wall with something to hold it up
    because she couldn't lay it down flat in the bed because of the pain. Well, I
    asked them for olive oil and they got me a vial of olive oil, and I start to sing
    a hymn, and after I sung the hymn I felt the moving of the Holy Spirit, and
    after I felt the movement of the Holy Spirit I pour the olive oil in my hand,
    and holding the bottle I prayed using the Holy Name of the Father and of
    His Son. Father Yahvah and of His Son Yashoa, the Messiah. After using
    and calling upon Yahvah, Yahrin, Voyin and upon His Son Yahvahshoa
    and in short Yashoa, I consecrate the oil in the power of the Spirit and I lay
    my hand on the woman and anoint her. After I finish anointing her feet,
    the woman exclaimed and said the pain gone. And she got up out of the
    bed and took me to the bathroom and give me a towel to wash my hands.
    And the Monday morning while I was at home where I was staying in Los
    Angeles, I saw her drive herself in a car and came and visited me and bring
    a present for me and give glory to Yahvah for such miraculous power.

Q. This first one that you did? Did it surprise you?

A. No, I wouldn't say that this is the first one. That wouldn't be the first one.
    I did some healing before.

Q. I am interested in the very first time you recognized that you had the power.

A. The very first time. I know that I had the power from the age of about
    seventeen. I know I got the power because my mother and grandmother
    and grandfather, they are Presbyterians, and a missionary came to
    the Presbyterian church, and they were having the Anglican visit the
    Presbyterian and the Presbyterian visit the Anglican. So during the time
    that the missionary came to the Presbyterian church –

Q. This is back in Westmoreland?

A. Yes, that is back in Westmoreland. The Anglican came over and they have an
    open-air meeting – not in the church – about five miles to six miles from the
    church, and I was sitting down beside my mother and my grandmother and
    my grandfather, and they call for testimonies, and everybody was testifying.
    So I sat beside my mother and I get up to testify, and my mother say, "No,
    you are not a member, sit down." So after she say that to me I sat down, and I
    just felt a great power lift me off the chair, and I was prostrate on the ground.

There I was, praying, and the people who were around and the missionary and other ministers, they said that in all their life and hearing prayers they have never heard anyone make such supplication and intercession to the Heavenly Father. And then the Presbyterian now go and visit the Anglican, and I was sitting in the front row of the Anglican church, and there is a white minister there, and they were singing a hymn, and while they were singing the hymn I felt the power of the Spirit again lift me off my seat and put me right in front of the altar where the railing is, and I knelt down. And after I knelt down there, I could not utter one word in English. Various tongues, various tongues I was speaking. I never go to Church of God, the church that receives the spirits and speak in tongues; I never go to Pentecost; I never go Revival or what they call Poco; I never go to them. I got the Spirit – from a Presbyterian church to an Anglican church, you see. And the white minister said that from he been travelling various countries in the world and preach, he had never heard such language like what I have spoken and so fluently, and I never go to school and study those languages. Alright. People in the district, sick, and I would pray for them and they get healed. I don't remember the first person, but I know from I receive the Spirit that time, I know that the power was in me.

Q. And you knew it was the power of healing?

A. And I know it was a power of healing and of glorifying Yahvah and preach the gospel.

Q. From when you know it was Yahvah?

A. No. I never say Yahvah at the time, you see. I never say Yahvah at the time because they were saying Jesus and Lord and God. But after I going on and I decide to do studies and begin to buy books and read books, I bought a book by the name of Six[th] and Seven[th] Books of Moses and when I read the Six[th] and Seven[th] Books of Moses I saw in it the holy names of the Father and of angels and so forth. And I was afraid of using them because people were saying that the Six[th] and Seven[th] Books of Moses was the devil book and all like that. But I know that I never believe them that it was the devil book, but to avoid the *ism* and so forth, I kept on using Jesus and Lord God –

Q. Excuse me. What led you to read them? What led you to read the Six[th] and Seven[th] Books?

A. Because I was seeking for knowledge.

Q. Oh, you were seeking for knowledge. But how did it come into you?

A. Well I went to a friend's home and I was shown one, and I got interested and start to read it, and he give me one. Yes. In the Six[th] and Seven[th] Books of Moses, Moses is a servant of Yahvah who led the children of Israel out of Egypt, and I don't see why his book in Jamaica should be prohibited literature in those days.

Q. It still is, isn't it?

A. Well, I don't think so because when Mr Manley get in power so as to let all different books come into the island, I think he removed those books from the prohibited list. So the Six[th] and Seven[th] Books of Moses and the Eight[h], Nin[th] and Ten[th] Books of Moses⁴ –

Q. I didn't know they had Eight[h], Nin[th] and Ten[th], I have only heard of Six[th] and Seven[th].

A. Yes, they have the Six[th] and Seven[th] Books of Moses and Eight[h], Nin[th] and Ten[th] Books of Moses, and they have what is called the Original Key to the Six[th] and Seven[th] Books of Moses.

Q. You can get those in Jamaica?

A. No. You can't get them in Jamaica. And then I started to widen my study because I have a yearning now for knowledge.

Q. From you were seventeen?

A. Yes.

Q. From you had that experience, you continued seeking literature.

A. Literature. Reading and so forth. And I grow big and came to Kingston and I was then doing auctioneer. My office was at 73 Slipe Road, and during those days I been preaching and healing people, you see. Sometimes I would give them herbs as I am led –

Q. As you are led, all of this comes to you in the Spirit?

A. Yes, I was led. I give them herbs, different herbs, and I heal a lot of people from Westmoreland, Hanover, all over.

Q. Your healing: is it a particular kind of illness? You do only some illnesses or you do anything?

A. Anything. Anything. While they come. And I can remember I was in Kingston here, and the Spirit told me to go to Clark's Town in Trelawny, and I went and I had an open-air meeting – it was largely attended – and there were some brethren down there that teach and preach Yahvah and Yashoa. There is a lodging there and I went to the lodging. And the morning that I having breakfast I heard that somebody was on the veranda waiting on me, and I went. And there was two men who came to me and told me that they were at the meeting last night and they enjoy my preaching very much and they can see that I have the spirit, but there is deeper depths I want to know. And I say yes. They said, well, they are having a set of meetings in the Anglican church in Clark's Town because it open for meditation all day. So we went in there and they brought to me the name of Yahvah and Yashoa, and clicking back to the Six[th] and Seven[th] Books of Moses, I remember that is those that are the names. And I put away the name of Jesus and Lord and God from that time. And then I began to do deep research now in the name and in the Hebrew and I discover that the name of God is a fake name. God is an object and Yahvah is a spirit. There is a difference between an object and a spirit. And I said, well if God is an object and God is not the Creator's name, why should I call upon the name of an object and leave the Creator's holy name that he has given. Then I began to study, and I see that Tetragrammaton is a four right angle consonant of the Hebrew. The vowels are taken out and leave the four consonants. It was so sacred and holy that the priests in those days never want the average man to call the Father's name, so therefore they only put in the vowels on special occasion. The vowels used to be handed down word of mouth to different priests. And then we get to know that the Tetragrammaton's four consonants are Y-h-v-h. English say, Y-h-w-h, but the ancient Hebrew have no "w" and the Hebrew alphabet only contains twenty-two letters and not twenty-six as the English alphabet, so therefore there is no "j" in the Hebrew and there is no "w" in the Hebrew. Good. So I began to use the name of the Father – Yahvah. You put the "a" between the "y" and the "h" and get "yah", and you put the "a" between the "v" and the "h" and you [get] the "vah". "Vah" means the root. He is the root of everything. And "yah" means the almighty, omnipotent, omnipresent. Anything beyond man. You see it. So when I look through the word "Yahvah" I see that man substitute the word God, because the name of the Father was too sacred and holy and that the word God came from an Assyrian deity – Got – and that the Germans say Gott and the English say God, meaning a deity, and that the Roman Catholics say Deus. "Deus" means deity. The Creator is no deity. God is an object, that is, an object everybody see, hand and touch. So that is not Yahvah. The Ten Commandments as it was written and handed down to Moses on Mount Sinai is changed. They change it up in the King James version, and substitute false names. The word "Baal" in Hosea 2:6, for instance: a reference Bible will show you that the word "Baal" means an idol, and the Creator is not an idol. They have substituted the Father's name. All these things are Roman Catholic. They set up this idol. And how the word "Jesus" came in. Jesus is an idol that they used to worship on Mount Olympus and the idol's name is Zeus. It said here Zeus, z-e-u-s, "Zeus is Greek mythology, the son of Kronus who became the chief deity." Now what is a deity? A deity is an object. That's their version. And Father of the gods: g-o-d-s. And then, "his secret place being Mount Olympus". See it there. So the Roman Catholic, they used to worship this idol on Mount Olympus, and the Roman Catholic say, I-Zeus, i-Zeus, Latin and Greek, and when King James split away from the Roman Catholic and formed his own church and called his scribe to translate from the St James version of the Roman Catholic Bible Seotarian(?) version, when they came to the word Izeus, I-Zeus, King James used "J" and "Jesus", all referring back to the idol on Mount Olympus. The Saviour said, "I come in my Father's name", that's what the Saviour said, John 5:43, and the Father's name at Psalm 68:4 said, "Extol Him that ride up on the heavens by his name YAH," but King James took off the "y" and put "j". King James of England was a wizard and most people don't know. In practising and playing with the dead and invoking the devil, they couldn't use Yahvah's name and Yashoa's name, so they have to use that which is given to them by the devil. So the world is drunken as Revelations 17 said: "Mystery Babylon the mother of harlot is abomination of the earth that have drunken the kings of the earth with the wine of her fornication." That means the bad doctrine. There are many doctrine which the Roman Catholic and all these Sunday church preach which is false. They are robbing and destroying the souls of people. They are the greatest murderer. A man who murder your soul is the greatest murderer. Yashoa said, "Fear not him, who only can kill the body but rather fear him who can kill both soul and body."

Q. Can you tell me some of the books? You mentioned some of the research that you had been doing to come to this position. Can you tell me some of the books that you studied?

A. Well I studied various books because I seek knowledge and I want to know, because unless you are able to find something for yourself and know something for yourself, know what you have, somebody will always pull a false one on you. I read for information various books. I read Hindu magic, East Indian's occultism and all those books. I read the Holy Qabalah.

Q. The Holy Qabalah.

A. The Holy Qabalah. I read Septugen [the Septuagint]. I read the Duway [the Douay-Rheims Bible] version. I read *The Master Key of Solomon, The Greater Key of Solomon, The Lesser Key of Solomon.*

Q. So you went to America. Where did you do your reading? There or here?

A. In America I do my reading. I do my studies in America, and the Father has blessed me with good memory and I retain.

Q. How did you get to go to the States?

A. Well after the brethren in America who study from the States – the headquarters of the church is in the States.

Q. Oh, we haven't reached the church as yet. The point you left me at was when some men came to you and suggested that you join them in a church in Trelawny, Clark's Town. Were they affiliated to a church?

A. Yes. They affiliate to this assembly – Yahvah Little Flock Assembly, the Mystic Centre. They affiliate to it, so they getting teaching post to them, and they study and they recommend me now to the headquarters that I am powerful in the Spirit, but I want more learning. Just as how Aquilla and Priscilla met Paul. Paul was powerful in the Spirit, but Paul wanted more learning, so Aquilla and Priscilla took Paul and established him deeper in the ministry. So I been healing people all over –

Q. Here as well as America?

A. Here as well as America. I healed many people.

Q. So you been healing from you were seventeen.

A. Yes.

Q. That is a good many years now. You been healing more than thirty years?

A. Yes. And I was incriminated once through this same work of healing. There are certain things in healing. I gave a man what is called a seal or talisman with the Father's name, sacred and holy, consecrated, and he took it to the police and the police they were not wise, quashie themselves, dumb-dumb, they arrested me and charged me for receiving money under false pretences. And sometime after, the man who did that, he was duly compensated for the evil that he had done.

Q. You are available any time, or you have hours, special hours?

A. Well I have special hours, but when a person come, if it is not my time, they can sit and wait until the Spirit move and lead me to them. Yashoa said when they went to the marriage feast and they told him that the wine was finished, "My hour is not yet come." So he gots to wait. When his hour come, he turned water into wine. So you see, salvation is in no other name but in the name of Yashoa. The disciples, they never preach Jesus, not even once. In the thirty-three and a half years that the Saviour spent on earth, he has never been called Jesus once, you see. His Father –

Q. What about Christ?

A. Christ came from the word "Crisnow" [?], the sun god that the Catholic they worship. Is not Christ. Is Messiah. They fool the people and said "Christ" means Messiah. When they were translating the Hebrew, most of the Hebrew word they could not find any equivalent in English, so they just substitute a word and put a meaning to it.

Q. Can you tell me a little bit about your religion? About how old you were when you went to study in America?

A. I was about thirty –

Q. This is after you had had your business? You were an auctioneer you said. It was after you had set up your auctioneer business?

A. Yes, after that. Well I went to America in 1961 and study and came back 1963.

Q. What are the major tenets of that religion?

A. Now the major tenets of that religion. Number one: salvation must be preached in all the earth beginning at Jerusalem first. Not Jerusalem, Yarushalem. The city is named after the Father, so is not "j", is "ya" – Yarushalem. You must preach Yashoa's name. In full form is Yavashoa. In short form is Yashoa. You must preach salvation in that name. Peter said on the day of Pentecost, "Neither is there salvation in any other name." There is no other name given under Heaven which men can be saved but the name of Yashoa. This is Acts 4:12. King James took out Yashoa's name and put in

Jesus, and the people are so mad that when you even try to enlighten them about the Hebrew and so forth they rebel. But any preacher that don't know a little Hebrew is like a baby born without a head.

Q. Do you have any relationship with those people who call themselves Jews here who go to the synagogue?

A. Well, the Jews here that is at Duke Street, they are the Orthodox Jews. They do not believe that the Messiah has come but we are the reformed Jews that believe that the Messiah came.

Q. So do you call yourself by that name?

A. Yes. Receiving the Holy Spirit through Yashoa's blood then I am a Jew. Spiritual Jew. Not one that is a Jew outwardly but one that is a Jew inwardly. Most people don't know also that they have black Jews, which is called the Emmanite Jew and the Falasha Jew. They are black people, and many of them are in Jamaica here and don't even know themselves that's what they are. So that is one of our tenet. Another one: we observe the Feast of the Tabernacle in Leviticus 23, the Feast of the Tabernacle, Yom Kippur and the Feast of Atonement. And we observe Passover. Now it coming on to April when we observe Passover, the fourteenth of Abib. We observe all the holy days like the Orthodox Jews. Only difference that we believe that Yashoa came and we don't need to do burnt sacrifice anymore because Yashoa have given himself as the sacrifice.

Q. Do you have any intellectual or any theological connection with Africa and African religious bodies?

A. Oh yes. You see most people don't know that when Moses ran away from Egypt after slaying the Egyptian and was wandering the land, straying from Egypt, he went up and he saw two girls were watering the sheep, and the men were taking advantage of them. Moses was a fighter – him understand his stick well – and Moses beat off all of them, and they have to sit down there watch him. And he drew water and helped the two girls to take care of their father's flock. They went home very early that evening, so the father asked them how is it that they came home so early. They say, "A man helped us." And he send for the man, and there it is, Moses was there. And being there with this set of people, Moses married to Jethro's daughter, and Jethro is an African, an African priest that know about Yahvah, Elsharieye, Yahvah Elohim, Yahvah Eloica, Yahvah Yiree, Yahvah Desai, Tetragrammaton,

Sabaoth, Tetragrammaton, Elohim, Agla, Yov, Pelee [continues to name and to speak in unknown tongue]. He know all about the Father and could speak to the Father. To really invoke the Father you have to know his name, because he bring his people to know his name. . . . [unknown tongue].

Q. You are saying that Jethro helped to educate Moses?

A. Yes, and helped Moses to know the Father. When Moses now learn from Jethro, one day Moses was out in the field and Father appear to Moses because Moses know his name and how to talk with him to invoke him and know the various seals.

Q. What about present-day Africa. Have you any connection at all with that, spiritually or theologically or –?

A. Yes, we have. We have plenty. I should be in Africa now because they want me over there. The brethren want me over there. We have thousands of members over there. The African teaching, you see – there are some that turn away from the teaching follow the Gentiles and making image worshipping it. That's why even in Ethiopia they turn away from Jahvah and worship idol and Father lock the heaven. If you read Jeremiah 14, you will see when they turn away from him and go to idol he lock the Heaven that no rain fall.

Q. Now we are accustomed to seeing all sorts of images and to associate them with African religions. You are saying that is not how it ought to be?

A. That is not how it ought to be. You have different kinds of voodoo and all kind of demons worship from this idol. Father said, "Thou shalt not make unto him any graven image or the likeness of anything that is in the heaven or in the earth or in the water." So when you make an image and bow down to it in your worship that is demons you are invoking and worshipping. Africa, India and many other countries, they practise this demon worshipping. But people who really worship the Father, they don't worship the Father by setting up an image. There are what is called seals and –

Q. I just want to get something clear. I am trying to get back to Jethro, who you say was an African and the African religions and the demon thing. Now are you saying that there was a time when Africans worshipped as Jethro did?

A. Correct. There was a time and Jethro know and Africa know about the Father before Moses.

Q. So this worshipping of what you call demon worship, voodoo and so on is a corruption of the original religion which Jethro knew?

A. Right. You also have the Emperor of Ethiopia. He know the Father's name, and his church people know it there, but they follow up paganism, Greek Orthodox Catholic corruption. If he had kept to the faith of his great-grandfather, he would not have been slain in the way in which he was killed. Yahvah said he is a jealous [god] and him shouldn't gone to bow down to the pope of Rome, the man of sin, the devil. He shouldn't gone to bow. The pope fi come up and bow to him. If he was like Solomon, wise as Solomon, you see, the pope should come up to him in Ethiopia and bow to him while he sit on his throne, but not him to go down there and bow to the pope. He give away his power and cause them to ride over him that he died in a dishonoured way. Until the Africans get back to the sacred and holy laws and statutes and precepts and ordinances of the Father, like how it was given to Moses, they will never be a nation of any value. If they are going to depend on Russia to doctrinate them to be something, they will never be, but will always be divided. They must go back to the divine order, the Commandments of the Father. All nation will have to bow to the Ten Commandments, the royal laws of the Heavenly Father, because they need to get wisdom, to get knowledge. Even King James's version of the Bible tell us that we must pray. Solomon pray for wisdom, knowledge and understanding. All these are seals, all these are special seals.

Q. But these seals are coming out of the church in America.

A. Yes. Not only in America. From the ancient order.

Q. What I mean is, you don't produce them?

A. No, no, I don't produce them, you see.

Q. Bishop, it seems to me that you are a very spiritual man and your healing is coming out of the Spirit. Now I know of people who heal, using herbs and sometimes things from the dispensary. Do you use this kind of thing?

A. Yes. Now listen. It is three type of healing, three ways of healing. The Saviour performed the three ways of healing, and any person that say that they are a healer and them only believe in laying hand upon a person, there is something wrong with them. They are not developed. And if anyone believe that it is just to speak the word and the person will heal, like how many of them say, "Put your hand on your radio", and they speak the word and they consider that is all, is not so. Is three ways of healing. When the Saviour was here and the centurion leave his sick servant at home and went to Yashoa and told him that his servant is sick, Yashoa said, "I will come and heal him." He said, "No, master, I am not worthy, I am a man with soldiers under me. I say to this one go and he go, and this one come and he come. But I am not worthy for you to come into my house. Just speak the word and my servant will be healed." Yashoa said, "I have not seen so great a faith in Israel, go thy way. And as you believe so be unto you." When the centurion went home he saw his servant strong and hearty, and he asked what time he got well, and they told him, and he remembered that it was about the same time that Yashoa spoke the word. So that is one way of healing. The second way of healing: Yashoa touch them. Connection. They came to him and he lay his hand and they heal. Woman came to him and touch the hem of his garment and healing effect. The third way of healing now: Yashoa spat upon the ground and after Yashoa spat upon the ground he mixed clay. That's medicine. When Hezekiah was sick, Yah send Isaiah to Hezekiah and told Hezekiah that he shall die. Hezeiah turn his face to the corner and wept and pray and Yahvah told him that he will set the sun fifteen degrees, and the sun did turn fifteen degrees, and Hezekiah get fifteen years more added to his life, and Yahvah told Isaiah to pick the fig leaf and put on Hezekiah boil. And he was healed. So is three ways of healing, and any healer in the island of Jamaica is not performing the three ways of healing, then they are not well-informed of the right way.

Q. Has a doctor ever referred a patient to you?

A. Well, a patient came to me, yes.

Q. Did they come referred by the doctor?

A. Not exactly, because I never read a letter and say, well then, "Doctor give me this to give you." Because you know some of these doctors they wouldn't ... you know. But some of them is wise. Some of these doctors have studied and – [While I turned the tape, he spoke about how necessary good health is and that therefore doctors are vital to spiritual health.]

    Our body is temple of the Holy Spirit. That means you can't delve in whoredom.

Q. You mentioned whoredom of women, but that does not mean that the men have to keep to themselves.

A. Of course, just the same. I can tell you that anytime a man who is spiritual, or a woman who is spiritual, start in illegal sex – when I say illegal sex, I mean sex without marriage – then their power cut, because you are not a clean vessel for the Spirit to work in. Your conscience is bothering you and you have to purify your conscience. That's why you see you have to examine yourself and confess your sins and beg forgiveness wherever you slip: to keep up your mind that the Spirit can operate on you. When the mind is clean, your thought is clean, and whether you invoke the Spirit by your thought or by prayer or by meditation or by concentration, the Spirit come to you.

Q. The body now. How in your view do the parts of the body work together?

A. Well, they work together in unity, and if one member of the body is affected, all other members of the body go with it. The greatest factory is our body. When you eat anything, the organs in our body, if it want vitamin A, it will produce; it want vitamin C, it extract it. Each organ do its own work, and when there is a breaking down of one, unless that one is quickly repaired, the whole body is out of order. So is unity. The Bible say unity is strength. Sometimes things that we eat, we shouldn't eat. Sometimes we eat too much of one thing and not enough of the other. Our diet should be balanced. Our body is just like that car. Sometimes the car drive but is not that it is in good order, it not performing aright. Well, so it is with our body. We'll find our body is sluggish; sometimes we find we are easy to contract a cold and various things like that. So therefore the resistance of our body may be weak, and we gots to rebuild up that resistance.

Q. And it would affect you spiritually. You have said the body is a case for the spirit.

A. Right. If you are in this house and it is leaking, what happens? You will wet. But if the roof is good, you will be alright. So sometimes now when you are in good health, and keep your mind in Yahvah, then the Spirit flow through you, you see, because one of the greatest transmitting station any human being can ever realize is our body. If you are properly tuned, you can sit down here and hear from any part of the world. I can remember that before President Kennedy was killed, I told them that President Kennedy is going to be assassinated. Months before it happen, I pick it up.

Q. You picked up the vibrations?

A. Yes. The Spirit told me, you see.

Q. So you are saying your body was at that time in a peak of working of unity, and so it was able to pick up something as far-ranging as that?

A. Yes. There is no mileage that is a barrier for the Spirit. There is nothing like that. When you have the Spirit, you connect at will. Father said, "Lo, I am with you always, I will not leave you." So His Spirit is with us, with his children who have received the Spirit at all times. Now there is a little thing I would like you to know. Is not everybody have the Spirit, the Holy Spirit, because Nicodemus though he had the spirit of life, yet he never filled with the Holy Spirit. It is not everybody filled with the Holy Spirit. You will have the spirit of life to a certain extent, but the baptism of the Holy Spirit is a different thing. The disciples, they had certain portion of the spirit of life and understanding, but they had to tarry at Jerusalem until they were imbued with the Holy Spirit before they have power.

Q. The spirit of life is different from the power?

A. The power, the Holy Spirit.

Q. What would you say is the spirit of life?

A. Solomon show that the horse, when it die, the spirit go back down into the earth, but man, when you die, your spirit go back to the Creator. Now the spirit of life is to keep the body going, keep the organs in order – but you are still a matter without deep understanding. When the Holy Spirit come up on you, then the Holy Spirit enlightens, you get knowledge and understanding. In the King James version, they put, Solomon pray and get wisdom, knowledge and understanding. Is not three things. They fool – want to confuse the people. Wisdom is another word for understanding. Wisdom and understanding is just the same. Knowledge now is different. Knowledge now, you would have to go and do some research and get it. But understanding: you can do the research, and you don't have the understanding of what you read.

Q. You can have knowledge but not understanding? The spirit of life is really that you are very healthy. You have the spirit of life, but you need to have the gift, then, for the power?

A. Right. [Takes a book, *The Greater Key of Solomon*.] Well, you see, without knowledge, you are a fool.... Now if you will read here. It says here: "When Yah appear to Solomon in Gibbon and said to him in the dream, 'What shall I give to thee', Solomon reflected, 'If I ask for gold, silver or jewels, Yah will give them to me. I will ask however for wisdom. If that is granted me all other good things are included'; therefore he replied, 'Give to thy servant an understanding heart.'" So you see, he said "wisdom" here, and then come down here, "an understanding heart". That is wisdom. You want to say "wisdom", or you want to say "understanding". That is wisdom. But it is in degrees. Before Solomon get his higher degree, he had certain amount of understanding, but he got more. "Then Yahvah said, 'Because thou has asked for wisdom and requested not wealth or dominion over thy enemies, by thy life wisdom and knowledge shall be thine and through them thou shalt obtain wealth and power.'"

Q. Are these the books [from which he was reading] they call the de Laurence books?

A. Well, it is not de Laurence who wrote the book. De Laurence is like Sangster's Book Store – gather information from all over the world. Ancient. Some of them is on the scroll. He will take it off and put it in book form and put his name as the publisher. But many of what people calling de Laurence book, is not de Laurence put them out. He collects knowledge. Just like the university sends out and collects knowledge all over the world, so de Laurence does. He has good there and bad.

Q. So he has good and he has bad?

A. Yes. He sell good books and bad books. If you want to study black magic, voodoo, necromancy, he will sell you the book because he collect it from the people all over the world who practise these things. He compiles them and put his name on it. Many books that you can't get other places you can get it from their company. It's like a supermarket. They gather everything and you can buy it from them. He just put his name to say, well is this place you get it from.

Q. Do you know of any cases of people working black magic through de Laurence? Throwing of stones on houses –

A. Well there are many people who send there and buy books that teach them about black magic. When they get the book from de Laurence, they study it and they can stone a man's house. If I want to stone a man's house, I can. If I should turn to evil and want to stone a man's house, I can.

Q. Which brings me to another point. How, in your view, does the world operate?

A. Well, the world operate by two forces – the agromania and the spengromania. Light and darkness.

Q. Agromania?

A. AGROmania and SpenGROmania. Light and darkness. Evil and good. The Father Yahvah and Satan, the deceiver. The devil. The devil kingdom is divided in many portions, because all those angels that cast out from Heaven with Satan, they want to set up their own kingdom. That's why you find the various nations and within the nation you find the various division and confusion, because the devil is divided. The only time that you will have peace on earth is when man really turn and believe that there is a supreme [being] and his order must be kept. Nature have two sides. Take your dictionary and look at the word "nature". Nature have two sides, the known and the unknown. Professors. Universities. Doctors all over trying to explore.

Q. You have given me a distinction between light and dark. Now you are giving me another distinction between the known and the unknown. The world is divided as well into the known and the unknown?

A. Right. Society have form themselves in such a way to suppress and rule and reign. Society do not give knowledge or permit knowledge to be given freely to whosoever will. Society took knowledge and try to harness it for themselves. But is impossible. You cannot harness knowledge. You cannot harness wisdom. So what they try to do, they go about and they collect knowledge from everybody, like a bank. University, in other words, is a bank. The bank have nothing unless you carry your dollar and put there, and I carry my one, this one carry their ten, and that one carry their twenty, until they have millions of dollars inside there to lend. But they themselves never have it, they may just open the bank and start out with a little "smalls". So it is university. University is a bank that go about and collect knowledge and lodge it inside there and somebody, your son or my son, have to go there and pay to get it. Some years to come, my grandson may have to pay to get some of my knowledge. . . . Many come down here questioning me. They want to write theses and all like that.

Q. So you have done a lot of talking to a lot of people about this matter?

A. Yes, I have done a lot of talking. I used to write in the paper but the paper
stop me now because I was enlightening the people with too much things.
These things that the society cover up, the Free Mason, the Masonic and
all those lodge have it as their secret and I just throw it out so whoever will
can pick it up. The Gleaner Company will not publish for me, because I am
giving facts, and when I put article in the paper, no theologian in the island
of Jamaica can condemn it.

The African Americans (I assume them to be, for if they were white Euro-
Americans, Bishop Kohath would have said so, as he did on other occasions in
his recital of his life story) who heard him preach thought Bishop Kohath had
valuable knowledge but thought that he needed more, and they knew where he
could get this further knowledge. They could not have known these things if they
themselves were not on or had not been on the same quest. What is the kind of
knowledge that these two peoples of the African diaspora seek? It clearly is not
the kind of knowledge available in the normal school and university system, for
these institutions were all around them and could be accessed.

Edward Blyden, in his inaugural address as president of Liberia College on
5 January 1881, comments on the kind of curricula that should be devised for
application to Africans. He questions the approach of Euro-American helpers: "In
their efforts to assist us to become sharers in the advantages of their civilization,
they have aimed at establishing institutions *a priori* for our development. That
is, they have, by a course of reasoning natural to them, concluded that certain
methods and agencies which have been successful among themselves must be
successful among Africans."[5] Blyden goes on to discuss the disadvantages for
Africans in following a programme designed for Euro-Americans:

> It was during the sixth period that the Atlantic slave-trade arose, and those the-
> ories – theological, social, and political – were invented for the degradation and
> proscription of the Negro. This epoch continues to this day, and has an abundant
> literature and a prolific authorship. It has produced that whole tribe of declamatory
> Negro-phobists, whose views, in spite of their emptiness and impertinence, are
> having their effect upon the ephemeral literature of the day – a literature which is
> shaping the minds of the Negro in Christian lands. His whole theory of life, quite
> contrary to what his nature intends, is being influenced consciously and uncon-
> sciously, by the general conceptions of his race entertained by the manufacturers
> of this literature.[6]

Blyden would exclude from the programme of study for the African the literature of this period. The Africans of the diaspora featuring in the interview, like Blyden, see distortions in the system of knowledge available through Euro-America and struggle to get out of it and into the correct learning. Bishop Muir, after studying with the African Americans, gets, among other things, the correct meaning of the word "God"; he learns that there is a difference between an object and a spirit and that the term "God", used in Western Christendom, denotes an object and cannot refer to the Creator, for the Creator is a spirit. This study, in addition, led him to the true name of the Creator. It led him, too, to a greater appreciation of Moses and of his own spirit-based healing, which can be advanced by his reading of books which deal with Moses's healing strategies, such as those published by de Laurence in Chicago.[7]

These Africans of the diaspora, disturbed by the nature of the knowledge available in the public space about them and feeling it to be untrue, seek enlightenment from the one said by this same general public to be the wisest man ever. They turn to the writings of Solomon, again as found in the publications of de Laurence. With this knowledge to which he is led, the African of the diaspora feels able to stand secure and strong enough to battle the forces of powerlessness, which, as we learn from Orlando Patterson, is a hallmark of the slave.[8] Graduating from these studies, he is now truly emancipated. Bishop Muir is now Moshe ben Kohath.

Bishop Kohath's interview does not tell us where in the United States he went to get the deeper knowledge he felt he needed and to which some caring African Americans sent him. We know, though, that this was available in New York City. There, Rabbi Wentworth Matthews of the Black Jews had established a rabbinical school, where he trained other men to lead congregations.[9] Whichever biography is true, all biographers agree that Matthews's youth was spent in Africa and in the West Indies; that he arrived in New York before 1920; and that in New York, he established the Commandment Keepers.[10] This sect grew and still exists today. If Bishop Kohath had been guided by the African Americans preaching Jashoa and Jahvah in Clark's Town, Trelawny, Jamaica, to go to New York, it is very likely that he attended Rabbi Mathews's rabbinical school and lived among the Commandment Keepers, often called the "Black Jews" of Harlem.

If he had been guided to go to Chicago, he could have studied under the

Reverend James E. White. This Reverend White ran a six-inch advertisement on 20 February 1943 and possibly days before and after in the *Chicago Defender*, in which he told the public that he offered lessons by which one could "develop and increase your spiritual powers with these illuminant courses", which he lists. The Reverend White also tells the public that he is an occultist and astrologer.[11] He praises astrology as the "science of sane living" pursued by the "ancients, the Hebrews, Egyptians, Chaldeans, Essenes and Hermetists". According to Baer, there were schools in the black community for the perfection of the gift of mediumship, where one learned psychology and the esoteric science. People interested in deeper knowledge, of the kind Bishop Muir sought, need not go to any institution of learning, be it Rabbi Matthews's or the local schools of mediumship; one could chose to study at home, for there were mail-order offerings for books such as the *Seven Books of Power* and *The Seven Steps to Power* – the advertisement for the latter taking up less print space than the former. Bishop Muir/Kohath's two years in the United States did not see him staying in one place, be it New York or Chicago; he was in Los Angeles, California, as well, where the kind of healing with which he was involved seemed to be a normal practice, for he was sent for by a woman who heard of his work and felt that she needed the kind of healing that he practised.

Baer coins the phrase "spiritual advisors" and puts under this label people who work with clients interested in "achieving socially desired ends such as financial property, prestige, love, health".[12] The practitioner, the "spirit advisor", helps the client to arrive at these goals through "magico-religious rituals and by acquiring esoteric knowledge which provides the individual with power over oneself and over others".[13] Spiritual advisors, we also hear, "have the tendency . . . to combine elements from a number of religious traditions into a new tradition".[14] In this genre, science and religion are bound together in diagnosis and in treatment. The Jamaican Bishop Kohath falls neatly into this group. He helps his clients to fulfil the desires mentioned above; he arrives at his theoretical position by a juxtaposition of Christian and Hebrew knowledge and the knowledge which de Laurence found and republished, and he analyses physical ailments in terms of a disturbance of the "spirit".

Spiritual healing, it is clear, was normalized in certain sections of the black population in the United States, where the woman cured by Bishop Kohath moved at the time when he was seeking appropriate knowledge. African

Americans have pursued this kind of knowledge since 1775 and Prince Hall's Negro Freemasonry, which itself was associated, in Kohath's thinking, with the Ethiopianist view of the black man in the cosmos.[15] Bishop Kohath, in his two years of searching for knowledge in African America, would not only have been able to read books and discuss esoteric issues openly with colleagues; he would have also seen the link between this knowledge and practice and political freedom for the children of Africa and the diaspora. This Jamaican needed the company of and exposure to African Americans to better understand the links between his healing practice, his Africanist interests and a mysticism which called him. As far as I know, there were no colleges in Jamaica where he could find people with his interests. I know only of one community of what Baer calls spiritual advisors in Jamaica which could compare with Rabbi Mathews's rabbinical college. The closest approximation is the spiritual community of Watt Town, St Ann, and that one appears to cater to a female clientele.[16] Neither Watt Town nor any other "spiritual" training institution in Jamaica places an advertisement in any newspaper as Reverend James E. White and others of his kind did in the *Chicago Defender*. It is also very unlikely that those books on esoteric knowledge advertised in the *Chicago Defender* and available by mail could have been so advertised in Jamaica and made available to Bishop Muir. As he has said, it is in the United States that he managed to read as many of the de Laurence publications as he was able to. These books made the proscribed list in Jamaica in 1940.

Because of its unrelenting racism, the United States encouraged a "black space" into being. Intellectual activity in it would be forced to contemplate the issue of origins. Intellectuals were free to use whatever they thought could help in this search. Several turned to the Bible. Clergymen like Bishop Turner found in it reason to believe that God is black; it led Crummell to write of the superiority of the Negro race; and it led Blyden to believe that God has created the black race to work with him to carry out his works.[17] These are highly literate men, published writers who have passed through white institutions of learning. With no serious governmental prohibition to what they could read, as happened in Jamaica, subgroups could develop in this black space, building apposite theories from old Germanic scripts collated and published by de Laurence. All these tendencies were more or less linked by the African-derived notion that man, like God, is a spirit, and the two spirits do communicate. African Americans have not been selfish with their findings: as we see in Bishop Kohath's interview, they travelled to Jamaica on a proselytizing mission. They continue to come, and African Jamaicans continue to accept their invitation to enter into their religious space.

Afterword

THESE SIX CHAPTERS, EACH REPRESENTING a moment in time between 1782 and 1996, support the notion of a "black Atlantic", a "black international", but is there any reason to believe, as was our hope, that this black Atlantic, this black international, could eventuate into a structure which could protect the interests of the human beings who comprise these abstract entities? In this presentation, I focused on the nature of the interaction between African Americans and African Jamaicans in the hope to better see if the interaction had the capacity to move into structured organization. In chapter 1, which dealt with the enslaved African Americans joining enslaved African Jamaicans on a Jamaican plantation, it was noted, from an examination of the slave list and, to a less successful extent, from interviews with residents carrying the surnames of the African Americans, that out of an interaction which was imposed, these people being slaves who had to go where and do what they were ordered to do, individuals from the two groups came together to make families and possibly to build chuches and worship together. In chapter 2, we saw the positive sentiment that African Americans felt on seeing the success of African Jamaican ex-slaves. Many of them celebrated the first of August as a holiday, apparently aware that they were celebrating the emanciapation of African Jamaicans from ensalvement. This identification of descendants of Africans enslaved in the United Sates with those in Jamaica kept the desire for emancipation in the United States strong. We saw, too, the intention of the Hamic Association in Jamaica, a group of merchants, "impressed with that indelible type which is the peculiar characteristic of the African race", to be linked to their counterparts of African America. Our records do not say if this desired link was made fact.

In chapter 3, we saw a human being, an African Jamaican, who had given up a national for an international persona and considered his home to be wherever in the black Atlantic he found himself. It is general knowledge that Marcus Garvey was able to convince African Americans to join him in a new world, the UNIA, where they would work on the problems which they aired in their newspapers. In chapter 4, we see a religious organization founded in Oklahoma by an African American, transported and planted in Jamaica, here to influence another and original form, the Rastafari. Black America continues to be the mother organization of this church, the Church of God and Saints of Christ, and African Jamaicans join their brethren there annually for some rites.

In chapter 5, we saw African Jamicans in interaction with African Americans in the Florida cane fields. We saw that while the African Jamaicans sympathize with the racist situation in which they know African Americans to have lived and continue to live unhappily in the late twentieth century, and while they acknowledge the several ways in which African Americans have helped them, they note with distaste aspects of African American behaviour, and so strongly that they blame African Americans for their condition. That African Jamaicans are, in many cases, treated as honorary whites and accept this treatment without the full understanding that this good treatment is due to the fact of the temporary nature of their stay contributes to their disdain of those descendants who happened to have been enslaved in the United States.

Chapter 6 points to a case where some African Americans visiting Jamaica proselytized an African Jamaican healer to make him one of them – a black Jew. We also noted in this interaction the search for "power" among blacks on both sides of the Atlantic and note too that the paths to this power seemed the same – a mix of Christianity, Hebrewism, astrology and herbs.

Taken as a whole, the moments of interaction of the African American and the African Jamaican in the late eighteenth century to the twentieth century show "where lines between the two not only cross but become blurred".[1] Those people who carry the surnames of the slaves brought from Georgia to St Mary, Jamaica, by Governor James Wright to work on his plantation have no notion of a connection to these American slaves, so blurred have the lines become. It seems, though, that with time and perhaps class, the connections have grown slack. By the late twentieth century, which is the time when the last of the farm workers whom we interviewed left Florida, the Jamaicans seemed to privilege nation over race. In this response of the African Jamaican farmworkers to their fellow African American workers lay a dilemma faced by nineteenth-century African American thought and action: to migrate to a black community as Bishop Holly did in going to Haiti, John Brown Russwurm to Liberia and an earlier Delaney to the Niger Valley, or to stay at home and fight, as was the position of Frederick Douglass?

The Civil War and the prospect of incorporation into the civil society popularized the stay-at-home option among African Americans in the post–Civil War period. A similar thing appears to have happened in African Jamaica. With a new constitution in 1944 and political independence in 1962, Jamaican political thought veered towards island nationalism, so that though travel to the United States remained attractive, African Jamaicans kept their eyes on the prize – earning money to spend back at home. Segregation was wrong, but it was not their business – they were only short-term visitors who would be going home soon. God would punish the white Americans who mistreated their black citizens. Mary C. Waters describes well their position: "when the West Indians lose their distinctiveness as immigrants or ethnics they become not just American but black Americans. Given the ongoing prejudice and discrimination this represents downwards mobility for the immigrant."[2] How can the black Atlantic, the black international, be made into a concrete organization able to handle the concerns of the descendants of Africans enslaved in the New World, given this circumstance? With time, even the empathy which had glued the several geographical areas into an imaginary entity will melt, with each left to fight for incorporation into their nation states.

What clear connections between African America and African Jamaica in the twentieth century exist are in the realm, as this work has shown, of the supernatural – the successful transport of the Church of God and Saints of Christ in the 1930s from Oklahoma to Jamaica, Bishop Muir's transformation into Moshe ben Kohath, a black Jew, and the pleasure that some farmworkers find in worship with African Americans. Diane Austin-Broos concludes from her detailed study or religion in Jamaica, that "twentieth century evangelical sects ... have populated weaker nation states",[3] and she shows Jamaica with its past of slavery and colonization to be a "weaker nation state". If this state continues to exist, it follows, the American evangelical influence on the Jamaican society will always be. But Austin-Broos makes no distinction between Afro and Euro evangelicals. Will the African American supernatural associations as the Euro be similarly able to "populate" African Jamaica? It might be useful for future researchers to distinguish American supernatural associations in terms of race and see whether their effect on the Jamaican polity is the same.

Notes

INTRODUCTION

1. Chris Dixon, *African America and Haiti: Emigration and Black Nationalism in the Nineteenth Century* (Westport, CT: Greenwood Press, 2000); Leon D. Pamphile, *Haitians and African Americans: Heritage of Tragedy and Hope* (Philadelphia: University of Pennsylvania Press, 2005).
2. Laura Putnam, *Radical Moves: Caribbean Migrants and the Politics of Race in the Jazz Age* (Chapel Hill: University of North Carolina Press, 2003).
3. Ifeoma Nwankwo, *Black Cosmopolitanism* (Philadelphia: University of Pennsylvania Press, 2005).
4. Millery Polyné, *From Douglass to Duvalier: U.S. African Americans, Haiti, and Pan-Americanism, 1870–1964* (Gainesville: University of Florida Press, 2010); Putnam, *Radical Moves*.
5. Mary C. Waters, *Black Identities: West Indian Immigrant Dreams and American Realities* (Cambridge, MA: Harvard University Press, 1999).
6. Paul Gilroy, *The Black Atlantic* (Cambridge, MA: Harvard University Press, 1993), ix.
7. Lloyd Best, "Independent Thought and Caribbean Freedom", *New World Quarterly* 3, no. 4 (1967): 30.
8. R.T. Smith, foreword to *Jamaica Genesis: Religion and the Politics of Moral Orders*, by Diana Austin-Broos (Chicago: University of Chicago Press, 1997), xv.
9. Harold Cruse, *The Crisis of the Negro Intellectual* (New York: William Morrow, 1967); Melvin B. Rahming, *The Evolution of the West Indian's Image in the Afro-American Novel* (Port Washington, NY: Associated Faculty Press, 1986).
10. Erna Brodber, *Louisiana* (London: New Beacon, 1994); Erna Brodber, *The Continent of Black Consciousness* (London: New Beacon, 2003).

CHAPTER 1

1. Ellen Gibson Wilson, *Loyal Blacks* (New York: Putnam's Sons, 1976), 25.
2. Anne C. Bailey, *African Voices of the Black Atlantic Slave Trade* (Boston: Beacon Press, 2005), 106.
3. Jeffrey J. Crow, "What Price Loyalism? The Case of John Cruden, Commissioner of Sequestered Estates", *North Carolina Historical Review* 58, no. 3 (1981): 215–33.

4. William Bull to Lloyd George Germain, CO 5/176, folio nos. 63–65d, in CO 5/410, 291–95. This and all other referenced communication between the governor of Georgia, the officers of the army and the Colonial Office are taken from G.K. Davies, *Documents of the American Revolution 1770–1783/Calendar of 1780–1783* (Shannon: Irish University Press, 1972–81), consulted in the Public Records Office, Kew, London.

5. Bull to Germain, CO 5/176, folio nos. 63–65.

6. Bull to Germain, CO 5/107, folio nos. 118–142d, entry 2001.

7. Bull to Germain, CO 5/397, folio no. 421.

8. Archibald Campbell to Whitehall, 20 September 1782, CO 137/82, 290, no. 17.

9. Robert Stansbury Lambert, *South Carolina Loyalists in the American Revolution* (Columbia: University of South Carolina Press, 1987), 268.

10. Wallace Brown, "American Loyalists in Jamaica", *Journal of Caribbean History* 26, no. 1 (1992): 121.

11. See "Judahs's List of Loyalists", manuscript 246, Institute of Jamaica.

12. General Alexander Leslie to Sir Guy Carleton, CO 5/108, folio no. 35.

13. Return of Registration of Slaves for Sir James Wright's Palmetto Grove Estate, St Mary, Jamaica Archives, Spanish Town, Jamaica.

14. Brown, "American Loyalists", 139.

15. Ibid., 123.

16. Data from Georgia Historical Society, compiled by Willa Mills Harris and Karen Elizabeth Oswold, 1976.

17. *Jamaica Almanack*, 1789.

18. Crop Accounts for Palmetto Grove estate, 1B/11/4/25, 184, and 1B/11/4/27, submitted in 1799 by Robert Anderson, Jamaica Archives.

19. Crop Accounts for Palmetto Grove estate, 1B/11/4/143/30, submitted by John Thompson in 1801, Jamaica Archives.

20. Crop Accounts for Palmetto Grove estate, 1B/11/4/37/192, submitted in 1806 by Thomas Tucker, Jamaica Archives.

21. Return of Registration of Slaves in 1817 and 1820 for Alexander Wright's Palmetto Grove estate, Jamaica Archives.

22. *Jamaica Almanack*, 1789.

23. Erna Brodber, *Woodside, Pear Tree Grove P.O.* (Kingston: University of the West Indies Press, 2004), 56.

24. Ibid., 58.

25. B.W. Higman, *Slave Population and Economy in Jamaica, 1807–1834* (Cambridge: Cambridge University Press, 1976), 106.

26. Wright to Townshend, 3 September 1782, CO 5/657, folio no. 257.

27. Leslie to Carleton, 18 November 1782, CO 5 108, 35.

28. Wilson, *Loyal Blacks*, 30, 31.
29. Shirley Gordon, *God Almighty, Make Me Free: Christianity in Pre-Emancipation Jamaica* (Bloomington: Indiana University Press, 1996), 42.
30. "Three Letters by Nathaniel Hall to the Countess of Huntington – August 15, 1782, October 26, 1782, July 10, 1783", in the West Indies Collection, University of the West Indies, courtesy of the Georgia Historical Society.
31. In 1831, the enslaved in the area were contemplating building themselves a larger Baptist church at Braehead, which is within walking distance of Palmetto Grove. See Brodber, *Woodside*, 92.
32. See Crop Accounts, 1B/11/7–87, 115, 125; IB/11/4/34 for the estates of Zachary Bailey Edwards of Dove Hall and Hugh Edwards of Top Hill, both in St Thomas in the Vale, the parish which then adjoined St Mary and bordered Palmetto Grove, Jamaica Archives.
33. Register of Property Tax, 1 August 1869 to 31 July 1870 for St Mary; "Statement of Land Tax and Arears paid in St Mary 1881–1881", Jamaica Archives.
34. Interviews of Eustace Wright of Kilancholy and Lescene Wright of Woodside, 2006.
35. Interview with Mrs Una Edwards of Palmetto Grove, 2006.
36. Title presented to the author by Monica Lee in 2006.
37. Erna Brodber, "The Bagnolds District of St Mary, Jamaica, and the Atlantic Crossings of the late Eighteenth Century", in *The Sea Is History*, ed. Carmen Birkle and Nicole Waller (Heidelberg: Universitätsverlag Winter, 2006), 67–82.
38. Registration of Slaves on the estates of Zachary Bailey of Dove Hall and Hugh Edwards of Top Hill for the yards 1817, 1820, 1823, Jamaica Archives.
39. Brodber, *Woodside*, 68; interview with Frank Mattie of Palmetto Grove, 2006.
40. This was a very young collection of slaves. Beck was the only person in Adam's age range, and she was five years younger than he. They were also young in that they were new to the estate, most being there by purchase. Adam would want to seek adult companionship and was likely to have been a visitor at the nearby Palmetto Grove estate. Granville was fifty years old and might have seemed a good candidate for the prize of being Markland's father, but he came to Hugh Edwards as likely to be close to the master, possibly his valet, with less time for courting than Adam.
41. Information offered in 2007 by Faye Hutchinson, who claims to be a great-granddaughter of Isaac Edwards.
42. Register of Marriages for St Catherine, St Thomas in the Vale and St Mary: 1B/11/8/11/14, 17, and 20 1816–66, Jamaica Archives.
43. Interview with Frank Mattie of Palmetto Grove, 2007.

CHAPTER 2

1.   David Walker, *Appeal to the Colored Citizens of the World but with Particular Reference and Very Expressly to Those of the United States of America*, with an introduction by James Turner (Baltimore: Black Classic Press, 1993), 61.

2.   Ira Berlin, *Slaves without Masters: The Free Negro in the Antebellum South* (Oxford: Oxford University Press, 1974), 136.

3.   Gad Heuman, *Between Black and White: Race Politics and the Free Coloured in Jamaica, 1792–1865* (Westport, CT: Greenwood Press, 1981), 7. I have added together the figures for free coloureds and free blacks.

4.   Penelope Campbell, *Maryland in Africa: The Maryland State Colonization Society, 1831–1857* (Champaign: University of Illinois Press, 1971), 3.

5.   Berlin, *Slaves without Masters*, 157.

6.   Ibid., 92; Campbell, *Maryland in Africa*, 4.

7.   Berlin, *Slaves without Masters*, 106.

8.   The *Liberator* in July 1839 advertises this coming event and on 21 August 1840 mentions its occurrence and the *Colored American* mentions it 6 February 1840 and 2 May 1840 as having happened in New York City in 1837, Providence in 1840, Newark in 1839–41, Boston in 1839 and Delaware and Philadelphia in 1840. See African American newspapers 1830–1850 in the collection at Schomburg Centre for Research on Black Culture in New York. Note also the poem "To the First of August" by Ann Plato in *Daughters of Africa*, ed. Margaret Busby (New York: Panther, 1992), 75.

9.   Brodber, "Bagnolds District", 67–82. See also Edward Brathwaite, *The Development of Creole Society in Jamaica, 1770–1820* (Oxford: Oxford University Press, 1971), 63–67.

10. *Votes of the House of Assembly 1841–1842*, 1B/11, Jamaica Archives, 104. See also *The Narrative of Nancy Prince*, with an introduction by Ronald G. Walters (New York: Markus Weiner, 1990), 50.

11. See William Main Doerflinger, *Songs of the Sailor and Lumbermen* (Glenwood, IL: Meyerbooks, 1990), 74; and, particularly, "Sally Brown", who had a farm in the isle of Jamaica where she "raised a farm in Jamaica sugar cane, rum and terbacker". W. Jeffrey Bolsters in *Black Jacks* (Cambridge, MA: Harvard University Press, 1997) documents the existence of black watermen in the antebellum United States and their contribution to a black Atlantic identity. See also David Cecelski, *The Waterman's Song: Slavery and Freedom in Maritime North Carolina* (Chapel Hill: University of North Carolina Press, 2001).

12. Julius Scott, "The Common Wind: Communications in the Era of the Haitian Revolution" (PhD diss., Duke University, 1986).

13. Hubert Harrison to David Webster, 19 August 1841, US Consular Reports from Kingston, National Archives and Record Administration, Washington, T31 Roll 7 vo. 17, 12 January 1842–11 December 1842.

14. Berlin, *Slaves without Masters*, 48.

15. Campbell, *Maryland in Africa*, 18, 19.

16. Hansard Parliamentary Debates, Great Britain, vol. 57, 11 March 1841, session of the House of Commons.

17. *Votes of the House of Assembly Jamaica 1843*, address to the Legislative Council, Jamaica Archives.

18. Ibid., appendix 3, Elgin to Downing Street, no. 148, September 1843.

19. *Votes of the House of Assembly 1841–1842*, appendix 5, Barclay to Higginson, 11 September 1840, 50–57.

20. Alexander Barclay, *Remarks on Emigration to Jamaica: Address to the Coloured Class of the United States* (New York: James Van Norden, 1840), 8.

21. Elgin to Downing Street, no. 148, September 1843.

22. *Votes of the House of Assembly 1841–1842*, appendix 5, Barclay to Higginson, 11 September 1840.

23. Ibid.

24. African American Newspapers, 1830–1850, microfilm entry 2106, Schomburg Centre for Research on Black Culture, New York Public Library.

25. Martin Luther King Jr, *A Testament to Faith: Essential Writings and Speeches*, ed. James M. Washington (San Francisco: Harper, 1986). See the editor's introduction, "Martin Luther King Jr, Martyred Prophet for a Global Beloved Community".

26. *Colored American*, 31 October 1840, African American Newspapers, 1830–1850, microfilm reel 1–6, January 1830 to July 1851, Schomburg Centre for Research on Black Culture, New York Public Library.

27. Ansell Hart, *The Life of George William Gordon* (Kingston: Institute of Jamaica, n.d.), 120.

28. George William Gordon, by colour and property, was easily distinguished from the mass of black-skinned and recently freed Jamaicans, but he championed their cause and was eventually hanged by the state for this.

29. Heuman, *Between Black and White*, 14.

30. Walker, *Appeal*, 44.

31. Gale L. Kenny, "Manliness and Manifest Racial Destiny: Jamaica and African American Emigration in the 1850s", *Journal of the Civil War Era* 2, no. 2 (June 2012): 152–78.

32. *Votes of the House of Assembly 1841–1842*, appendix 5, Barclay to Higginson, 11 September 1840.

33. "Return of Immigrants Who Have Arrived in the Island of Jamaica for 30th Sept. 1840"; *Votes of the House of Assembly 1841–1842*, appendix 1.

34. *Colored American*, letter written from Jamaica, 6 March 1841.

35. Prince, *Narrative*, 50.

36. *Votes of the House of Assembly 1841–1842*; Barclay to Lord John Russel in Governor's Dispatch, 1B/5/18 no. 463.

37. "The State of Agriculture: Stipendiary Magistrates Report" in CO 137/256 1841, Public Records Office, Kew, London.

38. Ibid.

39. *Parliamentary Debates Great Britain*, vol. 61, 1092–93.

40. Prince, *Narrative*, 52.

41. Ibid., 56.

42. *Colored American*, letter written from Jamaica, 6 March 1841.

43. Hall Pringle to Higginson, encl. 25 in no. 18, 23 November 1841, *Sessional Papers*, vol. 5, 1842.

44. H. Moresby to Higginson, encl. 7 in no. 18, 6 December 1841, *Sessional Papers*, vol. 5, 1842.

45. Douglas Hall, *Free Jamaica* (New Haven, CT: Yale University Press, 1959), 217.

46. *Votes of the House of Assembly 1843*, address to the Legislative Council, Jamaica Archives.

47. African American Newspapers, 1830–1850, microfilm item 3965, Schomburg Centre for Research on Black Culture, New York Public Library.

48. *Colored American*, letter written from Jamaica, 6 March 1841.

49. Prince, *Narrative*, 53.

50. Hubert Harrison to David Webster, 19 August 1841, US Consular Reports from Kingston, National Archives and Record Administration, Washington, T31 Roll 7 vo. 17, 12 January 1842–11 December 1842.

51. Quoted in Waibinte Wariboko, *Race and the Civilizing Mission* (Trenton, NJ: Africa World Press, 2011), 11.

52. *Colored American*, February 1839, microfilm, in African American Newspapers, 1830–1850, Schomburg Centre for Research on Black Culture, New York Public Library.

53. *Votes of the House of Assembly 1841–1842* appendix 5, 53, Jamaica Archives.

54. Peter C. Ripley, ed., *The Black Abolitionist Papers*, vol. 1, *British Isles, 1830–1865* (Chapel Hill: University of North Carolina Press, 1985).

55. Gordon, *God Almighty*.

56. Prince, *Narrative*, 50.

57. Gale L. Kenny, *Contentious Liberties: American Abolitionists in Post-Emancipation Jamaica, 1834–1865* (Athens: University of Georgia Press, 2010), 7.

58. Ripley, *Black Abolitionist Papers*, 28.

59. *North Star*, 12 January 1849.

60. CO 137/257, Stipendiary Magistrates Reports, St Ann.

61. CO 137/255, encl. 71, package 70, Metcalfe to Lord John Russel, 1 January 1841.

62. CO 137/255, encl. 72, Metcalfe to Stanley, March 1841.

63. CO 137/255, encl. 73.

64. Governor's Dispatch 460, Rt Hon W.E. Gladstone, May 1840, Jamaica Archives.

65. *Falmouth Post*, 5 November 1840.

66. *Votes of the House of Assembly 1841–1842*, appendix 5, Barclay to Higginson, 11 September 1840.

67. CO 137/255, encl. of William Wenyss Anderson's lecture which he read at Kingston before the Colonial Literary Society, Monday, 7 January 1840.

68. Kenny, "Contentious Liberties", 7.

69. *Liberator*, 7 March 1840, announcement of the meeting called to talk of conditions in Jamaica.

70. Ripley, *Black Abolitionist Papers*, 117–19.

71. Ibid., 189.

72. African American Newspapers, 1830–1850, microfilm entry number 3246, Schomburg Centre for Research on Black Culture, New York Public Library. Also note that if this was Arthur Tappan to whom the note was sent, then he was a white abolitionist. See also Brown, "American Loyalists".

73. Ripley, *Black Abolitionist Papers*, 28.

74. Ibid., 117–19.

75. CO 137/288/452, Charles Darling to Hon. W.E. Gladstone, 21 February 1846.

76. *Votes of the House of Assembly 1841–1842*, appendix 5, 53.

77. *North Star*, 12 January 1849.

78. African American Newspapers, 1830–1850, microfilm, encl. 2106, Schomburg Centre for Research on Black Culture, New York Public Library.

79. *North Star* 1, no. 23 (2 June 1848): 1.

80. *Colored American*, 6 March 1841.

81. *Proceedings of the National Convention of Colored People and Their Friends Held in Troy, N.Y. on the 6th, 7th, 8th and 9th October, 1847* (Troy, NY: Steam Press of J.C. Kneeland and Co., 1847), 23.

82. Ibid.

83. *Votes of the House of Assembly*, appendix 5, Barclay to Higginson writing from New York, 31 July 1840.

84. Ripley, *Black Abolitionist Papers*, 408. His wife also ran a school for girls.

85. Ibid., 441.

86. Clinton Hutton, "African Americans in Jamaica in the Nineteenth Century: John

Willis Menard in the Struggle for Definition of Post-Slavery Society", in *Jamaica Journal* 31, no. 1–2 (June 2008): 56–63.

CHAPTER 3

1.　Joseph B. Earnest, *Religious Development of the Negro in Virginia* (Charlottesville, VA: Michie Company, 1914).

2.　All the newspapers referenced were obtained from the African American collection in the Richmond Public Library.

3.　Orlando Patterson, *Slavery and Social Death* (Cambridge, MA: Harvard University Press, 1982), 8.

4.　Franklin W. Frazier, *Black Bourgeoisie* (New York: Free Press, 1987), 44.

5.　Erna Brodber, *Perceptions of the Caribbean Woman*, Women in the Caribbean Project (Cave Hill, Barbados: University of the West Indies, 1982), 29.

6.　The two early black medical schools were at Howard University and Meharry, but by the 1920s, there were five more.

7.　For further information on Bishop Turner, see Edwin S. Redkey, *Black Exodus* (New Haven, CT: Yale University Press, 1969).

8.　*Richmond Planet*, 26 June 1920, Ms 10, no. 275, reel 8, African American Newspaper Collection, Richmond Public Library, Virginia.

9.　For further information on the civilization versus colonization debate, see Wilson Jeremiah Moses, *The Golden Age of Black Nationalism* (Oxford: Oxford University Press, 1978), 15–31; Sterling Stuckey, *Slave Culture* (Oxford: Oxford University Press, 1987), 178, 179.

10.　Earnest, *Religious Development*, 129. Earnest is reporting from the *Richmond Times Dispatch* of 28 August 1904.

11.　*Southern Workman* 40 (May 1911): 202.

12.　*Richmond Planet*, Ms 10, no. 275, reel 6, African American Newspaper Collection, Richmond Public Library, Virginia.

13.　Reference to these books appears in Redkey, *Black Exodus*, 276.

14.　James T. Holly, the first black bishop in the Episcopalian Church, chose to migrate to Haiti; Frederick Douglass, a staunch anti-emigrationist, contemplated emigration to Haiti; and Abraham Lincoln proposed migration to Haiti to a group of significant free blacks in 1862.

15.　Brodber, "Bagnolds District". This work is about the settlement of a part of Jamaica by loyalists from Georgia and South Carolina after the war for American independence. They came with their slaves and some, like Mrs Burrowes, went back home from time to time with their slaves. I surmise that these slaves would be housed in the slave quarters of those hosting the likes of Mrs Burrowes. In such ways the slaves of Mrs Burrowes and other white slave-owning travellers would relate to each other. Even before the war, as Brathwaite's *Development of Creole Society* presents, there was a great deal of movement on both sides of the Atlantic as masters would visit their properties taking their slaves, their body servants, with them. Understandings were likely to develop between visiting slaves and local slaves making clear to them the commonalities they faced as chattel slaves.

16. Samuel B. Jones, "The British West Indian Negro: First Paper – Historical Survey", *Southern Workman* 40 (May 1911): 205.

17. Erna Brodber, *The Second Generation of Freemen in Jamaica, 1907–1944* (Gainesville: University of Florida Press, 2004), 61–62.

18. Ibid., 93.

19. Winston James, *Holding Aloft the Banner of Ethiopia* (New York: Verso, 1998), 358.

20. John S. Reynolds, *Reconstruction in South Carolina, 1865–1877* (New York: Negro Universities Press, 1905).

21. *Southern Workman* 40 (May 1911): 231. Also see Tony Martin, *Race First* (Westport, CT: Greenwood Press, 1976).

22. James, *Holding Aloft*, 12.

23. Cruse, *Crisis*; Moses, *Golden Age*.

24. Cruse, *Crisis*, 129.

25. For lists of African American pan-Africanists from 1850 and before, see Cruse, *Crisis*, 6; and Moses, *Golden Age*, 267.

26. Moses, *Golden Age*, 197.

27. Ibid.

28. *Richmond Planet*, January 1916, Ms 10, no. 275, reel 6, Schomburg Centre for Research on Black Culture. Also see Kenny, "Manliness".

29. Moses, *Golden Age*, 197.

30. Martin, *Race First*, 33.

31. Moses, *Golden Age*, 95.

32. Martin, *Race First*, 286.

33. W.E.B. Du Bois, *The Autobiography of W.E.B. Du Bois* (New York: International Publishers, 1968), 236.

34. Ibid., 238.

35. Ibid., 240.

36. Martin, *Race First*, 297.

37. Ibid., 331.

38. Ibid., 320.

39. Ibid., 316.

40. Du Bois, *Autobiography*, 289n33.

41. Ibid., 215.

42. Ibid., 289n33.

43. Ibid., 220. Du Bois was in touch with Max Weber and Franz Boas, both of whom were more psychological/qualitative in their practice of sociology, and could have used their methods had he wished to.

44. Ibid., 289n33.

45. Phillip S. Foner, ed., *Du Bois Speaks* (New York: Pathfinder Press, 1970), 244.

46. Du Bois, *Autobiography*, 291.

47. Ibid., 296.

48. Ibid., 395–96.

49. Ibid., 361, 253.

50. John Henri Clarke, *Marcus Garvey and the Vision of Africa* (New York: Vintage, 1974), 73.

51. Ibid.

52. Martin, *Race First*, 4.

53. Patterson, *Slavery*, describes the condition of the enslaved in the society in which they reside as "social death", he or she having no status there. I think the term can be applied to the condition of the African American of the post-slavery South, whose social existence was virtually nullified by Jim Crow laws.

54. Martin, *Race First*, 6.

55. With the Treaty of Versailles, which ended the First World War, Africa was once more divided among the "great" powers. This was only one of their treaties in which they shared Africa among themselves.

56. Anna Grimshaw, *The C.L.R. James Reader* (Hoboken, NJ: Blackwell, 1992), 289.

CHAPTER 4

1. Attributed to R. Williams, rector of the Church of Advent, New England, United States, in Wilson Jeremiah Moses, *Alexander Crummell* (Oxford: Oxford University Press, 1989), 32.

2. Edward W. Blyden, in *Christianity, Islam and the Negro Race* (Edinburgh: Edinburgh University Press, 1967), 120–21. In this essay, "Africans' Service to the World", it is mainly Africa that is touted as the "elect". Other essays in this compilation are wider in their range and speak to the diaspora as well.

3. Moses, *Golden Age of Black Nationalism*, 24.

4. Jill Leporte, *New York Burning* (New York: Vintage, 2006), 7.

5. Ibid., 23.

6. Patterson, *Slavery*, 1.

7. Ibid., 8.

8.   C.L.R James, *Black Jacobins* (New York: Vintage, 1989), 87.

9.   Gayward G. Wilmore, *Black Religion and Black Radicalism* (New York: Orbis, 1998).

10.   Barry Chevannes, *Rastafari: Roots and Ideology* (Kingston: University of the West Indies Press, 1995), 37.

11.   See chapter 1 in this collection.

12.   See Gordon, *God Almighty*.

13.   For a discussion of these two forms of religious expression in Jamaica, see Dianne M. Stewart, *Three Eyes for the Journey* (Oxford: Oxford University Press, 2005).

14.   Jacob S. Dorman, " 'I Saw You Disappear with My Own Eyes': Hidden Transcripts of New York Black Israelite Bricolage", *Nova Religio: The Journal of Alternative and Emergent Religions* 11, no. 1 (2007): 61–83.

15.   Howard Brotz, *The Black Jews of Harlem* (New York: Schocken, 1970), 12. Note too that Yosef Ben-Jochannan found the need to publish his two-volume work, *We the Black Jews* (Baltimore: Black Classic Press, 1983/1993), to counter a view in Brotz's work and that of other students of the Black Jews of New York – that the organization was an imitation of white Jewry – when, according to his work, these black Jews had brought their Jewry with them from Africa. In his words, "HEBREWISMS were among the indigenous AFRICANS of every last part of the continent the Greeks and Romans called 'AFRICA' before the birth of the very first HARIBU, HEBREW, ISRAELITE or JEW named ABRAHAM" (374).

16.   Wilmore is regarding this claim when he culls the words from Richard Wright's *Black Metropolis*: "The apex of white racial ideology was reached when it assumed that white domination was a God-given right." Wilmore, *Black Religion*, 198.

17.   Historical Committee of the Church of God and Saints of Christ, *The History of the Church of God and Saints of Christ* (Suffolk, VA: Historical Committee of the Church of God and Saints of Christ, 1992).

18.   Elly Wynia, *The Church of God and Saints of Christ* (New York: Garland, 1994), 27.

19.   Ibid., 32.

20.   I have been to the headquarters in Suffolk, Virginia, to the assembly in Richmond, Virginia, to the assembly in Kingston, Jamaica, and to Passover (several times) in Morant Bay, Jamaica, and have never seen a white face in the congregation.

21.   Walker, *Appeal*.

22.   Moses, *Alexander Crummell*, 32.

23.   Dr Love was an upper-middle-class Bahamian. His family had raised themselves from slavery to the ceiling allowed to black-skinned people. He migrated to Jamaica, where he ran a newspaper and kept in touch with black intellectuals throughout the world. He was one of Marcus Garvey's mentors.

24.   De Laurence was a publishing house in Chicago. Its publications were widely read

in the Caribbean, with some of the British island states – Jamaica for one – banning them.

25. Diane Austin-Broos, *Jamaica Genesis* (Chicago: University of Chicago Press, 1997).

26. For instance, Erna Brodber, ed., "The World Let Go Now" (39StaFc), in *Life in Jamaica in the Early Twentieth Century: A Presentation of 90 Oral Reports* (St Augustine, Trinidad: SALISES Documentation Centre, University of the West Indies, 1979). The respondent talks about the discussion in the Pentecostal church and compares it positively with the Anglican Church that she used to attend, where one was encouraged to be silent and not ask questions.

27. Austin-Broos, *Jamaica Genesis*. New faces, some white, do appear to head churches and do heal.

28. Ken Post, *Strike the Iron* (Atlantic Highlands, NJ: Humanities Press, in association with Institute for Social Studies, the Hague, 1981), 43.

29. Psalm 68:31 in the Bible.

30. In the durbar in Ghana, where the chiefs meet to welcome the new year, the display of gold on the persons of chiefs and queen mothers is remarkable. I witnessed this in 1994 in Akwapem, Ghana.

31. Lorenzo Greene, *A Diary: Working with Carter G. Woodson, 1928–1930* (Baton Rouge: Louisiana State University Press, 1989), 133–37.

32. Ibid.

33. Wikipedia, s.v. "Howard Z. Plummer", last updated 11 November 2008, https://en.wikipedia.org/wiki/Howard_Z._Plummer.

34. The information concerning the history of the church comes from *The Establishment of the Congregation of the Church of God and Saints of Christ in Jamaica 1931–2001*, a magazine produced by the local tabernacle at 23 Sligo Road, Kingston, Jamaica.

35. Chevannes, *Rastafari*, 126.

36. The "sankey" is a hymnal brought into Jamaica by American missionaries; the "Hymns Ancient and Modern" is that used by the Anglicans.

37. I have seen whole congregations doing this high-step exercise, which looks like a horse prancing, and been told that it is called the "holy prance".

38. Chevannes, *Rastafari*, xi.

39. Ibid., 89.

40. Ibid.

41. In a 30 June 2009 discussion in Castries, St Lucia, with Brother Joe, a young man who was establishing a black religious organization there, I noticed that his claim for black people to be seen as the elect of God takes these verses from Deuteronomy as his authority.

42. Telephone interview with Overseer Slack of the Bethel Church of God and Saints of Christ in Jamaica, 27 September 2009. He corroborates.

43. Chevannes, *Rastafari*, 27. Professor Chevannes read this chapter and find this construction, by which a figure in the Church of God and Saints of Christ is one of the foundations of Rastafari, credible.

44. See note 24 above.

45. Chevannes, *Rastafari*, 131.

46. Ibid., 89.

47. See chapter 2 in this collection.

CHAPTER 5

1. For discussion of the concept of multiple occupations as applied to rural black Jamaicans, see Brodber, *Second Generation*.

2. George Campbell, audiocassette interview, 8 February 1990, audio cassette interview no. 38, and Bert Campbell, audiocassette interview, no. 37, 21 February 1990, were part of a study on occupation that I was hired by the Social History Project at the University of the West Indies, Mona, to do. The cassettes reside in the West Indian Reference Library at the University of the West Indies, Mona. The transcripts of these interviews with farmworkers from the Woodside district are now housed in the documentation centre of the Sir Arthur Lewis Institute for Social and Economic Studies, University of the West Indies, Mona, Jamaica.

3. George Campbell showed me something like a miniature sculpture of an angel which he had found in a fish. He had kept this from before 1943. He thought it was a ship sent to him as a sign of the place from which his good fortune would come – thus his prayer for the sea to open up, presumably to let the ship in to bring him relief from his poverty.

4. This event took on international proportions as Jamaicans at home and in the United States raised protests and accused the US government of racism. See Fitzroy Andre Baptiste, "Amy Ashwood Garvey and Afro-West Indian Labour in the United States Emergency Farm and War Industries Programme of World War II, 1943–1945" (unpaginated typescript).

5. He says this with a great deal of pride.

6. Camp Murphy was where the recalcitrant were taken prior to being shipped back home.

7. As the Drake Professor in the English department, part of my assignment was to take two graduate students back home with me as apprentices. Ann Margaret Castro and Petal Samuel were the students who came. They spent two weeks interviewing farmworkers in Woodside, St Mary.

8. See Baptiste, "Amy Ashwood Garvey"; Post, *Strike the Iron*, vols. 1 and 2.

9.   See Baptiste, "Amy Ashwood Garvey".

10.   Ibid.

11.   As at note 2. Audiocassette interview, no. 33, 2 February 1990.

12.   "Schedule of Agreements", in appendix 79, 1B/5/80/1/1, Jamaica Archives, Spanish Town, Jamaica.

13.   "US-WI Labour Pact Urged", *Daily Gleaner*, 8 August 1956.

14.   For further information on the history of Woodside, see Brodber, *Woodside*.

15.   The many works of Elizabeth Thomas-Hope on Caribbean migration support this position, but see, in particular, "Population Mobility in the West Indies: The Role of Perceptual and Environmental Differentials" (PhD diss., Oxford University, 1977).

16.   "Schedule of Agreements".

17.   Ibid.

18.   *Proceedings of the Legislative Council (Jamaica)*, 1B/5/11a/19, Jamaica Archives, 282.

19.   Ibid., spring session, 30 March 1944.

20.   Ibid., 118.

21.   Ibid., 28–29.

22.   Hansard, 1B/15/80/2/1, 19. Coke gives notice of a resolution he wants to present on 10 and 12 April 1945.

23.   Hansard, 1B/5/8/2/2.

24.   Hansard, 1B/5/80/2/3, 244, 328–29, 434.

25.   *Daily Gleaner*, 12 November 1955.

26.   Ibid.

27.   Post, *Strike the Iron*, writes in detail of the negotiations surrounding the lease of the bases.

28.   *Daily Gleaner*, 13 January 1961.

29.   *Proceedings of the Legislative Council (Jamaica)*, 1B/5/11a/19, spring session, 30 March 1944. Mr Lowe comments, "last year the arrangement was that they should not be sent to the South, touching only their in transit to home. But when they reached Florida they were asked to work."

30.   Vincent, interviewed by Anne Margaret Castro, transcript no. 15; but not all the farm owners in the North were "fatherly". Kenroy experienced both types. The one who had the apple orchard 150 miles from Canada was not as kind as the one in Massachusetts. Kenroy, interviewed by Anne Margaret Castro, transcript no. 8, 7–9.

31.   Samuel, as above, transcript no. 13.

32.   James, interviewed by Petal Samuel, transcript no. 7.

33.   A.P., interviewed by Petal Samuel, transcript no. 1.

34.   Ibid., 30.

35. Ephraim, interviewed by Petal Samuel, transcript no. 4; Sibrant, interviewed by Petal Samuel, transcript no. 14.
36. Ephraim interview as at note 35, 6.
37. James interview as at note 32.
38. A.P. interview as at note 33.
39. Ellis, interviewed by Petal Samuel, transcript no. 3, as at note 30.
40. Raphael, interviewed by Petal Samuel, transcript no. 11.
41. Ephraim interview, 4.
42. Dr Catherine John of the English department of the University of Oklahoma shared with me this experience related to her by a Jamaican, now a citizen of the United States, who had been on the farm work programme in Florida.
43. Gus, interviewed by Petal Samuel, transcript no. 5, 14.
44. Ibid., 13.
45. James interview, as at note 37.
46. Ibid. Marcus Garvey came to a similar understanding after he visited Africans of the diaspora in Central, South and Latin America. He said, "I have given my time to the study of the Negro here there and everywhere, and I have come to realize that he is still the object of degradation." Martin, *Race First*, 6.
47. George Beckford's *Persistent Poverty* (Oxford: Oxford University Press, 1972) and Michael Manley's *The Politics of Change: A Jamaican Testament* (Washington, DC: Howard University Press, 1974) both address the poverty of the descendants of Africans enslaved in the New World and by inference African Americans in terms of international capitalism. Along with this and his other books, Michael Manley made several speeches around Jamaica in the 1970s on election platforms discussing his ideas with the public.
48. A.P. interview, as at note 38.
49. Roy, interviewed by Petal Samuel, transcript no. 12, 8.
50. Elcot, interviewed by Anne Margaret Castro, transcript no. 2, 13.
51. Roy interview, 7.
52. Sibrant, interviewed by Petal Samuel, transcript no. 14, 13.
53. Ibid., 16.
54. A.P. interview, 21.
55. Ephraim interview, 14.

CHAPTER 6

1. Erna Brodber, *Myal* (London: New Beacon, 1988).
2. These are ideas arising out of my research for the book *Continent of Black Consciousness* (London: New Beacon, 2003).

3. Elmer T. Clark, *The Small Sects of America* (New York: Abingdon-Cokesbury Press, 1949).

4. These books are still on the banned list. "Daniel Young, Trinidad 1931", Obeah Histories, accessed 10 October 2018, https://obeahhistories.org/Daniel-young-trinidad-1931.

5. Edward Blyden, "Aims and Methods of a Liberal Education for Africans", in *Christianity, Islam and the Negro Race* (Edinburgh: Edinburgh University Press, 1967), 72.

6. Ibid., 82.

7. L.W. de Laurence is a virtually mythical figure who strikes fear into many Jamaicans. Poltergeists and just about any unexplained phenomena are attributed to his activity.

8. Patterson, *Slavery*, 1, calls "total powerlessness from the viewpoint of the slave" one of the constituent elements of slavery.

9. Arthur Dobrin, "A History of the Negro Jew in America" (manuscript, 18 February 1965, Schomburg Centre for Research on Black Culture).

10. Dobrin, "History"; Brotz, *Black Jews*; Joseph R. Washington, *Black Sects and Cults* (New York: Anchor, 1973).

11. *Chicago Defender*, 20 February 1943, 10. The *Chicago Defender*, founded in 1905, was certainly around in the early 1960s when Kohath was in America. In the 1950s, it was the largest black-owned newspaper in the world. It reached more than one hundred thousand paid-up customers daily. This continued to be so with the occasional name change.

12. Hans A. Baer, "Prophets and Advisors in Black Spiritual Churches", *Journal of Ethno-Medicine and Psychiatry* 2 (June 1981): 148.

13. Ibid.

14. Ibid.

15. Moses, *Golden Age*, 24.

16. Erna Brodber, "Mother T" (interview on audiocassette, African Caribbean Institute, Kingston, Jamaica).

17. Edwin Redkey, *Black Exodus*, Yale Publications in American Studies (New Haven, CT: Yale University Press, 1969), tells that Bishop Turner trained as a pastor in Baltimore, Maryland, and was appointed chaplain to the black troops serving in the Civil War. In *Alexander Crummell*, Moses tells us that Crummell studied at Yale and eventually graduated from Cambridge University; he was an Episcopalian priest. Edward Blyden, author of *Christianity Islam and the Negro Race* (Edinburgh: Edinburgh University Press, 1967), was president of Liberia College.

AFTERWORD

1.   Nwankwo, *Black Cosmopolitanism*, 17.
2.   Waters, *Black Identities*, 5.
3.   Austin-Broos, *Jamaica Genesis*, 244.

Bibliography

Austin-Broos, Diana. *Jamaica Genesis: Religion and the Politics of Moral Orders*. Chicago: University of Chicago Press, 1997.

Baer, Hans A. "Prophets and Advisors in Black Spiritual Churches". *Journal of Ethno-Medicine and Psychiatry* 2 (June 1981): 145–70.

Bailey, Anne C. *African Voices of the Black Atlantic Slave Trade*. Boston: Beacon Press, 2005.

Baptiste, Fitzroy Andre. "Amy Ashwood Garvey and Afro-West Indian Labour in the United States Emergency Farm and War Industries Programme of World War II 1943–1945". Typescript.

Barclay, Alexander. *Remarks on Emigration to Jamaica: Address to the Coloured Class of the United States*. New York: James Van Norden, 1840.

Beckford, George. *Persistent Poverty*. Oxford: Oxford University Press, 1972.

Berlin, Ira. *Slaves without Masters: The Free Negro in the Antebellum South*. Oxford: Oxford University Press, 1974.

Best, Lloyd. "Independent Thought and Caribbean Freedom". *New World Quarterly* 3, no. 4 (1967): 13–35.

Birkle, Carmen, and Nicole Waller, eds. *The Sea Is History*. Heidelberg: Universitätsverlag Winter, 2006.

Blyden, Edward. *Christianity, Islam and the Negro Race*. Edinburgh: Edinburgh University Press, 1967.

Bolster, W. Jeffrey. *Black Jacks*. Cambridge, MA: Harvard University Press, 1997.

Brathwaite, Edward. *The Development of Creole Society in Jamaica, 1770–1820*. Oxford: Oxford University Press, 1971.

———. *Contradictory Omens*. Kingston: Savacou Publications, 1974.

Brodber, Erna. "The Bagnolds District of St Mary, Jamaica, and the Atlantic Crossings of the Late Eighteenth Century". In *The Sea Is History*, edited by Carmen Birkle and Nicole Waller, 67–82. Heidelberg: Universitätsverlag Winter, 2006.

———. *The Continent of Black Consciousness*. London: New Beacon, 2003.

———, ed. "Life in Jamaica in the Early Twentieth Century: A Presentation of 90 Oral Reports". Kingston: SALISES Documentation Centre, University of the West Indies, 1979.

————. *Myal*. London: New Beacon, 1988.

————. *Perceptions of the Caribbean Woman*. Women in the Caribbean Project. Cave Hill,
Barbados: University of the West Indies at Cave Hill, Barbados, 1982.

————. *The Second Generation of Freemen in Jamaica, 1907–1944*. Gainesville: University
of Florida Press, 2004.

————. *Woodside, Pear Tree Grove P.O.* Kingston: University of the West Indies Press,
2004.

Brotz, Howard M. *The Black Jews of Harlem – Negro Nationalism and the Dilemmas of
Negro Leadership*. New York: Schocken, 1964/1970.

Brown, Wallace. "American Loyalists in Jamaica". *Journal of Caribbean History* 26, no. 1
(1992): 121–46.

Campbell, Penelope. *Maryland in Africa: The Maryland State Colonization Society, 1831–
1857*. Champaign: University of Illinois Press, 1971.

Carnegie, James. *Some Aspects of Jamaica's Politics, 1918–1983*. Cultural Heritage Series
4. Kingston: Institute of Jamaica, 1973.

Carrington, Selwyn. *The British West Indies during the American Revolution*. Dordrecht:
Foris, 1988.

Cecelski, David. *The Waterman's Song: Slavery and Freedom in Maritime North Carolina*.
Chapel Hill: University of North Carolina Press, 2001.

Chevannes, Barry. *Rastafari: Roots and Ideology*. Kingston: University of the West
Indies Press, 1995.

Clark, Elmer T. *The Small Sects in America*. New York: Abingdon-Cokesbury Press,
1949.

Clarke, John Henri. *Marcus Garvey and the Vision of Africa*. New York: Vintage, 1974.

Cronon, E. David. *Black Moses: The Story of Marcus Garvey and the Universal Negro
Improvement Association*. Madison: University of Wisconsin Press, 1955.

Crow, Jeffrey J. "What Price Loyalism? The Case of John Cruden, Commissioner of
Sequestered Estates". *North Carolina Historical Review* 58, no. 3 (1981): 215–33.

Cruse, Harold. *The Crisis of the Negro Intellectual*. New York: William Morrow, 1967.

Davies, G.K. *Documents of the American Revolution, 1770–1783/Calendar of 1780–1783*.
Shannon: Irish University Press, 1972–81.

De Laurence, L.W. *100 Years of Service to the Mystic Community: De Laurence's Catalogue*.
Chicago: De Laurence, n.d.

Diouf, Mamadou, and Ifeoma Kiddoe Nwankwo, eds. *Rhythms of the Afro-Atlantic
World: Rituals and Remembrances*. Ann Arbor: University of Michigan Press, 2010.

Dixon, Chris. *African America and Haiti: Emigration and Black Nationalism in the Nineteenth Century*. Westport, CT: Greenwood Press, 2000.

Doerflinger, William Main, comp. *Songs of the Sailor and Lumbermen*. Glenwood, IL:
Meyerbooks, 1972/1990.

Dorman, Jacob S. "'I Saw You Disappear with My Own Eyes': Hidden Transcripts of New York Black Israelite Bricolage". *Novo Religio: The Journal of Alternative and Emergent Religions* 11, no. 1 (2007): 61–83.

Du Bois, W.E.B. *The Autobiography of W.E.B. Du Bois*. New York: International Publishers, 1968.

Dunn, Richard S. *A Tale of Two Plantations: Slave Life and Labor in Jamaica and Virginia*. Cambridge, MA: Harvard University Press, 2014.

Earnest, Joseph B. *Religious Development of the Negro in Virginia*. Charlottesville, VA: Michie Company, 1914.

Foner, Phillip S., ed. *Du Bois Speaks*. New York: Pathfinder Press, 1970.

Frazier, Franklin W. *Black Bourgeoisie*. New York: Free Press, 1987.

Gibson Wilson, Ellen. *Loyal Blacks*. New York: Putnam's, 1976.

Gilroy, Paul. *The Black Atlantic*. Cambridge, MA: Harvard University Press, 1993.

Gordon, Shirley. *God Almighty Make Me Free: Christianity in Pre-Emancipation Jamaica*. Bloomington: Indiana University Press, 1996.

Greene, Lorenzo. *A Diary: Working with Carter G. Woodson: 1928–1930*. Baton Rouge: Louisiana State University Press, 1989.

———. *Selling Black History for Carter G. Woodson – A Diary,1930–1933*. Columbia: University of Missouri Press, 1996.

Grimshaw, Anna. *The C.L.R. James Reader*. Hoboken, NJ: Blackwell, 1992.

Hall, Douglas. *Free Jamaica*. New Haven, CT: Yale University Press, 1959.

Harris, Joseph E., ed. *Global Dimensions of the African Diaspora*. Washington, DC: Howard University Press, 1982.

Hart, Ansell. *The Life of George William Gordon*. Kingston: Institute of Jamaica, n.d.

Herskovits, Melville J. *The Myth of the Negro Past*. Gloucester, MA: Peter Smith, 1970.

Heuman, Gad. *Between Black and White: Race Politics and the Free Coloured in Jamaica, 1792–1865*. Westport, CT: Greenwood Press, 1981.

Higman, B.W. *Slave Population and Economy in Jamaica, 1807–1834*. Cambridge: Cambridge University Press, 1976.

Historical Committee of the Church of God and Saints of Christ. *The History of the Church of God and Saints of Christ*. Suffolk, VA: Historical Committee of the Church of God and Saints of Christ, 1992.

———. *The Re-establishing Years*. Suffolk, VA: Historical Committee of the Church of God and Saints of Christ, 1982.

Hutton, Clinton. "African Americans in Jamaica in the Nineteenth Century: John Willis Menard in the Struggle for Definition of Post-Slavery Society". *Jamaica Journal* 31, no. 1–2 (June 2008): 56–63.

James, C.L.R. *Black Jacobins*. New York: Vintage, 1989.

James, Winston. *Holding Aloft the Banner of Ethiopia*. New York: Verso, 1998.

——. *The Struggles of John Brown Russwurm: The Life and Writings of a Pan-Africanist Pioneer, 1799–1851*. New York: New York University Press, 2010.

Jasanoff, Maya. *Liberty's Exiles: American Loyalists in the Revolutionary World*. New York: Vintage, 2011.

Jochannan, Ben. *We the Black Jews*. Baltimore: Black Classic Press, 1983.

Jones, Samuel B. "The British West Indian Negro – Customs, Manners, and Superstitions". *Southern Workman* 40 (October 1911): 580–89.

Kasinitz, Phillip. *Caribbean New York: Black Immigrants and the Politics of Race*. Ithaca, NY: Cornell University Press, 1992.

Kenny, Gale L. *Contentious Liberties: American Abolitionists in Post-Emancipation Jamaica, 1834–1865*. Athens: University of Georgia Press, 2010.

——. "Manliness and Manifest Racial Destiny: Jamaica and African American Emigration in the 1850s". *Journal of the Civil War Era* 2, no. 2 (June 2012): 152–78.

Lambert, Robert Stansbury. *South Carolina Loyalists in the American Revolution*. Columbia: University of South Carolina Press, 1987.

Lawson, Winston Arthur. *Religion and Race: African and European Roots in Conflict – A Jamaican Testament*. New York: Peter Lang, 1996.

Lepore, Jill. *New York Burning: Liberty, Slavery and Conspiracy in Eighteenth Century Manhattan*. New York: Vintage, 2006.

Lewis, Rupert. "Robert Love: A Democrat in Colonial Jamaica". *Jamaica Journal* 11, no. 1–2 (1977): 59–63.

Lewis, Rupert, and Maureen Lewis, eds. *Garvey – Africa, Europe, the Americas*. Kingston: Institute of Social and Economic Research, University of the West Indies, 1986.

Manley, Michael. *The Politics of Change: A Jamaican Testament*. Washington, DC: Howard University Press, 1974.

Martin, Tony. *Race First*. Westport, CT: Greenwood Press, 1976.

Meehan, Kevin. *People Get Ready: African American and Caribbean Cultural Exchange*. Jackson: University of Mississippi Press, 2009.

Moses, Wilson Jeremiah. *Alexander Crummell*. Oxford: Oxford University Press, 1989.

——. *The Golden Age of Black Nationalism, 1850–1925*. Oxford: Oxford University Press, 1978.

Nwankwo, Ifeoma. *Black Cosmopolitanism*. Philadelphia: University of Pennsylvania Press, 2005.

Pamphile, Leon D. *Haitians and African Americans: Heritage of Tragedy and Hope*. Gainesville: University of Florida Press, 2001.

Paton, Dianna, and Maarit Forde, eds. *Obeah and Other Powers: The Politics of Caribbean Religion and Healing*. Durham, NC: Duke University Press, 2012.

Patterson, Orlando. *Slavery and Social Death: A Comparative Study*. Cambridge, MA: Harvard University Press, 1982.

Plato, Ann. "To the First of August". In *Daughters of Africa*, edited by Margaret Busby, 75–76. New York: Panther, 1992.

Polyné, Millery. *From Douglass to Duvalier: U.S. African Americans, Haiti, and Pan-Americanism, 1870–1964*. Gainesville: University of Florida Press, 2010.

Post, Ken. *Strike the Iron*. Vols. 1 and 2. Atlantic Highlands, NJ: Humanities Press, in association with the Institute of Social Studies, the Hague, 1981.

Prince Nancy. *The Narrative of Nancy Prince*. Introduction by Ronald G. Walters. New York: Markus Weiner, 1990.

Proceedings of the National Convention of Colored People and Their Friends Held in Troy, N.Y. on the 6th, 7th, 8th and 9th October, 1847. Troy, NY: Steam Press of J.C. Kneeland and Co., 1847.

Putnam, Laura. *Radical Moves: Caribbean Migrants and the Politics of Race in the Jazz Age*. Chapel Hill: University of North Carolina Press, 2003.

Rahming, Melvin B. *The Evolution of the West Indian's Image in the Afro-American Novel*. Port Washington, NY: Associated Faculty Press, 1986.

Redkey, Edwin S. *Black Exodus*. New Haven, CT: Yale University Press, 1969.

Reynolds, John S. *Reconstruction in South Carolina, 1865–1877*. New York: Negro Universities Press, 1905.

Ripley, Peter C., ed. *The Black Abolitionist Papers*. Vol. 1, *British Isles, 1830–1865*. Chapel Hill: University of North Carolina Press, 1985.

Scott, Julius. "The Common Wind: Communications in the Era of the Haitian Revolution". PhD dissertation, Duke University, 1986.

Stein, Judith. *The World of Marcus Garvey: Race and Class in Modern Society*. Baton Rouge: Louisiana State University Press, 1986.

Smith, M.G. *Dark Puritan: The Life and Work of Norman Paul*. Kingston: Department of Extra-Mural Studies, University of the West Indies, 1963.

Stewart, Dianne M. *Three Eyes for the Journey: African Dimensions of Jamaican Religious Experience*. Oxford: Oxford University Press, 2005.

Stuckey, Sterling. *Slave Culture*. Oxford: Oxford University Press, 1987.

Thomas-Hope, Elizabeth. "Population Mobility in the West Indies: The Role of Perceptual and Environmental Differentials". PhD dissertation, Oxford University, 1977.

Walker, David. *Appeal to the Colored Citizens of the World but in Particular and Very Expressly to Those of the United States of America*. With an introduction by James Turner. Baltimore: Black Classic Press, 1993.

Wariboko, Waibinte. *Race and the Civilizing Mission*. Trenton, NJ: Africa World Press, 2011.

Washington, James M., ed. *A Testament to Faith: Essential Writings and Speeches of Martin Luther King, Jr*. San Francisco: Harper, 1986.

Washington, Joseph R. *Black Sects and Cults*. New York: Anchor, 1973.

Waters, Mary C. *Black Identities: West Indian Immigrant Dreams and American Realities.*
     Cambridge, MA: Harvard University Press, 1999.

Wilmore, Gayraud S. *Black Religion and Black Radicalism: An Interpretation of the Reli-
     gious History of African Americans.* 3rd ed. New York: Orbis, 1998.

Wynia, Elly M. *The Church of God and Saints of Christ: The Rise of the Black Jews.* New
     York: Garland, 1994.

JOURNALS

Colored American

Jamaica Journal

Journal of Caribbean History

Journal of the Civil War Era

Journal of Ethno-Medicine and Psychiatry

Liberator

New World Quarterly

North Carolina Historical Review

Novo Religio: The Journal of Alternative and Emergent Religions

Southern Workman

ARCHIVAL SOURCES

Jamaica Government Archives

Hansard Parliamentary Debates, Great Britain, September 1837 session of the House of
     Commons. 1841.

Parliamentary Debates, Great Britain, Vol. 61, Jamaica Archives/University of the West
     Indies, Mona, WI Collection.

Return of Registration of Slaves 1817, 1820, 1823 and 1826 (Saint Mary) t-diagram/map
     1he.

Votes of the House of Assembly 1841–1842, appendix 5, Barclay to Higginson, 11 September
     1840, 50–57.

Votes of the House of Assembly 1843, Address to the Legislative Council.

National Archives, Washington

Consular Reports (Kingston) T31 Roll 17, Vol. 7, January 1841–19 December 1842.

Schomburg Center for Research in Black Culture, New York Public Library

African American Newspapers, 1830–1850 (microfilm).

Colored American, February 1839, in African American Newspapers, 1830–1850 (microfilm).

Colored American, 31 October 1840, African American Newspapers, 1830–1850 (microfilm), reel 1–6, January 1830–July 1851.

Dobrin, Arthur. "A History of the Negro Jew in America". Unpublished paper, 18 February 1965, Schomburg Collection, New York.

UNPUBLISHED PAPERS

Hannah, Lewis (Evangelist) US. "Exh: Ark of the Covenant". 6 April 2009

"Judahs's List of Loyalists". Institute of Jamaica (manuscript 246). Institute of Jamaica (manuscript).

INTERVIEWS/CONVERSATIONS

Ann Marie Grant, Montego Bay, Jamaica, 2010.

Brother Joe, St Lucia, 30 June 2009.

Elder Eawell O. Slack, Kingston, Jamaica, 2010.

Elder Ezra Locke, Temple Beth-El, Suffolk, VA, USA, 2010.

Hannah Lewis, Miami, Florida, USA (by telephone), 2010.

"Mother T". Unpublished interview (with cassette tape). African Caribbean Institute, Kingston, Jamaica.

Mrs Doris Spence, Port St Lucie, Florida, USA, 2008.

Monica Lee, Palmetto Grove, St Mary, 2006.

Mrs Una Edwards, Palmetto Grove, St Mary, 2006.

Eustace Wright, Kilancholy, St Mary, 2006.

Lascene Wright, Woodside, St Mary, 2006.

Frank Mattie, Martin Gully, St Mary, 2007.

Faye Hutchinson, Islington, St Mary, 2007.

The people named below are from Woodside, St Mary. To maintain their privacy, only names by which they are commonly called were used in the interviews as well as the transcripts, thus there are no surnames listed. They were interviewed in 2013:

A.P.	Leon
Elcott	Lloyd
Ellis	Leon

Ephraim	Raphael
Gus	Roy
Hopeton	Sibrant
James	Vincent
Kenroy	

Interviewees from Oracabessa, St Mary, July 1990:
Harold Sinclair, Collorain.
Bert Campbell, Main Street.
George Campbell, Canoe Pond.

Index

abolitionists, 29–30, 34–35, 46, 47, 48–49

Africa: divided by Treaty of Versailles, 160n55; as site of freemen colonization, 32, 56–58

African Americans: and connection with Jamaican coloureds, 53; and influence on Jamaican culture, 2; intelligentsia of, 70, medicinal cures for, 55–56; and perception of Jamaicans, 50; and political cartoons, 63; post-Reconstruction social organizations of, 54–55; and race relations, 58–62, 64–65

African American migrants to Jamaica in the 1840s, 31, 37, 40, 41; Baltimore passenger list, 38; Philadelphia immigrants, 38

African Americans and black Jamaicans, interaction between: during the 1780s, 83–84; in Florida, 115–24; Jamaica Hamic Association, 51; proselytizing, 147; through structured organization, 148

African Americans, names on Palmetto Grove Plantation of, 4–5

African American conventions and organizations, 37, 55

African Canadians, 47

African Communities League, 69

African diaspora, 58, 63, 81, 83, 125; and authority figures, 55; social history of the, 3–5; Spanish speakers of the, 2; theosophy of, 98

African Jamaicans: economic independence of, 48–49; post-emancipation experiences of, 39–44, 65, 89– 90, 148; treated as honorary whites in Florida, 149

African Methodist Episcopal Church, 72

African Repository (newspaper), 37

agricultural innovation in Jamaica, 46–47

agricultural labour programmes, 103

agricultural labourers, recruitment qualifications of, 105

American Civil War, 150

American Colonization Society, 31, 49, 81

American Negro trends, 68

American presence in Jamaica before 1840, 31

American War of Independence, African American experience during, 1–3

Anderson, Robert, 13, 18

Anderson, William Wenyss, 47, 49

Anglican proselytization, 18

Anglo-American Caribbean Commission, 102

anti-emigration position of African Americans, 43

Atlanta Exposition (1895), 69

Austin-Broos, Diane J., 89, 150

colour stratification in, 36–37; disenfranchisement post–Morant Bay Rebellion, 36; emancipation and labour shortage, 30–34, 41; post-emancipation experiences, 39–41, 45; resettlement of loyalists to, 17; wages paid post-emancipation, 42–43, 44

Jamaica Almanack, 11, 15

Jamaica League, 65

Jamaican Hamic Association, 51–53, 148

Jamaican government and US employers of farm labour, 107

Jamaicans in farm work programme, 103–4, 106; interaction with Americans, 111, 120; relations between African Americans and, 115–24

Jamaica League, 65

"Jamerican" identity, 3

James, Winston, 65

Jefferson, Thomas, 30

Jellep, Peter, 51

Jim Crow laws, 160n53

Jones, Samuel B., MD, 65

"Joy to the savage realms, O Africa" (poem), 80

Kenroy (Jamaican farm worker in US), *110*, 111

Kerr, James, P., 56

Kerr, William, 3

Kew plantation, South Carolina, 3

Kilancholy, Jamaica, 11, *12*, 13, 23

Kilancholly, Jamaica, polling division lists, 12

King, Martin Luther, Jr, 35

Kingston riot (1840), 39

The Klansman (Dixon), 61

Knibb, William, 83

Knights of Pythia, 54

Ku Klux Klan, 59, 68, 79, 120

labour protest, 101

labour shortage post-emancipation era, 32–33, 42

Lend-Lease Act, 102

The Leopard's Spots (Dixon), 61

Leslie, General Alexander, 2, 3, 11, 16

Leslie, Robert, 9

Levy, Hugh Henry, 91

Levy, Rose, 91–92

Lewis, George, 3, 84

Lewis, Reverend Dr, 72

Liberator (newspaper), 37, 44

Liberia, 31, 57, 63, 78, 149; emigration of African Americans to, 49–50

Liberia College, 143, 166n17

Life's Demands, or, According to the Law (Griggs), 62

Lincoln, Abraham, 158n14

Linda Pinkham's medicine, 56

Lisle, George, 84

Livingston, W.P., 97

Locke, Elder, 87

L'Ouverture, Touisaint, 63, 79

Love, Dr Robert, 89, 97, 161n23

Loving Sisters of Worship, 54

loyalists, 2; resettlement to Jamaica, 3, 17; slaves of, 3

Mackinnon, W.A., 33

manumission: laws in the US, 30; in Maryland, 31–32; offered during American War of Independence, 1

Martin, Tony, 70, 72

Marx, Karl, 73

Maryland and emigration of free Negros, 31–32